THE CONCEPTUAL PRACTICES OF POWER

THE

CONCEPTUAL

PRACTICES

OF

POWER

A
FEMINIST
SOCIOLOGY
OF
KNOWLEDGE

DOROTHY E. SMITH

UNIVERSITY OF TORONTO PRESS
TORONTO

Originally published by Northeastern University Press, 1990. Simultaneously published in Canada by University of Toronto Press.

ISBN 0-8020-2753-9 (cloth)
    0-8020-6796-4 (paper)

Canadian Cataloging in Publication Data

Smith, Dorothy E., 1926–
  The conceptual practices of power

Includes bibliographical references.
ISBN 0-8020-2753-9 (bound) ISBN 0-8020-6796-4 (pbk.)

1. Sociology – methodology. 2. Knowledge, Sociology of. 3. Ideology. 4. Feminist criticism.

HM24.S59   1990   301'.01   C90-093529-4

Designed by Daniel Earl Thaxton

Composed in Trump by Composing Room of Michigan, Grand Rapids, Michigan. Printed and bound by Arcata Graphics/Fairfield, Fairfield, Pennsylvania. The paper is Sebago Antique, an acid-free sheet.

MANUFACTURED IN THE UNITED STATES OF AMERICA

ACKNOWLEDGMENTS

I acknowledge with thanks the following:

Kluwer Academic Publications for permission to reprint as chapters 6 and 7 "No one commits suicide: Textual analyses of ideological practices," originally published in *Human Studies*, 1983; Press Gang Publishers Ltd. for permission to reprint as chapter 5 "The statistics on mental illness: What they will not tell us about women and mental illness," originally published in *Women Look at Psychiatry*, ed. Dorothy E. Smith and Sara J. David (Vancouver, 1975); and *Sociological Inquiry* for permission to reprint in rewritten form as chapter 1 "Women's perspective as a radical critique of sociology" (vol. 44 [1974]: 1–13), and as chapters 3 and 4 "The social construction of documentary reality" (vol. 44 [1974]: 257–68).

I also owe a great deal to Deborah Kops of Northeastern University Press, whose support and grasp of what I'm trying to do has been very important, and to Larry Hamberlin, copy editor, who made me work very hard. His rigorous attention to both the detail and the cogency of the text has benefitted it greatly, perhaps most of all at those points where we disagreed and I was forced to clarify. Finally, without the support and help of my friends George Smith and Susan Turner, this book would not have existed.

CONTENTS

◪

FIGURES

THE CONCEPTUAL PRACTICES OF POWER

INTRODUCTION

Gail Scott has written a passage that expresses the problematic of this book:

> We women have two ways of speaking. The first begins in our mother's womb as we listen to the rhythms of her body (likewise for our brothers). As girls, we continue to develop this largely oral tongue in our ongoing relationship and identification with her (here, said Freud, our brothers start to differ). But at the same time we are developing another relationship to the "fathertongue" of education, the media, the law—all patriarchal institutions. Consequently, we end up with a split relationship to language: there is the undernurtured woman's voice, badly heard outside in what my mother always called a "man's world," and the other language, the one we try to speak in order to bridge the gap.[1]

Scott is working with a theory I don't share; she is in debt, I think, to a theory, evolved by Julia Kristeva and based on the constitutional conventions of Jacques Lacan, that identifies the entry of the subject into language as at once the constitution of the subject and the subject's subordination to the law of the father. Kristeva creates a realm of language prior to and underneath and before the "fathertongue": the babble of women to their children, the speech that is not speech. Scott and I disagree on theory, but not on what she is talking about. That experience of a split relationship to language, of the undernurtured woman's voice outside the "man's world"—that is mine, too.

I understand the split differently and not as language alone. I understand the "fathertongue" as the mode of participation in the relations of ruling; I understand our use of the language and conceptual practices of the fathertongue as entering us into those relations as agents or objects. For the novelist the undernurtured language of women is to be discovered as a method of writing; for the sociologist a more ambiguous problem emerges. The fathertongue would seem to be the essential language of our discipline in the sense simply that it cannot otherwise be written. Perhaps this is so; but in the work developed here I've chosen to risk other possibilities: that we, too, can speak in the relations mediated by texts that are organized conceptually and as knowledge, and that we are not condemned forever to a "borrowed language."

This book begins by examining the properties of a patriarchal sociology from the standpoint of women's experience; it seeks to characterize just what it is in sociological practices of writing that alienates and occludes the standpoint of experience, and to identify what we do when we think in ways that place us on the wrong side of the split. It explores sociological practices of writing as ideology, addressing them as instances of a class of practices—called here *ideological*—that subdue the lived actualities of people's experience to the discourses of ruling. Here language is not addressed as a phenomenon artificially differentiated from its local historical uses. Rather, the focus is on the socially organized and organizing practices of using language that constitute objectified knowledges. The analyses developed here are specifically concerned with those forms of objectified knowledge that are embedded in and integral to the relations of ruling—the kind of knowledge that bureaucracies produce and sociologists depend on (census data, labor statistics, demographic information, epidemiological data, and so forth).

Thus the practices of thinking and writing that are of special concern here are those that convert what people experience directly in their everyday/everynight world into forms of knowledge in which people as subjects disappear and in which their perspectives on their own experience are transposed and subdued by the magisterial forms of objectifying discourse.

The book as a whole is a reflexive inquiry—what we make here an object of investigation is what we ourselves are immersed in. The ideological practices explicated here are our own. Explicating such practices enables us to become aware of how, in deploying them, we participate in the relations of ruling. Feminism, a commitment to women, does not alone protect us from being implicated in the relations of ruling, the language of which is the "fathertongue."

I have relied heavily on analyses of the ideological practices of psychiatry in this inquiry—partly because at an earlier stage of my life as a sociologist I specialized in this area and am therefore particularly familiar with it, partly because it has had a distinctive political significance for women. Though I have not incorporated it here because it does not bear on ideological powers and practice, one of my earliest feminist analyses was an essay on women and psychiatry that understood the latter as an enforcer of women's dependent and subordinate situation in the home.[2] That essay conjoined two moments in my own life, one predating, one postdating the advent of the women's movement.

When my marriage was working badly a good many years ago, I went for three or four years to a number of different psychiatrists. My husband did not. The work those psychiatrists and I were committed to was that of working through and thereby eradicating whatever it was in me that made me discontented and difficult in my marriage. That process ended at a point I now see as having more significance than I recognized at the time. I stopped going to therapists, and at the same time I wrote a long paper on becoming mentally ill. Examining in-depth interviews collected by John Clausen some years earlier of accounts of "paths to the mental hospital,"[3] it traced a dialectic between someone's need to act out of desperation, fear, or rage and the social invalidation consequent upon being identified as mentally ill, an invalidation that progressively denies the possibility of socially coordinated and hence socially effective courses of action.[4] I had never been diagnosed as mentally ill nor gone so far down the road of despair and disorganization that I could not get back, but I knew enough about it as an insider to write about it and so somehow or other (though I wrote theoretically and not about myself) to decide not to do it any more.

The second moment was early on in the women's movement, when being bold still gave us the shakes. Meredith Kimball (a psychologist) and I insisted that women had to be represented in a series of six public lectures that the late Ernest Becker had organized in Vancouver, British Columbia. While other speakers got an evening all to themselves, we two women were bundled into one. But that was enough. I don't remember exactly what we said, but I remember the exhilaration of speaking of psychiatry's oppression of women, of breaking with the professional complicity that normally silences such critique, and beyond that of proposing that psychiatry's own methods of knowing ensured psychiatry's ignorance of people.

I have come to see the problem of psychiatry's ignorance as analyzable as using the same ideological practices that I first explored in the context of sociology. This line of thinking and investigation builds on what I have learned in analyzing the alienative practices of sociology. Three substantive chapters analyze ideological practices in different sites of the institutions of psychiatry: Chapter 5 explores the professional and bureaucratic relations that generate the statistics on mental illness and seeks to understand the underlying relations that implicate this method of knowing people in enforcing familial forms of patriarchy. Chapter 6 analyzes the conceptual work of transposing accounts grounded in primary experience into the narrative forms of psychiatry. Chapter 7 analyzes the ideological organization of Quentin Bell's interpretation of the last few months of Virginia Woolf's life as displaying the mental illness that led to her suicide. It also explores the reader's own interpretive competence and hence implication in the intended interpretation of Bell's narrative.

As Scott formulates the "fathertongue," the only option for women is to slide away sideways from the ruling institutions and find modes of speaking the "mothertongue" into texts. The fathertongue is a condition of speaking beyond what we learn from our mothers; it is ineluctable; we may bridge the gap between the mother- and father-tongues, but Scott does not envisage changing the fathertongue (and by implications the relations that it is embedded in and organizes) so that it would speak differently. I do propose such an alternative. Exploring ideological practices provides us both with an alternative method and with discoveries to be made in using it. Indeed, the possibility of exploring ideological practices as I do in this book depends upon having worked out an alternative method that at least enables awareness of what we're doing and what we're joined to when we take them up. Of course, I don't think speaking differently comes all at once, but the aim of this book is to work toward a different method of thinking and knowing the society we live.

The general strategy of the book is an exploration, beginning in chapter 1 with what I have come to see in taking up the standpoint of women in our everyday/everynight worlds and disclosing the abstracted, conceptual mode of the ruling relations that is contrasted to and opposes it. The following three chapters isolate those ideological practices with which sociology alienates its own modes of consciousness from those of people's lived experience, the social organization and relations of objectified knowledge, and the structures of power that underpin them. The final three chapters, devoted to different aspects of psychiatry, deepen the analyses of ideological practices and their implication in the relations of ruling; they also sharpen the method of analysis by focusing on a particular institutional configuration at a number of different sites. These final chapters illuminate, I hope, the distinctive modes of psychiatric oppression and elucidate the ways in which we, as participants in those relations and as competent users of Scott's "fathertongue," play our part. The conclusion summarizes an alternative, reflexive, and materialist method of developing a systematic consciousness of our own society through which we can become conscious both of the social organization and relations of the objectified knowledges of the ruling institutions and of our tacit and unconscious complicity in them when we speak the "fathertongue."

CHAPTER

I

WOMEN'S EXPERIENCE AS A RADICAL CRITIQUE OF SOCIOLOGY

◗ The Disjuncture between Sociology
and Women's Experience

I have introduced this book as a reflexive critique of the ideological practices by which we create and express objectified forms of knowledge that are constituents of power in contemporary societies. It is a reflexive critique in this sense: At the line of fault along which women's experience breaks away from the discourses mediated by texts that are integral to the relations of ruling in contemporary society, a critical standpoint emerges. We make a new language that gives us speech, ways of knowing, ways of working politically. At the moment of separation from established discourses, the objectified forms of knowledge they embody become critically visible. Still, we are committed to the enterprise of speaking on this terrain; we know how to proceed—and must proceed—on the same terrain. The aim, then, of this book is to explore practices of knowing, particularly the objectified forms that are properties of institutional organization and that become visible at the point of rupture, but at the same time are practices in which we participate, that we know from inside, and that shape the practices through which we have sought to establish women's interests and experience on the terrain of ruling.

We begin by exploring the moment at which the rupture can appear historically. It is explored as an insider's experience, an experience distinctively of women, though by no means the experience of all women. It is, however, an experience organized by the concept of woman as the primary organizer of an emerging political discourse. This concept of woman provides not so much an organizer of experience as an opening in a discursive fabric through which a range of experience hitherto denied, repressed, subordinated, and absent to and lacking language, can break out. The first break enlarges the breach beyond any notion of what it might lead to at the outset.

This breach is also within sociology, the medium I work in—a systematically developed consciousness of the societies we live, written in and of the time at which we live them. In my life, the moment of rupture breached my relation to a discipline that I had seen as a means of knowing about the shape of my world beyond the immediately known. It directed me toward a rewriting of the methods of knowing that I worked with. For in calling into question the objectified modes of knowing characteristic of the relations of ruling, I began to be able to see the problems of a sociology that worked in this mode. Still, I needed to work out methods of doing sociology that would not fall back into the same old methods, that would not make worlds that exist only in texts, that would not forget the site of experience, the presence of actual subjects, and the actualities of the world we live in.

The enterprise of this book has a double character. It begins with the discovery of learning how to explore the social from within without allowing it to be swallowed up into the wholly subjective. That means exploring as insiders the socially organized practices that constitute objectified forms of knowledge. It means exploring what we already know how to do and participate in, and that, of course, means finding methods of exploration that don't fall into the same objectifying mode. Thus we look for a method of inquiry where inquiry itself is a critique of socially organized practices of knowing and hence is itself an exploration of method.

The opening up of women's experience gives sociologists access to social realities previously unavailable, indeed repressed. But can a feminist sociology be content to describe these realities in the terms of our discipline, merely extending our field of interest to include work on gender roles, the women's movement, women in the labor force, sexuality, the social psychology of women, and so forth? Thinking more boldly or perhaps just thinking the whole thing through further brings us to ask how a sociology might look if it began from women's standpoint and what might happen to a sociology that attempts to deal seriously with that standpoint. Following this line of thought has consequences larger than they seem at first.

It is not enough to supplement an established sociology by addressing ourselves to what has been left out or overlooked, or by making women's issues into sociological issues. That does not change the standpoint built into existing sociological procedures, but merely makes the sociology of women an addendum to the body of objectified knowledge.

The first difficulty is that how sociology is thought—its methods, conceptual schemes, and theories—has been based on and built up within the male social universe, even when women have participated in its doing. This sociology has taken for granted not only an itemized inventory of issues or subject matters (industrial sociology, political sociology, social stratification, and so forth) but the fundamental social and political structures under which these become relevant and are ordered. There is thus a disjunction between how women experience the world and the concepts and theoretical schemes by which society's self-consciousness is inscribed. My early explorations of these issues included a graduate seminar in which we discussed the possibility of a women's sociology. Two students expressed their sense that theories of the emergence of leadership in small groups just did not apply to what had happened in an experimental group situation they had participated in. They could not find the correlates of the theory in their experiences.

A second difficulty is that the worlds opened up by speaking from the standpoint of women have not been and are not on a basis of equality with the objectified bodies of knowledge that have constituted and expressed the standpoint of men. The worlds of men have had, and still have, an authority over the worlds that are traditionally women's and still are predominantly women's—the worlds of household, children, and neighborhood. And though women do not inhabit only these worlds, for the vast majority of women they are the primary ground of our lives, shaping the course of our lives and our participation in other relations. Furthermore, objectified knowledges are part of the world from which our kind of society is governed. The domestic world stands in a dependent relation to that other, and its whole character is subordinate to it.

The two difficulties are related to each other in a special way. The effect of the second interacting with the first is to compel women to think their world in the concepts and terms in which men think theirs. Hence the established social forms of consciousness alienate women from their own experience.

The profession of sociology has been predicated on a universe grounded in men's experience and relationships and still largely appropriated by men as their "territory." Sociology is part of the practice by which we are all governed; that practice establishes its relevances. Thus the institutions that lock sociology into the structures occupied by men are the same institutions that lock women into the situations in which we have found ourselves oppressed. To unlock the latter leads logically to an unlocking of the former. What follows, then, or rather what then becomes possible—for it is of course by no means inevitable—is less a shift in the subject matter than a different conception of how sociology might become a means of understanding our experience and the conditions of our experience (both women's and men's) in contemporary capitalist society.

◖ Relations of Ruling
and Objectified Knowledge

When I speak here of governing or ruling I mean something more general than the notion of government as political organization. I refer rather to that total complex of activities, differentiated into many spheres, by which our kind of society is ruled, managed, and administered. It includes what the business world calls *management*, it includes the professions, it includes government and the activities of those who are selecting, training, and indoctrinating those who will be its governors. The last includes those who provide and elaborate the procedures by which it is governed and develop methods for accounting for how it is done—namely, the business schools, the sociologists, the economists. These are the institutions through which we are ruled and through which we, and I emphasize this *we*, participate in ruling.

Sociology, then, I conceive as much more than a gloss on the enterprise that justifies and rationalizes it, and at the same time as much less than "science." The governing of our kind of society is done in abstract concepts and symbols, and sociology helps create them by transposing the actualities of people's lives and experience into the conceptual currency with which they can be governed.

Thus the relevances of sociology are organized in terms of a perspective on the world, a view from the top that takes for granted the pragmatic procedures of governing as those that frame and identify its subject matter. Issues are formulated because they are administratively relevant, not because they are significant first in the experience of those who live them. The kinds of facts and events that matter to sociologists have already been shaped and given their character and substance by the methods and practice of governing. Mental illness, crimes, riots, violence, work satisfaction, neighbors and neighborhoods, motivation, and so on—these are the constructs of the practice of government. Many of these constructs, such as mental illness, crimes, or neighborhoods, are constituted as discrete phenomena in the institutional contexts of ruling; others arise as problems in relation to the actual practice of government or management (for example, concepts of violence, motivation, or work satisfaction).

The governing processes of our society are organized as social entities external to those persons who participate in and perform them. Sociologists study these entities under the heading of formal organization. They are objectified structures with goals, activities, obligations, and so on, separate from those of the persons who work for them. The academic professions are similarly constituted. Members of a discipline accumulate knowledge that is then appropriated by the discipline as its own. The work of members aims at contributing to that body of knowledge.

As graduate students learning to become sociologists, we learn to think sociology as it is thought and to practice it as it is practiced. We learn that some topics are relevant and others are not. We learn to discard our personal experience as a source of reliable information about the character of the world and to confine and focus our insights within the conceptual frameworks and relevances of the discipline. Should we think other kinds of thoughts or experience the world in a different way or with horizons that pass beyond the conceptual, we must discard them or find some way to sneak them in. We learn a way of thinking about the world that is recognizable to its practitioners as the sociological way of thinking.

We learn to practice the sociological subsumption of the actualities of ourselves and of other people. We find out how to treat the world as instances of a sociological body of knowledge. The procedure operates as a sort of conceptual imperialism. When we write a thesis or a paper, we learn that the first thing to do is to latch it on to the discipline at some point. This may be by showing how it is a problem within an existing theoretical and conceptual framework. The boundaries of inquiry are thus set within the framework of what is already established. Even when this becomes, as it happily often does, a ceremonial authorization of a project that has little to do with the theory used to authorize it, we still work within the vocabularies and within the conceptual boundaries of "the sociological perspective."

An important set of procedures that serve to separate the discipline's body of knowledge from its practitioners is known as *objectivity*. The ethic of objectivity and the methods used in its practice are concerned primarily with the separation of knowers from what they know and in particular with the separation of what is known from knowers' interests, "biases," and so forth, that are not authorized by the discipline. In the social sciences the pursuit of objectivity makes it possible for people to be paid to pursue a knowledge to which they are otherwise indifferent. What they feel and think about society can be kept out of what they are professionally or academically interested in. Correlatively, if they are interested in exploring a topic sociologically, they must find ways of converting their private interest into an objectified, unbiased form.

◖ Sociology Participates in

the Extralocal Relations of Ruling

Sociologists, when they go to work, enter into the conceptually ordered society they are investigating. They observe, analyze, explain, and examine that world as if there were no problem in how it becomes observable to them. They move among the doings of organizations, governmental processes, and bureaucracies as people who are at home in that medium. The nature of that world itself, how it is known to them, the conditions of its existence, and their relation to it are not called into question. Their methods of observation and inquiry extend into it as procedures that are essentially of the same order as those that bring about the phenomena they are concerned with. Their perspectives and interests may differ, but the substance is the same. They work with facts and information that have been worked up from actualities and appear in the form of documents that are themselves the product of organizational processes, whether their own or those of some other agency. They fit that information back into a framework of entities and organizational processes which they take for granted as known, without asking how it is that they know them or by what social processes the actual events—what people do or utter—are construed as the phenomena known.

Where a traditional gender division of labor prevails, men enter the conceptually organized world of governing without a sense of transition. The male sociologist in these circumstances passes beyond his particular and immediate setting (the office he writes in, the libraries he consults, the streets he travels, the home he returns to) without attending to the shift in consciousness. He works in the very medium he studies.

But, of course, like everyone else, he also exists in the body in the place in which it is. This is also then the place of his sensory organization of immediate experience; the place where his coordinates of here and now, before and after, are organized around himself as center; the place where he confronts people face to face in the physical mode in which he expresses himself to them and they to him as more and other than either can speak. This is the place where things smell, where the irrelevant birds fly away in front of the window, where he has indigestion, where he dies. Into this space must come as actual material events—whether as sounds of speech, scratchings on the surface of paper, which he constitutes as text, or directly—anything he knows of the world. It has to happen here somehow if he is to experience it at all.

Entering the governing mode of our kind of society lifts actors out of the immediate, local, and particular place in which we are in the body. What becomes present to us in the governing mode is a means of passing beyond the local into the conceptual order. This mode of governing creates, at least potentially, a bifurcation of consciousness. It establishes two modes of knowing and experiencing and doing, one located in the body and in the space it occupies and moves in, the other passing beyond it. Sociology is written in and aims at the latter mode of action. Robert Bierstedt writes, "Sociology can liberate the mind from time and space themselves and remove it to a new and transcendental realm where it no longer depends upon these Aristotelian categories."[1] Even observational work aims at description in the categories and hence conceptual forms of the "transcendental realm." Yet the local and particular site of knowing that is the other side of the bifurcated consciousness has not been a site for the development of systematic knowledge.

◖ Women's Exclusion

from the Governing Conceptual Mode

The suppression of the local and particular as a site of knowledge has been and remains gender organized. The domestic sites of women's work, traditionally identified with women, are outside and subservient to this structure. Men have functioned as subjects in the mode of governing; women have been anchored in the local and particular phase of the bifurcated world. It has been a condition of a man's being able to enter and become absorbed in the conceptual mode, and to forget the dependence of his being in that mode upon his bodily existence, that he does not have to focus his activities and interests upon his bodily existence. Full participation in the abstract mode of action requires liberation from attending to needs in the concrete and particular. The organization of work in managerial and professional circles depends upon the alienation of subjects from their bodily and local existence. The structure of work and the structure of career take for granted that these matters have been provided for in such a way that they will not interfere with a man's action and participation in that world. Under the traditional gender regime, providing for a man's liberation from Bierstedt's Aristotelian categories is a woman who keeps house for him, bears and cares for his children, washes his clothes, looks after him when he is sick, and generally provides for the logistics of his bodily existence.

Women's work in and around professional and managerial settings performs analogous functions. Women's work mediates between the abstracted and conceptual and the material form in which it must travel to communicate. Women do the clerical work, the word processing, the interviewing for the survey; they take messages, handle the mail, make appointments, and care for patients. At almost every point women mediate for men at work the relationship between the conceptual mode of action and the actual concrete forms in which it is and must be realized, and the actual material conditions upon which it depends.

Marx's concept of alienation is applicable here in a modified form. The simplest formulation of alienation posits a relation between the work individuals do and an external order oppressing them in which their work contributes to the strength of the order that oppresses them. This is the situation of women in this relation. The more successful women are in mediating the world of concrete particulars so that men do not have to become engaged with (and therefore conscious of) that world as a condition to their abstract activities, the more complete men's absorption in it and the more effective its authority. The dichotomy between the two worlds organized on the basis of gender separates the dual forms of consciousness; the governing consciousness dominates the primary world of a locally situated consciousness but cannot cancel it; the latter is a subordinated, suppressed, absent, but absolutely essential ground of the governing consciousness. The gendered organization of subjectivity dichotomizes the two worlds, estranges them, and silences the locally situated consciousness by silencing women.

🔲   Women Sociologists and the Contradiction

between Sociology and Experience

Bifurcation of consciousness is experienced as women move between these two modes with a working consciousness active in both. We are situated as sociologists across a contradiction in our discipline's relationship to our experience of the world. Traditional gender roles deny the existence of the contradiction; suppression makes it invisible, as it has made other contradictions between women and men invisible.

Recognizing, exploring, and working within it means finding alternative ways of thinking and inquiry to those that would implicate us in the sociological practice of the relations of ruling.

The theories, concepts, and methods of our discipline claim to be capable of accounting for the world we experience directly. But they have been organized around and built up from a way of knowing the world that takes for granted and subsumes without examining the conditions of its own existence. It is not capable of analyzing its relation to its conditions because the sociological subject as an actual person in an actual concrete setting has been canceled in the procedures that objectify and separate her from her knowledge. Thus the linkage that points back to its conditions is obliterated.

For women those conditions are a direct practical problem to be somehow solved in doing sociological work and following a sociological career. How are we to manage career and children (including of course negotiating sharing that work with a man)? How is domestic work to get done? How is career time to be coordinated with family caring time? How is the remorseless structure of the children's school schedule to be coordinated with the equally exigent scheduling of professional and managerial work? Rarely are these problems solved by the full sharing of responsibilities between women and men. But for the most part these claims, these calls, these somehow unavoidable demands, are still ongoingly present and pressing for women, particularly, of course, for those with children. Thus the relation between ourselves as practicing sociologists and ourselves as working women is always there for us as a practical matter, an ordinary, unremarked, yet pervasive aspect of our experience of the world. The bifurcation of consciousness becomes for us a daily chasm to be crossed, on the one side of which is this special conceptual activity of thought, research, teaching, and administration, and on the other the world of localized activities oriented toward particular others, keeping things clean, managing somehow the house and household and the children—a world in which the particularities of persons in their full organic immediacy (feeding, cleaning up the vomit, changing the diapers) are inescapable. Even if this isn't something that currently preoccupies us, as it no longer preoccupies me, our present is given shape by a past that was thus.

We have learned, as women in sociology, that the discipline has not been one that we could enter and occupy on the same terms as men. We do not fully appropriate its authority, that is, the right to author and authorize the acts of knowing and thinking that are the knowing and thinking of the discipline. Feminist theory in sociology is still *feminist* theory and not just plain sociological theory. The inner principles of our theoretical work remain lodged outside us. The frames of reference that order the terms upon which inquiry and discussion are conducted have originated with men. The subjects of sociological sentences (if they have a subject) are still male, even though protocol now calls for a degendering of pronouns. Even before we became conscious of our sex as the basis of an exclusion (they have not been talking about us), we nonetheless could not fully enter ourselves as the subjects of its statements. The problem remains; we must suspend our sex and suspend our knowledge of who we are as well as who it is that in fact is speaking and of whom. Even now, we do not fully participate in the declarations and formulations of its mode of consciousness. The externalization of sociology as a profession is for women an estrangement both in suppressing dimensions of our experience as women and in creating for our use systems of interpreting and understanding our society that enforce that suppression.

Women who move between these two worlds have access to an experience that displays for us the structure of the bifurcated consciousness. For those of us who are sociologists, it undermines our commitment to a sociology aimed at an externalized body of knowledge based on an organization of experience that excludes ours.

🔖 Knowing a Society from Within:

A Woman's Perspective

An alternative sociological approach must somehow transcend this contradiction without reentering Bierstedt's "transcendental realm." Women's standpoint, as I am analyzing it here, discredits sociology's claim to constitute an objective knowledge independent of the sociologist's situation. Sociology's conceptual procedures, methods, and relevances organize its subject matter from a determinate position in society. This critical disclosure is the basis of an alternative way of thinking sociology. If sociology cannot avoid being situated, then it should take that as its beginning and build it into its methodological and theoretical strategies. As it is now, these strategies separate a sociologically constructed world from that of direct experience; it is precisely that separation that must be undone.

I am not proposing an immediate and radical transformation of the subject matter and methods of the discipline nor the junking of everything that has gone before. What I am suggesting is more in the nature of a reorganization of the relationship of sociologists to the object of our knowledge and of our problematic. This reorganization involves first placing sociologists where we are actually situated, namely, at the beginning of those acts by which we know or will come to know, and second, making our direct embodied experience of the everyday world the primary ground of our knowledge.

A sociology worked on in this way would not have as its objective a body of knowledge subsisting in and of itself; inquiry would not be justified by its contribution to the heaping up of such a body. We would reject a sociology aimed primarily at itself. We would not be interested in contributing to a body of knowledge whose uses are articulated to relations of ruling in which women participate only marginally, if at all. The professional sociologist is trained to think in the objectified modes of sociological discourse, to think sociology as it has been and is thought; that training and practice has to be discarded. Rather, as sociologists we would be constrained by the actualities of how things come about in people's direct experience, including our own. A sociology for women would offer a knowledge of the social organization and determinations of the properties and events of our directly experienced world.[2] Its analyses would become part of our ordinary interpretations of the experienced world, just as our experience of the sun's sinking below the horizon is transformed by our knowledge that the world turns away from a sun that seems to sink.

The only way of knowing a socially constructed world is knowing it from within. We can never stand outside it. A relation in which sociological phenomena are objectified and presented as external to and independent of the observer is itself a special social practice also known from within. The relation of observer and object of observation, of sociologist to "subject," is a specialized social relationship. Even to be a stranger is to enter a world constituted from within as strange. The strangeness itself is the mode in which it is experienced.

When Jean Briggs[3] made her ethnographic study of the ways in which an Eskimo people structure and express emotion, what she learned emerged for her in the context of the actual developing relations between her and the family with whom she lived and other members of the group. Her account situates her knowledge in the context of those relationships and in the actual sites in which the work of family subsistence was done. Affections, tensions, and quarrels, in some of which she was implicated, were the living texture in which she learned what she describes. She makes it clear how this context structured her learning and how what she learned and can speak of became observable to her.

Briggs tells us what is normally discarded in the anthropological or sociological telling. Although sociological inquiry is necessarily a social relation, we have learned to dissociate our own part in it. We recover only the object of our knowledge as if it stood all by itself. Sociology does not provide for seeing that there are always two terms to this relation. An alternative sociology must preserve in it the presence, concerns, and experience of the sociologist as knower and discoverer.

To begin from direct experience and to return to it as a constraint or "test" of the adequacy of a systematic knowledge is to begin from where we are located bodily. The actualities of our everyday world are already socially organized. Settings, equipment, environment, schedules, occasions, and so forth, as well as our enterprises and routines, are socially produced and concretely and symbolically organized prior to the moment at which we enter and at which inquiry begins. By taking up a standpoint in our original and immediate knowledge of the world, sociologists can make their discipline's socially organized properties first observable and then problematic.

When I speak of *experience* I do not use the term as a synonym for *perspective*. Nor in proposing a sociology grounded in the sociologist's actual experience am I recommending the self-indulgence of inner exploration or any other enterprise with self as sole focus and object. Such subjectivist interpretations of *experience* are themselves an aspect of that organization of consciousness that suppresses the locally situated side of the bifurcated consciousness and transports us straight into mind country, stashing away the concrete conditions and practices upon which it depends. We can never escape the circles of our own heads if we accept that as our territory. Rather, sociologists' investigation of our directly experienced world as a problem is a mode of discovering or rediscovering the society from within. We begin from our own original but tacit knowledge and from within the acts by which we bring it into our grasp in making it observable and in understanding how it works. We aim not at a re-iteration of what we already (tacitly) know, but at an exploration of what passes beyond that knowledge and is deeply implicated in how it is.

🔖 Sociology as Structuring Relations
between Subject and Object

Our knowledge of the world is given to us in the modes by which we enter into relations with the object of knowledge. But in this case the object of our knowledge is or originates in the co-ordering of activities among "subjects." The constitution of an objective sociology as an authoritative version of how things are is done from a position in and as part of the practices of ruling in our kind of society. Our training as sociologists teaches us to ignore the uneasiness at the junctures where multiple and diverse experiences are transformed into objectified forms. That juncture shows in the ordinary problems respondents have of fitting their experience of the world to the questions in the interview schedule. The sociologist who is a woman finds it hard to preserve this exclusion, for she discovers, if she will, precisely that uneasiness in her relation to her discipline as a whole. The persistence of the privileged sociological version (or versions) relies upon a substructure that has already discredited and deprived of authority to speak the voices of those who know the society differently. The objectivity of a sociological version depends upon a special relationship with others that makes it easy for sociologists to remain outside the others' experience and does not require them to recognize that experience as a valid contention.

Riding a train not long ago in Ontario I saw a family of Indians—woman, man, and three children—standing together on a spur above a river watching the train go by. I realized that I could tell this incident—the train, those five people seen on the other side of the glass—as it was, but that my description was built on my position and my interpretations. I have called them "Indians" and a family; I have said they were watching the train. My understanding has already subsumed theirs. Everything may have been quite different for them. My description is privileged to stand as what actually happened because theirs is not heard in the contexts in which I may speak. If we begin from the world as we actually experience it, it is at least possible to see that we are indeed located and that what we know of the other is conditional upon that location. There are and must be different experiences of the world and different bases of experience. We must not do away with them by taking advantage of our privileged speaking to construct a sociological version that we then impose upon them as their reality. We may not rewrite the other's world or impose upon it a conceptual framework that extracts from it what fits with ours. Their reality, their varieties of experience, must be an unconditional datum. It is the place from which inquiry begins.

◖ A Bifurcation

of Consciousness

My experience in the train epitomizes a sociological relation. I am already separated from the world as it is experienced by those I observe. That separation is fundamental to the character of that experience. Once I become aware of how my world is put together as a practical everyday matter and of how my relations are shaped by its concrete conditions (even in so simple a matter as that I am sitting in the train and it travels, but those people standing on the spur do not), I am led into the discovery that I cannot understand the nature of my experienced world by staying within its ordinary boundaries of assumption and knowledge. To account for that moment on the train and for the relation between the two experiences (or more) and the two positions from which those experiences begin I must posit a larger socioeconomic order in back of that moment. The coming together that makes the observation possible as well as how we were separated and drawn apart as well as how I now make use of that here—these properties are determined elsewhere than in that relation itself.

Furthermore, how our knowledge of the world is mediated to us becomes a problem of knowing how that world is organized for us prior to our participation in it. As intellectuals we ordinarily receive it as a media world, a world of texts, images, journals, books, talk, and other symbolic modes. We discard as an essential focus of our practice other ways of knowing. Accounting for that mode of knowing and the social organization that sets it up for us again leads us back into an analysis of the total socioeconomic order of which it is part. Inquiry remaining within the circumscriptions of the directly experienced cannot explore and explicate the relations organizing the everyday matrices of direct experience.

If we address the problem of the conditions as well as the perceived forms and organization of immediate experience, we should include in it the events as they actually happen and the ordinary material world we encounter as a matter of fact: the urban renewal project that uproots four hundred families; how it is to live on welfare as an ordinary daily practice; cities as the actual physical structures in which we move; the organization of academic occasions such as that in which this chapter originated. When we examine them, we find that there are many aspects of how these things come about of which we, as sociologists, have little to say. We have a sense that the events entering our experience originate somewhere in a human intention, but we are unable to track back to find it and to find out how it got from there to here.

Or take this room in which I work or that room in which you are reading and treat that as a problem. If we think about the conditions of our activity here, we can trace how these chairs, this table, the walls, our clothing, our presence come to be here; how these places (yours and mine) are cleaned and maintained; and so forth. There are human activities, intentions, and relations that are not apparent as such in the actual material conditions of our work. The social organization of the setting is not wholly available to us in its appearance. We bypass in the immediacy of the specific practical activity a complex division of labor that is an essential precondition to it. Such preconditions are fundamentally mysterious to us and present us with problems in grasping social relations with which sociology is ill equipped to deal. We experience the world as largely incomprehensible beyond the limits of what we know in a common sense. No amount of observation of face-to-face relations, no amount of commonsense knowledge of everyday life, will take us beyond our essential ignorance of how it is put together. Our direct experience of it makes it (if we will) a problem, but it does not offer any answers. We experience a world of "appearances," the determinations of which lie beyond it.

We might think of the appearances of our direct experience as a multiplicity of surfaces, the properties and relations among which are generated by social organizations not observable in their effects. The relations underlying and generating the characteristics of our own directly experienced world bring us into unseen relations with others. Their experience is necessarily different from ours. If we would begin from our experienced world and attempt to analyze and account for how it is, we must posit others whose experience is not the same as ours.

Women's situation in sociology discloses to us a typical bifurcate structure with the abstracted, conceptual practices on the one hand and the concrete realizations, the maintenance routines, and so forth, on the other. Taking each for granted depends upon being fully situated in one or the other so that the other does not appear in contradiction to it. Women's direct experience places us a step back, where we can recognize the uneasiness that comes from sociology's claim to be about the world we live in, and, at the same time, its failure to account for or even describe the actual features we experience. Yet we cannot find the inner principle of our own activity through exploring what is directly experienced. We do not see how it is put together because it is determined elsewhere. The very organization of the world that has been assigned to us as the primary locus of our being, shaping other projects and desires, is determined by and subordinate to the relations of society founded in a capitalist mode of production. The aim of an alternative sociology would be to explore and unfold the relations beyond our direct experience that shape and determine it. An alternative sociology would be a means to anyone of understanding how the world comes about for us and how it is organized so that it happens to us as it does in our experience. An alternative sociology, from the standpoint of women, makes the everyday world its problematic.

◗   The Standpoint of Women

as a Place to Start

The standpoint of women situates the inquirer in the site of her bodily existence and in the local actualities of her working world. It is a standpoint that positions inquiry but has no specific content. Those who undertake inquiry from this standpoint begin always from women's experience as it is for women. We are the authoritative speakers of our experience. The standpoint of women situates the sociological subject prior to the entry into the abstracted conceptual mode, vested in texts, that is the order of the relations of ruling. From this standpoint, we know the everyday world through the particularities of our local practices and activities, in the actual places of our work and the actual time it takes. In making the everyday world problematic we also problematize the everyday localized practices of the objectified forms of knowledge organizing our everyday worlds.

A bifurcated consciousness is an effect of the actual social relations in which we participate as part of a daily work life. Entry as subject into the social relations of an objectified consciousness is itself an organization of actual everyday practices. The sociology that objectifies society and social relations and transforms the actualities of people's experience into the synthetic objects of its discourse is an organization of actual practices and activities. We know and use practices of thinking and inquiring sociologically that sever our knowledge of society from the society we know as we live and practice it. The conceptual practices of an alienated knowledge of society are also in and of the everyday world. In and through its conceptual practices and its everyday practices of reading and writing, we enter a mode of consciousness outside the everyday site of our bodily existence and experiencing. The standpoint of women, or at least, *this* standpoint of women at work, in the traditional ways women have worked and continue to work, exposes the alienated knowledge of the relations of ruling as the everyday practices of actual individuals. Thus, though an alienated knowledge also alienates others who are not members of the dominant white male minority, the standpoint of women distinctively opens up for exploration the conceptual practices and activities of the extralocal, objectified relations of ruling as what actual people do.

CHAPTER

2

THE
IDEOLOGICAL
PRACTICE
OF
SOCIOLOGY

❚ Sociology's Methods

of Alienating Experience

Women have recognized the alienating effects of our participation in language that does not express our experience. The issue goes beyond that of entering women's experience into the language. When we begin from women's standpoint in the actualities of our every-day/everynight world, we confront a sociology that is written from, and writes, a standpoint outside experience. Sociological methods of thinking and research write over and interpret the site of experience. This alienation is more than in the relation between women's experience and sociological utterance; it is also in how that speaking and writing transposes and displaces a speaking and writing grounded in experience. Sociological methods of analyzing experience and of writing society produce an objectified version that subsumes people's actual speech and what they have to tell about themselves; its statements eliminate the presence of subjects as agents in sociological texts; it converts people from subjects to objects of investigation. These practices or methods are by no means confined to sociology, for sociological practices are, as we shall see in later chapters, iso-morphic with those of other zones of the relations of ruling. They are among the practices that construct an alienated conscious vis à vis the standpoint of women. This chapter explores sociology's participation in them as its ideological practices.

◼ Ideology and Objectivity

in Social Science

Established sociology uses the concept of ideology as a category to express the deviant inverse of an objective inquiry or an objective account. *Ideology* identifies the biasing of sociological statements by special interests or perspectives. A sociology from the standpoint of women must, it seems, be ideological. Ideology and social science are opposed terms. Both denote statements about society and social relations, and as such they cannot be told apart. But one is held to be false and the other true. One is held to be distorted, biased by the interests and partial perspectives of those who make the statements; the other is objective.

The sociology of knowledge as an area of study within established sociologies identifies ideology with a situationally determined and interested social theory. If the perspectives and concepts of the knower are determined, for example, by class interests, by gender or racial standpoints, then sociological claims to objective knowledge are invalidated; sociological knowledge is irremediably ideological, and *knowledge* a term that must be continually resolved back into *ideology*. This difficulty is our heritage from Karl Mannheim[1] and from Marxists—but not, I shall hold, from Marx.

A feminist sociology must, it seems to me, begin with actual subjects situated as they actually are; it must be, therefore, an insider's sociology, a sociology of society as it is and must be known by people who are active in it.[2] Hence there can be no theory, no method, and no knowledge as a product of these that is not made by men and women and made from a definite standpoint in the society and in the interests of those who make it. To disclose the interests and perspectives of sociological knowers does not as such invalidate a knowledge that is grounded in actualities. Showing that people are interested is insufficient as a reason for saying that what they claim to know is biased by their interest and therefore invalid as knowledge. Curiously, objectivity in the social sciences is to be guaranteed by the detachment of the social scientist from particular interests and perspectives; it is not guaranteed by its success in unfolding actual properties of social relations and organization.

The practice of objectivity in the social sciences is less concerned with such values as "truth" and "knowledge" than it is with the constitution of a phenomenal world and a body of statements about it. These are the currency of the sociological discourse. The practice of objectivity in the social sciences allows that science to detach its corpus of statements from the subjectivities of those who have made them. It has very little to do with the pursuit of knowledge of society. Equating the opposition of values and objectivity to the opposition of ideology and science is a convention of a profession requiring that the presence of the subject and the subject's interest in knowing be canceled from the "body of knowledge" as a condition of its objective status. It is indeed required of professional social scientists that they be able to pursue, as professionals, versions of society at variance with their political values.[3]

The standpoint of women denies the Cartesian knower as constitutive of knowledge; such a knower is necessarily situated in a body (whose existence this knower may doubt, though the very capacity to doubt presupposes an embodied subject). Standard sociological concepts of ideology are devices deployed in the organization of an objective knowledge of society to cancel the presence of embodied subjects as knowers. But the standpoint of women insists that we are always located in particular, actual places, knowing the society only from within. I've suggested indeed that this is how it must be known if it is to be known at all.[4] Knowing is always a relation between knower and known. The knower cannot be collapsed into the known, cannot be eliminated; the knower's presence is always presupposed. To know is always to know on some terms, and the paradox of knowing is that we discover in its object the lineaments of what we know already. There is no other way to know than humanly, from our historical and cultural situation. This is a fundamental human condition. If to be situated as such entails ideology, then we can't escape it. Constructing a spot outside the world for the knowing subject to stand in is the accomplishment of definite socially organized practices. (These will be explored in the following chapter.)

To begin from the standpoint of women is to insist on the validity of an inquiry that *is* interested and that begins from a particular site in the world. It is to be committed to an inquiry that violates the conditions of sociological objectivity and yet insists that there is something to be discovered, to be known, a product of inquiry that can be relied on. Sandra Harding has argued that those who have developed methods of feminist inquiry in the social sciences have fallen short of the final step, the repudiation of the very possibility of a master narrative, of knowledge, and its replacement by multiple partial knowledges discovered from multiple sites and perspectives, with multiple interests in knowing, none prevailing, each equally valid.[5] But such a degree of ontological tolerance defeats the essential character of inquiry as a project. Suppose, as I've suggested elsewhere, we're not after "the truth," but that we do want to know more about how things work, how our world is put together, how things happen to us as they do. If we set out to discover, we want our inquiry to produce a knowing that can be relied on in an ordinary and un-problematic way. We want to be able to say, "Look, this is how it works; this is what happens." We want to be able to say, "Look, I can show you." We want to *know* because we also want to be able to act and in acting to rely on a knowledge beyond what is available to us directly. We want to be able to have arguments about how things work that refer to an ontological ground in the world we have in common, and we want, therefore, to be able to arrive at an agreement on the basis of what is there for both of us. Harding would deny us this project; but if this project is denied, then so is the point and meaning of inquiry, the project of discovering, of finding out, of seeking to know.

There is, however, an alternative to inconclusive, mutually respectful agreements to differ, alternating presumably with political contentions about whose version is to prevail in practice. Marx, in *The German ideology*,[6] proposes to ground social science in the activities of actual individuals and the material conditions thereof, more specifically in the forms of cooperation or social relations that arise from and organize their activities. Marx views history and social relations as processes that exist only in people's activities. His use of the concept of ideology identifies procedures that mask and suppress this grounding of a social science: Ideological procedures fix time in an abstract conceptual order. They derive social relations and order from concepts (the "nature of man," "species being," and so forth). Through a selective treatment of actualities they construct accounts of history and society as expressions of concepts. They substitute concepts for the concerting of the activities of people as agents and forces in history. Thus Marx's use of the concept of ideology differs radically from that used and sometimes attributed to him by some sociologists and Marxists.[7] His own method insists on the discovery of relations and processes that arise in and only in the actual activities of actual people. Society, therefore, happens. It is examinable. It goes on. Ideology as a method of reasoning about and interpreting society and history obstructs inquiry by giving primacy to concepts and their speculative manipulation. It fails to explore actualities and discover how to express them conceptually.[8]

◧ Marx's Conception

of "Ideology"

This chapter redraws the distinction between ideology and social science after Marx as a critique of social science. *Ideology* will identify for us practices that design how actualities are inscribed in the texts of sociological discourse. This strategy presupposes that it is indeed possible to explore the actualities of social organization and relations; it presupposes the possibilities of knowing something, at least, about how things actually work and happen in society.

In returning to Marx I have been concerned with the uses of his work for this inquiry and not with explicating or elaborating his theory. Although I have tried to be faithful in presenting what he said, this cannot be treated as an exegesis or relied upon as an interpretation. I have approached his work to find out how to think about society as actual people live it; at every encounter I have developed not simply his text but the understanding that is my preliminary use of it as a means to think with.

In *The German ideology* and early in his career Marx uses an analysis of the ideological properties of others' work to define and separate from it the methods of a science grappling with a real world.[9] The ideological critique is fundamental to his procedure, particularly at the earlier stages of his theoretical development.[10]

In Marx's critical procedure ideology is not equivalent to the totality of another's theory, beliefs, or ideas. His method identifies as ideological definite procedures or methods of thinking and reasoning about social relations and processes. *Ideology* names a kind of practice in thinking about society. To think ideologically is to think in a distinctive and describable way. Ideas and concepts as such are not ideological. They are ideological by virtue of being distinctive methods of reasoning and interpreting society.

Feminists have pointed out that Marx has stressed the sphere of economic activity, hence of the production of objects for consumption, to the neglect of the sphere involved in reproducing human life.[11] His theory thus fails to embrace patriarchal forms of oppression. Nonetheless, his ontology offers us a radical break with the types of social and sociological theory that begin with assumptions about human nature assigning agency, reason, creativity, and the recognition of rights to men and subordination, passivity, and a being ruled by body and feeling to women.[12] The radical break is not to offer us an alternative theory of human nature; it is rather to repudiate methods of thinking about society and social relations grounded in concepts of human nature or species being. The premises of the new materialism are not imaginary but actual people's activities and the material conditions thereof.[13]

The new materialism of *The German ideology* is far from being the reductive ontology it has often been taken for. The framework of the argument developed there is sketched in the *Theses on Feuerbach*. These outline a materialism synthesizing idealism and the old reductive materialism. The former neglects the sensuous, living aspect of existence, the latter the subjective. The new materialism unites these in an ontology of actual individuals and their activities. Consciousness is thus always the consciousness of people, whose feelings and thoughts arise as they are active in the social relations coordinating their activities with those of others. Their activities and how they are organized are their lives, their existence. Qualities attributed to them as properties of their humanity and resulting from their being as species are imaginary premises for which a materialist method substitutes the realities of people's actual practices.

Marx contrasts the new materialism with methods of thinking characterized as ideological. To treat assumptions about human nature (among other concepts) as active forces in social and historical processes is an ideological practice. Yet for the new materialism, which views consciousness as integral to people's activities and the coordination of their activities, such ideological practices are not wholly arbitrary. Concepts, ideology, and ideological practices are integral parts of sociohistorical processes. Through them people grasp in abstraction the real relations of their own lives. Yet while they express and reflect actual social relations, ideological practices render invisible the actualities of people's activities in which those relations arise and by which they are ordered.

Far from introducing here an irremediable relativism, Marx views concepts and categories as expressions of social relations and hence as opening up a universe for exploration that is "present" in them but not explicated.[14] The problem of what we are calling *ideological practices* is that they confine us to the conceptual level, suppressing the presence and workings of the underlying relations they express. Thus Marx criticizes the "bourgeois economists" for treating as fact what has to be explained. Terms such as *division of labor, exchange,* and *competition* are the primitives of their theories. Such terms express social relations organizing the actual activities of people, but the social relations themselves are presupposed without being explored or analyzed. Ideological theories conceal the presence and workings of these relations. What I am calling ideological practices or procedures are the methods of reasoning that effect that concealment.

Marx's critique of political economy is an explication of just those relations that are presupposed when the categories of political economy are treated as given. If categories and concepts of social science are taken to express social relations as organizations of actual activities, as Marx proposes, then a critical treatment of the ideological aspects of our thinking and our theoretical practice thus (following Marx's example) offers the possibility of passing beyond ideology to an inquiry aimed at discovering the actualities of people's social relations.

◖ Ideology as a Rupture between Concept

and the Actual Relations It Reflects

An analysis of ideology extrapolated from Marx's practice and applied to the social sciences explores the relation between a social scientific concept and the actual activities it expresses, between the "forms of thought" through which social scientists make what people do observable to social science, on the one hand, and what people actually do and the actual ways in which their lives are organized, on the other. If there is, as Louis Althusser has argued,[15] a major "epistemological break" between Marx's early work up to the *Economic and philosophic manuscripts of 1844* and his work from *The German ideology* on, it lies less in a final break with Hegel than in his radical proposal of the activities of actual living individuals as the ontological ground of social science.[16] "Where speculation ends—in real life—there real, positive science begins: the representation of the practical activity of men [*sic*]."[17] The practical activity of actual living individuals both is and produces the phenomena with which the social scientist is concerned.

Thus whatever becomes observable to the social scientist under whatever form of thought has no existence other than as it arises in what people do. People do not dream up the ordering of their relations and then put them into practice. That ordering is an effect of people's practical activities in the context of their actual material conditions. Conditions become conditions only in the context of a practice and are themselves the product of practical activities. The ideas, concepts, and categories in which the ordering of people's activities becomes observable to us are embedded in and express social relations. Thus those social relations are already given to us in the basic terms of our thinking about society and history. Categories and concepts, "forms of thought," reflect or express an organization of people's activities. "The categories of bourgeois economy consist of such like forms. They are the forms of thought expressing with social validity the conditions and relations of a definite historically determined mode of production."[18]

The actual practices of people ordered as social relations appear in social scientific discourse worked up conceptually as observables. We can think of a social scientific observable as having two sides: the concept or category that is a constituent of social scientific discourse, and its anchorage in the actual ordering of people's activities. Knowledge of society and social relations presupposes conceptual procedures. The phenomenal substructure of the observable is "in" the ordering of people's activities and arises only through them. The conceptual aspect of the observable reflects or expresses, then, what is already organized in the practices of actual individuals.

The relation between a concept and the social relations it reflects, evident in the construction of an observable, is schematized in figure 2.1. The arrow represents the relation of "reflection." The co-order-

actual co-ordered activities → concept = observable

Figure 2.1   The inner structure of the social scientific observable

ing of people's activities is prior to any conceptual expression; the conceptual structure expresses a social organization of the actual activities of actual people; it may be, indeed, in the original outside the text, a constituent of them. Social relations exist not as mutually defining sets of terms, as Bertell Ollman conceives them,[19] but in the ongoing co-ordering of individuals' activities.

This interpretive procedure is very different from those established in the sociology of knowledge, where the term ideology is used to identify social scientific formulations or theories that are determined by their social basis. There, the method of analysis "reads through" the statements of an author to underlying and unexpressed social factors—interests, perspectives and the like—held to be at work in and biasing the thinker's assertions. Thought is held to be a function of the life situation of the thinker.[20] We can in effect forget about the thinker and move directly from the statements to the interests or perspectives identified with that life situation, into which the thinker is collapsed. The presence of the subject is redundant, needed only as a vehicle for the causal nexus. Subjectivity is not a necessary term in the relation.

Marx works differently. Concepts and categories are already expressive of the actual social relations ordering people's activities. What we might in more contemporary terms call an *observable* has thus two sides: a surface, the concept or category abstracting from and expressing a social relation, and an underside that is the "real world" social relation in which the concept or category arises. For example, in discussing Hegel's theory of history in the second preface to *Capital*, Marx describes the ideal as "reflecting" the material world and the latter as "translated" by the human mind into forms of thought.[21] Nor does this conception conform to a correspondence or referential notion of the relation between concepts and sociohistorical process. Further, if we treat his terms seriously, the relations he thus names are not relations of determination; they are relations of meaning theorized as fully indexical in the ethnomethodological sense; the categories and concepts have meaning to the extent that they are grounded in actual social relations.

Here we can see the link we need between beginning from the subject's experience, to which we are committed when we take up the standpoint of women, and the method of thinking about society that Marx developed. For as he formulates the relation between the concepts of social science—in his case, of political economy—concepts "translate" what people already know as a matter of their experience. Thus, for example, Aristotle was blocked from developing his analysis of values because he could not see that "to attribute value to commodities, is merely a mode of expressing all labor as equal human labor, and consequently as labor of equal quality."[22] Grasping the relation between labor and value depends upon being able to see all labor as equal human labor. This was unavailable to Aristotle because "Greek society was founded upon slavery, and had, therefore, for its natural basis, the inequality of men and of their labor-powers."[23] In an analogous manner, we can see how the defects of Marx's own capacity to theorize gender relations and the forms of oppression women experience were grounded in his experience *as a man* of a society founded upon the oppression of women having for its natural[24] basis the inequality of women and men.

As can be seen, the relation Marx theorizes between a subject (the knower) and the conditions of that subject's knowledge is situational in quite a different sense than that of the "sociology of knowledge" paradigm. What can be known and translated into the forms of thought is already given in the conditions of experience created by the practical activities of people. People already have a working knowledge of the organization of the relations in which they participate, at least as far as it comes within their reach. Forms of thought expressing these relations or embedded in them make whatever sense they make insofar as this working knowledge explicates them, fills them out, provides what Harold Garfinkel calls "the background knowledge of social structure" that he holds to be essential to making sense of talk.[25] Concepts such as "individualism," "equality of power," "competition," "commodities," and so forth, are available to be thought about because their character and the distinctions they make apparent are already structured in actual social relations. People grasp them as particular forms of the ordering of their own practical activities.

This version of the relation between forms of thought and people's actual co-ordering of their activities preserves, rather than suppresses, the presence of the subject. It is later Marxists, following the simple-minded but vigorous positivism of Engels, and Mannheim's subtler and finally idealistic integrations, that in different ways cancel the subject. According to this line of thinking, the underlying social relations do not determine how they can be thought, but rather provide the conditions of the sense of concepts that express them. What *can* be thought is already organized in people's actual activities and is given explicit expression at the level of discourse through the concept. Take, for example, a very ordinary piece of sociological currency, the concept of *role*. It follows from this interpretation of Marx's view that this concept could not be thought unless people already knew how to make a separation between person and role as a practical accomplishment. The possibility of conceiving a difference between role and person arises (let us say) with the development of forms of organization that stand independent of individuals and that are performed, but not appropriated, by them. These arise late in European history. Thus people in, say, 900 A.D. in Europe would not have known how to take person and role apart conceptually because they did not have a social organization that constituted them as separable phenomena. E. H. Kantorowicz in his study of medieval political theology[26] shows various theoretical devices for distinguishing person and image, but he also illustrates the institutional incapacity to differentiate role and person in his account of a late eleventh-century man who argued that in his capacity as baron he could marry while in his capacity as bishop he must remain celibate. In the period of which he writes, it would appear that neither the concept nor the practice was available to its thinkers (it had of course existed earlier, notably in Rome).

Marx's example instructs us not to treat a concept as a theoretical primitive, in the logical sense, nor as interpretable solely in terms of other concepts. Rather, we are called on to explore the ground of a concept in the actual ordering of what living people do. The conditions of our thinking, our conceptual strategies, are made problematic.

To think ideologically, by contrast, identifies methods of reasoning that confine us to a conceptual level divorced from its ground; we remain then "on this side of" the concept; the internal relation in the observable between concept and the actualities of co-ordered activities is ruptured. Concepts then become a boundary to inquiry rather than a beginning. The topic of how it is possible for us to think these things and to talk about these things cannot be addressed. Ideologically construed, the concept confines thinkers to the boundaries already given in their experience. Thus to think ideologically is indeed to think in situationally determined modes, since ideology deprives us of access to, hence of critique of, the social relational substructure of our experience.

Forms of thought are the means by which people represent their experience to themselves and to each other. Sociological observables make us conscious of the sociohistorical processes and relations in which our lives are implicated in ways that cut consciousness off from its bedrock in social relations. Though the sociological observable is derived from and expresses or reflects actual social relations, their production moves from a ground where we know what we know as participants, to a discursive entity methodically constructed to suppress its ground in our active engagement with the world. What people already know as a matter of experience—their tacit knowledge, to use Michael Polanyi's term[27]—is translated into the forms of thought under which people make their experience conscious.

Consciousness itself, as Marx and Engels use this term, is not merely something going on in people's heads. Consciousness is produced by people and is "from the very beginning a social product, and remains so as long as men [sic] exist at all."[28] People produce consciousness for each other. Language is "practical consciousness, that is, consciousness as it exists for other men [sic]." Consciousness is originally only "consciousness of existing practice."[29] But, according to Marx and Engels, as talking, thinking, and writing become distinctly differentiated and specialized activities (in legal, administrative, managerial, and discursive forms of social organization), the relationship of social forms of consciousness to the social relations they reflect changes. The possibility of the separation of concept from its ground in the actual co-ordering of people's activities depends upon forms of social organization in which a concept and the practices it regulates and reflects can be taken apart.

Concepts thus become a kind of "currency"—a medium of exchange among ideologists and a way of thinking about the world that stands *between* the thinker and the object. The ideologist "remains in the realm of theory and does not view men [sic] in their given social connection, not under their existing conditions of life, which have made them *what* they are, he never arrives at the really existing active men [sic]."[30]

When concepts are detached from the relation in which they make the world of living people observable, they become a means of operating selectively upon it and of sorting it out in ways that preserve the ideal representation. Ideology can be viewed as a procedure for sorting out and arranging conceptually the living actual world of people so that it can be seen to be as we already know it ideologically. Social science is not its only site of operation. As we shall see in later chapters, ideological practices are pervasive features of the organization of the juncture between the relations of ruling and the actualities of people's lives they organize and govern. In social science, however, ideological practices are at war with a knowledge—or perhaps better, a *knowing*—that begins from the site of people's experience. Ideological practices ensure that the determinations of our everyday, experienced world remain mysterious by preventing us from making them problems for inquiry. The concept becomes a substitute for reality. It becomes a boundary, a terminus through which inquiry cannot pass. What ought to be explained is treated as fact or as assumption.

☐ Sociological Method

as Ideology

A passage in *The German ideology* with special relevance to the ideological practice of sociology describes three "tricks" that bring about "the hegemony of the spirit in history." If we do away with their specifically Hegelian reference, we find a recipe for making up an ideological representation of what people think. Here is my version:[31]

Trick 1 Separate what people say they think from the actual circumstances in which it is said, from the actual empirical conditions of their lives, and from the actual individuals who said it.

Trick 2 Having detached the ideas, arrange them to demonstrate an order among them that accounts for what is observed. (Marx and Engels describe this as making "mystical connections." These will be addressed in the following section.)

Trick 3 Then change the ideas into a "person"; that is, set them up as distinct entities (for example, a value pattern, norm, belief system, and so forth) to which agency (or possibly causal efficacy) may be attributed.

And redistribute them to "reality" by attributing them to actors who can now be treated as representing the ideas.

In a later passage Marx summarizes this procedure in a caustic example of how to be "profound and speculative in the German manner":

> First of all, an abstraction is made from the fact; then it is declared that the fact is based upon the abstraction. . . .
> *Fact:* The cat eats the mouse.
> *Reflection:* Cat-nature, mouse-nature, consumption of mouse by cat—consumption of nature by nature—self-consumption of nature.
> *Philosophic presentation of the fact:* Devouring of the mouse by the cat is based upon the self-consumption of nature.[32]

Through these "tricks" a fact can be represented as an expression of a principle originating in the same fact. The procedure discards the presence of the subject and reconceptualizes actual activity as an abstract noun capable of functioning as an agent. The original relation between the fact and the reflection, wherein the principle arises as an abstraction from the fact, is then reversed. The fact becomes an expression of the principle. An *ideological circle* is created.

Methodological prescriptions to be found in works on theory construction look uncomfortably like this recipe for making ideology. Take for example Hans Zetterberg's recommended procedure: "Sociological definitions are constructed by combining primitives of several actors. Let us assume that our primitives are verbal actions such as 'descriptions,' 'evaluations,' and 'prescriptions.' As a first operation consider any procedure used to find a 'central tendency.' . . . Central tendencies of the same action types among an aggregate of individuals become their 'social beliefs,' 'social valuations,' and 'social norms.' "[33]

Zetterberg is telling us how to take something that people actually said and make it over so that it can be treated as an attribute of an "aggregate." The process of getting from the original individuals who described, judged, and prescribed to the end product of "social beliefs," "social valuations," and "social norms" goes something like this:

1 Individuals are asked questions, presumably in an interview.
2 Their answers are then detached from the original practical determination in the interview situations and from the part the sociologist played in making them. They become data. Note that the questions are not data.

The data (the recorded responses) are coded to yield "descriptions," "evaluations," and "prescriptions" (trick 1).

3   The various intervening procedures of analysis would be tedious to elaborate here. They lead up to the statistical manipulation of the data to find the "central tendencies" (trick 2).

4   The original individuals are now changed into the sociologist's aggregate. Their beliefs, their values, and their norms are now attributed to this "personage" as "social beliefs," "social values," and "social norms." It is then perfectly within the bounds of ordinary sociological thinking that social beliefs, norms, and values be treated as causing behavior, though Zetterberg does not recommend this as the next step (trick 3 and conclude).

Ideology, as I've interpreted Marx's version, is a method. Contemporary sociology commands techniques for transforming concepts into the currency of discourse that were undreamed of in Marx's time. There is clearly an immediate problem with phenomena the only practical substrate of which is the social organization and relations of sociological discourse itself. This arises most obviously in connection with experimental work. But there are similar problems outside the laboratory. It is, for example, good, ordinary sociological practice to take a concept such as social class or power and locate it in the real world by creating indicators for it. There are procedures available for creating special classes of sociological events that stand in the relation of indicators to the concept (there are also instructions for making use of "naturally" occurring events in a similar way). A virtual reality vested in texts is thereby constituted, cutting social science off from the actual relations and organization of people's lives.

◗   An Alternative

and Materialist Method

We know that people are there as subjects somewhere in the original of what is theorized or conceptualized. Zetterberg's recommendations introduce a device for eliminating their presence from the sociological text, just as Marx's three "tricks" do. The sociological formulation constructs an absence. The problem is to find an alternative. The first of the three tricks suggests that we might begin with its opposite as a preliminary basis for an alternative. Inverted, it would stipulate procedures preserving the presence of the subjects locally and historically in any sociological version. Sociological statements must be grounded in and refer back to the actual socially organized practice of real people; sociological formulations must explicate tangible organization and relations discovered in a course of inquiry into the actualities of people's worlds.

The organization of people's activities in contemporary society typically produces a multiplicity of forms in which people do not appear as subjects; they can be identified in terms such as *formal organization, bureaucracy,* and so forth (*knowledge* itself is one such term—to be explored in depth in chapter 3). Rather than incorporating these concepts unanalyzed and unexplored, an alternative and materialist sociology opens up inquiry into just how people's activities are socially organized to suppress their presence as actual subjects. We move, then, to an exploration of how the activities of actual individuals are organized to produce that effect. Marx's *Capital* gives us a model of such a procedure. It begins with a careful specification of just how relations among people come to take on the appearance of relations between things—namely, commodities and money. His analysis of the fetishism of commodities shows just how the presence of actual producers is severed from the product as it enters into relations in which it is exchanged for money in such a way that commodity and money appear as "agents." If people do not appear as agents in their own effects, then that is also something that is itself an organization of people's actual activities. Thus if people's activities can come to have properties of a system, that effect must be specified with reference to the social practices and relations in and through which subjects are active in accomplishing their own invisibility. To treat human action in terms of systems necessitates an account of how people may be separated from their actions so that what they do or "expect" may become the components or parts of a system. If the system assumes the prerogatives of agency vis à vis the actors, then its "causal" hegemony must also be describable in terms that show how that is brought about in socially organized practices.

Sociological concepts may be treated in a preliminary way as markers of areas for investigation. Inquiry can move from concept or formulation to the discovery of what people are actually doing and what the relations co-ordering those activities are. Take, for example, the kinds of things that are said about technology, representing it as a force thrusting us blindly forward into a technologically determinate but humanly indeterminate future. If we follow this procedure, technological changes must be transposed out of that generalizing language and into a description of the work of actual people in actual work contexts, with given kinds of equipment, organized as an enterprise or in relations that produce the sense of forces operating without the will or intention of those active in the process. The everyday organization of the work of technological innovation is related to capitalist enterprises having uses for the products other than those of the people who make or eventually use them. Such an approach transforms the way in which questions about technological change are asked. It addresses technological change as practical activities embedded in definite social relations—something that people actually bring about. It addresses also the problem of how technological change can be represented to us as a force with its own internal dynamic. Conceptual procedures preserving the presence of actual subjects as active in social relations and organization is our first and elementary rule of sociological inquiry.

Working on the relation between concepts and what people do as a point of critical tension commits the sociologist further than may be expected. Much sociological practice and many methodological recommendations tend to preserve theory permanently in a theoretical status. Since Emile Durkheim's *Rules of sociological method*, the phenomenal universe of sociology has detached itself from the naïveté of a subject's direct encounter with the actualities of the everyday/everynight world.[34] The sociological encounter with the world must be conceptually mediated. According to the extreme view, the theoretical model need have no relation to actuality other than predicting events (whether these are "naturally" occurring or contrived by the sociologist experimentally). More general is the practice of constructing observables, in the form of variables, into various kinds of formal relations, such as relations between dependent and independent variables; relations of causality, interaction, feedback, and so on; or the kinds of relations constituted in factor or cluster analyses. The ontological status of the variables is indeterminate; there is certainly no stipulation that formal relations among them should reflect the way in which they were generated.

The alternative view represented here is that sociologists ought to make *existence claims* for their theories.[35] Theories that make exis-

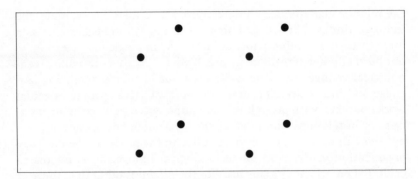

Figure 2.2   The set of observables

tence claims must be appraised as to their representational adequacy. A relation of adequacy is one in which the structure of the object of study determines the structure of the theory. Such a relation may be finally impossible in the natural sciences, though it is crucial to their practice. But in the social sciences theory and actuality have possibilities of inner coherence that natural scientific theories do not have. The organization and relations that are expressed theoretically order the actual activities of individuals. The inner connection between social relation and concept that Marx posited works both ways: if concepts express social relations, social relations may also be systematically expressed conceptually, and a ground for theory as an explication of actual relations is provided. The social scientist must work with the constraint of actuality and is not privileged to draw relations between observables arbitrarily. A theoretical account is not fixed at the outset, but evolves in the course of inquiry dialectically as the social scientist seeks to explicate the properties of organization discovered in the way people order their activities. Hence the structure of a theoretical account is constrained by the relations generated in people's practical activities.

To begin with the theoretical formulations of the discipline and to construe the actualities of people's activities as expressions of the already given is to generate ideology, not knowledge. Here is a visual metaphor. Imagine a set of observables arranged in a space as in figure 2.2. Their relations in that space are fixed. The sociologist may draw connections between them by any arbitrary rule or guesswork. Suppose them to be variables—say, "democracy," "education," and "working-class authoritarianism"; or "conformity," "rank," "influ-

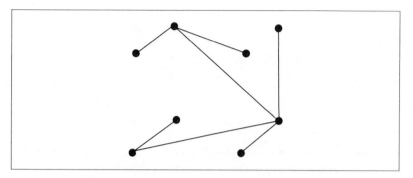

Figure 2.3   Making mystical connections

ence," and "observability." Suppose them to be anything you please, provided that it is an observable (it does not have to be constituted as a variable). The relations may be drawn any which way, as in figure 2.3.

Many alternatives are possible, and a number of these alternative "mystical connections" will in fact yield relations predicting to observables. This is because, as Marx and Engels said, "by virtue of their empirical base these ideas are really connected with one another."[36] Thus the theories may work, in the sense of predicting to the real world, precisely because beyond the text there is an actual co-ordering of activities that is reflected in them. But there is no formal restriction on how relations may be drawn, nor even necessarily on the (causal) direction among them. Terence Hopkins, for example, formulates a number of theories that relate two variables, centrality and rank, in small groups.[37] In one such theory the relation is mediated by three further variables: observability, conformity, and influence. Though the general order of the five variables is preserved, the relations between them can be drawn in a number of different ways. There is no intrinsic reason why they should be drawn in one way rather than another since the relations are purely formal (though in fact Hopkins preserves a causal direction from centrality to rank that restricts the alternatives). The possibility of writing mystical connections along these lines once the concept has been separated from its ground is greatly enhanced by the use of computers; this way, as Zetterberg points out, "chain patterns of great complexity can be simulated."[38]

Suppose, however, we insist only on connections that represent

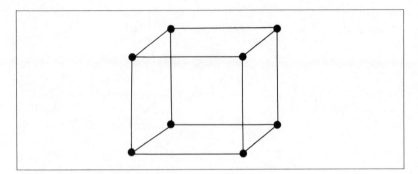

Figure 2.4   The box conceived

how those observables are "really connected with one another" and can specify the social organization determining that arrangement. Then at once many of the options are closed. Each observable takes its place as an essential feature of a total structure (fig. 2.4). The partially visible box, the box conceived, accounts for the sociological observables because it explicates an actual social organization underlying their sociological expression. Grasping the underlying organization makes sense of the arrangement of dots representing Hopkins's sociological observables. And note that our box here represents a real box and not the theoretician's magic black box (which normally conceals the problem of how things really work). It is drawn in perspective, in a definite relation to the observer; therefore it accounts for how the observables appear to us. From another position, it would appear differently.

Of course, these drawings are merely means of visualizing the point. They bear no formal weight in themselves. They illustrate how it is possible for formal theoretical models to be validated predictively even when the model is not constrained by "how things actually work." When existence claims are not made for the theoretical model, the relations that may be found to hold between observables are indefinitely open, as is the relation between the model itself and the reality it purports to reflect. This ideological practice—the drawing of mystical connections—precludes the development of a body of knowledge resulting from the explication and theorizing of the actual relations coordinating the particular sites of people's lives. The problem of how people can come to an agreement upon the representational adequacy of a theory remains, and it cannot be resolved in anticipation of the attempt. In the current practice of sociology the making of mystical connections is so prevalent that we take it for granted. Making mystical connections confines us to this side of the observables, that is, to the side where they exist as appearances—or rather, to where observables are constituted as appearances by methodological procedures restricting the sociologist to the conceptual level and cutting off their grounding in actual social relations. The procedures do not permit (let alone require) that we account for how they appear at all.

◖ A "New" Materialist Analysis

of Social Consciousness

Marx, of course, hasn't provided an insider's method. He operates with a dual ontology: what is outside the head—what the head thinks about, analyzes, and transforms into headstuff—exists as people's actual activities; the practices of thinking are addressed at the level of meaning, not of activities in time and place. The standpoint of women, as I've worked from it, insists that as thinking heads—as social scientists—we are always inside what we think about; we know it in the first place as insiders. So here we go beyond Marx, extending his materialist method to an exploration of "social consciousness." For knowledge itself is made problematic when we insist that there are knowers "doing knowing" and that we can explore, make explicit, *know*, the socially organized practices in and through which we accomplish knowledge.

Implicit in Marx's treatment of ideology and knowledge is the possibility of extending his materialism of actual individuals and their ongoing activities to thought and knowledge itself. Ideology, as Marx defines it, separates thought from the actualities of society and history and thus "makes language into an independent realm."[39] Although Marx views consciousness as inseparable from actual individuals, although he analyzes ideology as practices, and although he gives social consciousness a preliminary materialist formulation, he stops short at the investigation of the social relations and organization of consciousness. But we need not. Social forms of consciousness exist only in actual practices and in the concerting of those practices as an ongoing process. If consciousness appears as distinct from and determining social action and relations, that appearance is a product of the activity of real individuals and their material conditions. Marx's epistemology grounds the concepts and categories in and through which the nature of capitalism is disclosed in that historical mode of production itself. In capitalism, a system of economic relations emerges as a differentiated and objectified form. Capitalism itself creates the conditions of political economic analysis.[40] The independent system of relations mediated by money and commodities underlies the category of the "economy" as relations that can be seen apart from other dimensions of social existence. Analogously, the objectified and organizational forms that externalize consciousness create possibilities for inquiry that did not exist for Marx.

The practice of objectification in the social sciences is a property of an objectified discursive organization. As professionals, we know how to practice and preserve the rupture between the actual, local, historically situated experience of subjects and a systematically developed consciousness of society. If we are to claim full and proper membership in our discipline, we must be competent performers of this severance. Pursuing an Archimedian point enabling us to stand, in a textually grounded order, outside the world we inhabit as bodily and actual beings, we are constrained to divorce ourselves from the paramount reality of our experience. We deploy special methods of collecting accounts of actualities as data that substitute for the world as it is experienced. Data become stand-ins at the level of social scientific discourse for the actualities of people's lives. The procedures we use to understand and explain that body of data are at odds with those with which we interpret the everyday/everynight world in which we act, live, and know.

The conceptual structure of the social sciences is given primacy; it is externalized as that which is to be discovered in the process of passing beyond particular events. The immediate and concrete features of experience become a resource for the expression of the conceptual version; the particularities fall away and only what can be grasped and interpreted divested of its material basis remains. Take, for example, a passage such as this from the work of a social scientist (not, as it happens, a sociologist, but the procedure is the same, and I tried to play fair by reaching out at random for the nearest book):

"Structure can be defined as the design of organization through which the enterprise is administered. This design, whether formally or informally defined, has two aspects. It includes, first, the lines of authority and communication."[41]

In this passage, the term "structure" identifies a conceptual order. It is the "design of the organization." What might be actually observed as what people do in an organization is treated as mere appearance; the conceptual reality is to be discerned through that appearance. As social scientists we ordinarily begin with and return to the conceptual structure. We do not return to or give primacy to the actual, living individuals in their concrete situations of action from which we would, as social scientists, seek a hasty escape, moving perhaps from a set of particular events to find in them a schema that will interpret them and, in interpreting, forget about the original particulars. I myself have passed up and down what I could as a social scientist interpret as "chains of command," sitting in my office at the telephone and making a series of telephone calls to various members of the university administration. In giving an account of what I had done, it would not occur to me to describe the actual concrete activities as what I had done and it seems even in this context almost ridiculous to refer to them. I "naturally" move instead directly to the description in terms of chains of command or the like, that is, I move directly into the conceptual mode. This is a distinctive mode of action, a distinctive practice, and its ideological properties are fundamental and not merely added to it as a rationalization or justification. It is important to recognize how sociology is rendered ideological by taking that mode of constituting social reality for granted.

Sociologists have believed, perhaps because they have wanted or hoped to, that they were doing science, that the procedures they used in returning the concept to the actual world of living individuals were referential. That is, they took it that such concepts of their discipline as power, legitimacy, authority, elite, social class, and so forth, referred to phenomena that were discoverable in the world of actual events and living people. But even lacking the formal positivist commitment, sociologists have sought to use the actualities of people's lives as they know them to embody the conceptual order of social scientific discourse. The actualities of living people become a resource to be made over into the image of the concept. The work becomes that of transposing the paramount reality into the conceptual currency in which it is governed. Sociological procedures legislate a reality rather than discover one.

The conditions of our existence are constantly changing. Events enter our immediate experience. If someone intended them, their intention is present only in the event. We cannot track back through them to an author. Buildings are torn down, factories close and open, bombs are dropped, villages are razed, high-rise apartments go up. There was nothing in the scope of the experience of the people of New Guinea that could enable them to comprehend the airplanes, the air strips, the ships, and the astonishing people that arrived during World War II. For most of us also there is nothing in our experience that will do that either. We do not have to invent a cargo cult because we live it.[42] This break between an experienced world and its social determinations beyond experience is a distinctive property of our kind of society. Norman Geras has formulated this as a necessary movement on the part of the social scientist from the experienced to a reality beyond or behind or against them: "It is because there exists, at the interior of capitalist society, a kind of internal rupture between the social relations which obtain and the manner in which they are experienced, that the scientist of society is confronted with the necessity of constructing reality against appearances."[43] Our strategy recognizes the same break, but the movement of inquiry does not pose an opposition between appearance and reality, with experience depreciated as an illusion penetrated by the social scientist, master of reality. Rather, the knower's experience of the world is taken as an ineluctable ground of any knowledge of society we may have; inquiry explores reaches beyond that experience that are already present in it but are inexplicable by remaining within the boundaries of experiencing.

The texts of the relations of ruling—newspapers; television; census and economic reports; policy documents; the reports of commissions, task forces, ad hoc committees, and so forth—bring a virtual reality into the presence of the sociological reader. The social facts with which we work are constituted prior to our examination by processes of which we know little. They are constituted already in a mode that separates them from the actualities and subjective presences of individuals. The ordinary forms in which the features of our society become observable to us as *its features*—rates of unemployment and of illiteracy, birth rates, family violence, leisure, stress, motivation, and so on—these are already constructed, some as administrative products, others by our sociological predecessors. They are the coinage of our discipline. Our primary world as professionals is thus already made up. Much conceptual work is a secondary ideological efflorescence. Consider, for example, the following: "There are two kinds of domestic violence for which we would like to estimate future rates and thus two kinds of problems that make such estimates very difficult, if not impossible. The first kind is individual violence—murders, suicides, assaults, child-beatings—and the second is collective violence—riots, civil insurrections, internal wars, and the like."[44]

In this context sociological work appears to be almost parasitic upon the primary administrative work that constitutes murders, suicides, and so forth. Living individuals in their actual contexts of action have already been obliterated before their representation reaches the sociologist. Feminism makes us particularly attentive to the mode in which "domestic violence" is presented. The above passage identifies no agents; the presence of women and men and children as subjects in these relations of violence are suppressed; the presence of the oppressed, in riots, civil insurrections, and so forth, are obliterated. The other side, the representatives of the state, do not do violence; police, national guard, military—their forms of physical coercion are not identified. The mode is objectified. Who acts and how disappears. We cannot see what is going on.

The procedures by which this is done are definite social practices that must be understood and explained if sociologists are to be returned to the actualities of the world they claim to know. Marx has, as I've pointed out, set an example of the procedure in his analysis of the constitution of commodities at the beginning of his work on *Capital*. If, then, it appears that there is an objective mode in which events or actions can be represented as having happened without an author—if acts appear to stand independently of their subjects and of those who constituted them as such—then this itself must have been somehow done and must be a topic for examination. Just as the appearance of commodity as a "thing" independent of actual people must be accounted for, so the appearance of acts and events without doers and of facts and information without knowers must be accounted for. For these must also be the products of the practical activities of actual individuals.

We are right here, then, at this stable point in our everyday working world, at the sink washing dishes and trying to think about the next day's lecture, at the computer in an office, reading the newspaper in the coffee shop, struggling in the library to get the census data to make a kind of sense it isn't made to make; from right here, our knowledge of the world beyond can be seen as mediated to us in a variety of ways, most of them on paper. Here, then, we have a difficulty that Marx did not—or rather that did not yet appear to him as a difficulty. Marx takes his knowledge of his world for granted. Although he collects a great deal of information from a variety of sources, including government statistics and so on, the status of the information and facts that he accumulates gives him no difficulty. Perhaps here is something that he, like Aristotle, was blind to because his world was put together in ways that conceal from him the effects of his dependence on the virtual realities of his documentary materials. At all events, the standpoint of women enables us to question the social relations constitutive of an objective knowledge of society. The textual mediations of our knowledge of society do give us difficulty. The observables vested in texts that bring the society into the everyday/everynight worlds of our direct experience are a product of the complex organization of the media, of formal administrative process, of the "scientific" media of research methodologies, professional journals, and the like. Bearing the relations in which they originate and in which they are embedded, they bring into being a universe of facts, images, data, findings, models, and so forth, standing in for and treated as a reality. There is an organized practical work that makes possible the structure of statements such as "Moscow does this," "Beijing does that," "Washington does the other." These statements refer back to and depend upon a particular institutional structure of government, an unexplicated substructure that is a condition to the making, and making sense of, such statements. That substructure includes, however, at the point at which the statement is made, how the governmental process is mediated to the speaker and hearer through the organization of the media.

Marx's method of working with the categories of political economy presupposed a direct relationship between category or concept and the relations expressed. But in this kind of society, this relationship is complicated in that much of what we recognize as that which we know, much that is classifiable as what here has been called an *observable,* is already worked up and produced in a process mediating its relation to what people have done in the place where the process begins. Concepts and categories reflect social relations mediated and organized by concepts and categories. That mediating process itself is a course of practical activity. It begins with conceptually governed practices of finding, selecting from, and ordering original events or states of affairs that are already independently structured in their actuality. It includes the making of an account and then making that account public (by publishing it or presenting it at a symposium, for instance). Thus the universe on paper that social scientists encounter and rely on is *already ideologically structured.*

The study of ideology goes beyond anything that Marx foresaw because the character of ideological practice has been transformed. It is more now than a reflection of reality. It is itself a form of reality—a form of concrete action produced by living individuals. It is in this context that knowing what has been done and how it was done becomes a problem, and *how we know it* becomes a major research topic. Marx's insistence on returning to what people do, on seeing how social forms are produced by actual living individuals, directs us not to a theoretical but to an empirical examination of the social production of ideology.[45] Marx's work suggests that analysis of the ideological properties and uses of social scientific theory and method could be more than critical. Indeed, it must be. The relation he holds between concept and what people actually do makes possible a reversal of the ideological procedure. Concept becomes a means of rediscovering the practical activities behind or underlying their textual representation. "Actually, when we conceive things thus, as they really are and happen, any profound philosophical problem is resolved quite simply into an empirical fact."[46]

Marx's critical procedure is intended to remedy the ideological properties of theory and observable. It addresses the problem as it was and as it was possible to think it in his time. In our kind of society ideological practice is not remediable by a critique alone. Examination of the relation between the ideological uses of the forms of thought and the actualities of living individuals is subject to that very rule that Marx recommends, namely, to think of this relation not merely in the conceptual or theoretical mode but as an enterprise in discovering how it is mediated in people's practical activities, hence as an explication of our everyday experience. A shift in the direction of attention is not enough to disclose the lineaments in actuality of the "profound philosophical problem" and resolve it. The critique is rather a problem for investigation and discovery, a sociological work in itself. Inquiry and investigation explore and make explicit and visible what we know only as insiders in and through our practices of knowing. Inquiry here addresses our own practices as knowers. We know them tacitly and in practice; by making them objects of investigation, they are brought into view reflexively as a knowledge not just of the world but of ourselves, of our own doings in it.

CHAPTER

3

THE
SOCIAL
ORGANIZATION
OF
TEXTUAL
REALITY

◖ Objectified Knowledge
as a Social Practice

The standpoint of women, which locates us in the particularities of our experience, is profoundly contradictory to objectified forms of knowledge. This has indeed been a theme of feminist theorizing of the differences in women's and men's experience of intellectual life. As we saw in the previous chapter, established ideological practices separate the locally known and experienced from the objectified versions of society that have been the holy grail of established sociology. What Marx's new materialism offers feminism is a method of exploring everyday social relations without constructing an alienated world of abstractions. The standpoint of women allows us to explore as insiders the social relations in which we play a part, including the social relations of objectified knowledge.

Objectified forms of knowledge, integral to the organization of ruling, claim authority as socially accomplished effects or products, independent of their making. Because they are in fact forms of social organization, though, we can explore them as matters within our reach, as aspects of our ordinary competence, as social relations in which we participate, though they do not begin and end with our participation.

Our knowledge of contemporary society is to a large extent mediated to us by texts of various kinds.[1] The result, an objectified world-in-common vested in texts, coordinates the acts, decisions, policies, and plans of actual subjects as the acts, decisions, policies and plans of large-scale organizations. The primary mode of action and decision in the superstructures of business, government, the professions, and the scientific, professional, literary, and artistic discourses is utterance—verbal and, more importantly, textual. The realities to which action and decision are oriented are *virtual* realities vested in texts and accomplished in distinctive practices of reading and writing. We create these virtual realities through objectifying discourse; they are our own doing. Employing them, we separate what we know directly as individuals from what we come to know as trained readers of texts.

The traditional sociology of knowledge has focused on the social determinations of knowledge. It asks, How does social situation or class membership render a knower's perspective partial or interested? Knowledge must somehow transcend the local, historical settings to which the knower is necessarily bound if it is to be "pure." Knowledge itself thus escapes the sociologist of knowledge, whose concern is only the impediments to knowledge created by the social detritus that the knower drags into the relation between knower and known. It is a kind of intellectual housecleaning operation, putting in right order the settings in which the real business is to be done. Knowledge isn't the business of sociology once the housecleaning is done or at least the source of the dirt has been pointed out.

By contrast, the problem concerning us here shifts the emphasis from the situated imperfections of the knower to the status of knowledge as socially and materially organized, as produced by individuals in actual settings, and as organized by and organizing definite social relations. The social organization and accomplishment of the knowledge itself is the focus of inquiry. How can there be "knowledge" that exists independently of knowers? What are the socially organized practices of knowers who in concerted ways obliterate their presence as subjects from the objectified knowing we call *knowledge?* How does a knower, embodied and situated in a local and particular world, participate in creating a knowledge transcending particular knowers and particular places? These are the issues we raise of objectified knowledge from the standpoint of women. To investigate these and related issues is to inquire into the *social organization of knowledge,* rather than its sociology.

Knowledge can be investigated as the ongoing coordinated practices of actual people. This means addressing ideas, concepts, beliefs, and so forth as expressions of actual social practices, as things that are spoken, written, heard, or read in definite local historical contexts.[2] Also important is the physicality of the text, the words or other symbols on paper, on film, on the computer monitor. The material possibilities created by the mechanical reproduction of meaning are integral to the objectified forms of knowledge constituent to the contemporary organization of ruling.[3]

Objectified forms of knowledge structure the relation between knower and known. The knower's relation to the object known is structured by the social organization accomplishing it as knowledge. In contemporary societies this structuring goes deep. The production of knowledge is often a complex organizational and technical process that gives the knowledge produced its distinctive shape. That social and technical organization is not apparent in the final product. Thus, a textually mediated reality incorporates the social organization of its production and the courses of action separating it from people's lived actualities. Furthermore, its character as knowledge involves the knower's own constitutive practices of reading and interpretation. Objectivity is accomplished through her practical knowledge of its social organization.

In the textual mode, a knower's only access to the object of knowledge is through its textual presence. The shaping of that presence by the social organization of its production is hidden but effective; the knower is related to the object of her knowledge through it. Exploring knowledge as socially organized makes this mediated relationship of knower to known accessible to inquiry.

Let me clarify the difference between knowing arising from a subject's direct experience and a factual account as a constituent of externalized and objectified relations by contrasting two contending accounts of a single event, a confrontation between police and street people, that took place in Berkeley, California, in 1968.[4] One version appeared as a letter in an underground newspaper, the second was a response to that letter proceeding from the office of the mayor and incorporating a report from the chief of police. The versions are of course widely different in moral and political character. They also differ in how the original event is represented as known. This is the difference I am focusing on here.

The letter in the underground newspaper is written from the standpoint of an actual experience. A man who was on the margins of the events tells his story as he saw it. He accuses the police of attempting to provoke the people on the street in order to justify harassing and arresting them, describing what he saw as a brutal and arbitrary use of police force. The teller of the tale gives information about where he was and what he saw and heard from where he was standing on the street. He describes at one point moving from one corner of the street to another. His description of the incident is spatially and temporally bounded by this observational structure and by the action that took place within its scope. What he tells is restricted by what he has seen and heard from where he saw and heard it. It is not connected to previous events or to later ones. His version enters textual time when it is published in the newspaper but does not itself depend upon a textual reality constituted independently of it.

The official version from the mayor's office is in this respect markedly different. The standpoint is organizational; it is based upon an inquiry conducted by the chief of police with unnamed police officers and reported to the major. That organizational standpoint is more than a historical feature establishing the proper connection between the mayor and the original events that entitle him to write authoritatively about them; it is built into how the account is put together. The account is specifically detached from particular subjectivities, in part by being presented as the product of an official inquiry, but in part by grounding itself in the observations of police officers in their official capacity and by their anonymity as specific subjects. It treats police officers as interchangeable; it does not establish which individual saw or was active in what or attempt to preserve the continuity of the person with respect to how that person's knowledge of events came to be.

The continuity that the official account creates is an administrative continuity of reports and records. It displays moreover an internal temporal structure quite different from that of the witness speaking from the local historical site of his experience. Events described in the letter are articulated in the mayor's version to an "administrative" knowledge that locates those events in sequences of organizational action extending before and after them. In the letter, the witness sees a young man being roughly searched by the police and then sent on up the street. In the mayor's version, this young man is a juvenile known to the police who is later charged with being a minor in possession of alcoholic beverages. Such an account relies essentially on organizational procedures. A complex division of labor among police, court, and probation officers provides for the possibility of a description that makes reference in this way beyond the immediate event to a future in which the young man has been charged and found guilty. The description is also necessarily subtended by the organizational maintenance of files and records enabling the coordination of different stages and moments in the course of action here so summarily described. The knowledge that is taken for granted in this version is produced by precisely those processes upon which we are focusing here. Prior to the official version of events, prior to the inquiry upon which it is based, is an administratively constituted knowledge incorporated into records, files, and other forms of systematic collection of "information." Between the two accounts, there is little disagreement on the particulars of the story. But the official version reconstructs the witnessed events as moments in extended sequences of institutional action, locating them in textual time, dependent on textual realities already institutionally accomplished. What the witness saw and thought was going on is shown to be only a partial and imperfect knowledge of proper police procedure.

The modes of knowing revealed in this analysis of a bureaucratically controlled text are situated in the extralocal relations and apparatuses of ruling. In these relations the power of men over women is united with that of dominant classes over the mass of people. The objectified forms, the rational procedures, and the abstracted conceptual organization create an appearance of neutrality and impersonality that conceals class, gender, and racial subtexts. Institutionally differentiated spheres of bureaucratic, managerial, and professional control manage the local situations that people experience as a totality. Housing comes under one jurisdiction; public health another; mental illness yet another. Issues of wages and working conditions are incorporated into elaborated structures in which class struggle is displaced onto struggles within legal and bureaucratic processes. The domestic situation of women is parceled out into issues of housing, mental illness, child neglect, poverty, welfare, and family violence. The actualities of class, gender, and race are dispersed over a range of sites within the institutions of ruling. Though not every instance conceals specific gender and class issues, investigating the actual social organization of knowledge brings the social relations organizing power into the light. If we don't examine and explicate the boundaries set by the textual realities of the relations of ruling, their invisible determinations will continue to confine us.

◘   Knowing and Knowledge:

The Subject in the Objective

Knowing, of course, is always a "subjective" activity, that is, an activity of a particular subject. But *knowing* in this sense cannot be equated with perception or cognition; it always involves a social dimension, the coordination of activities among knowers vis à vis an object that is known in common. Moving from *knowing* to *knowledge* calls for attention to the disappearing subject. Knowing is still an act; knowledge discards the presence of the knowing subject. We are to look therefore for the actual socially organized practices and relations expressed in that concept of knowledge. In particular we will be concerned with the practices accomplishing the disappearance of subjects and hence, as we shall discover, with the properties of objectified knowledge that accomplish its distinctive and overriding power.

Knowledge as a specialized form of social organization appears to be independent of the presence and activities of subjects. It is in this sense externalized. Bruno Latour and Steve Woolgar described the attainment of factual status by a scientific finding as the progressive "forgetting" of the originating researchers and research.[6] As the findings of a piece of research become taken for granted, they are finally incorporated into the texts of the discourse without reference to their source. Factual conventions of writing present the statement without the modifier that locates it in a particular subjectivity; to qualify a statement with the modifier "I know" is to deprive it of factual status. Achieving facticity obliterates the historical and specific source; the work, the local setting, and the authorship of particular scientists are forgotten. Within the text, the reader finds what is presented thus as a given.

Yet knowledge exists only in the activities and participation of subjects as knowers. The contradiction between knowledge as independent of particular knowers and knowledge as arising in the activities of particular subjects is addressed here as an effect of social organization. We begin with the premise that a woman as knower is always a particular individual embodied and active in the local historicity of her everyday/everynight world. The externalization of a knowledge in which she participates and becomes a knower is the accomplishment of social organization in which she is active. Alfred

Schutz has described the personal disciplines of the scientific theorist who, in entering the domain of scientific theory, suspends interest in his personal life, his biography, and his pragmatic relevances.[7] Though Schutz writes an insider's ethnography of the practices of consciousness implicated in the domain, it is limited by its exclusive focus on the subjectivity of the knower. From the standpoint of women we can see that his mode of consciousness is sustained on the one hand by the conditions under which he is able to forget about his local and personal existence: he has a wife who does the work enabling that forgetting. On the other hand, we can also see the social relations of scientific discourse within which such practices of consciousness are active, including the distinctive methods of writing and reading scientific texts, the way subject-object relations are structured in such texts, the role of reading and scientific talk in scientific research,[8] and so forth. The theorist's practices of consciousness that involve suspending interest in personal matters, local pragmatic concerns, and the like, aren't merely a matter of self-imposed discipline or decision; participation in the scientific domain presupposes a specific organization of the local sites of his work that frees him to enter a universe of texts in which personal matters and particularities have no place.

Suspending the presence of particular subjects is the accomplishment of organized practices in and of the everyday world. It is not peculiar to the domain of scientific discourse. The objectification of knowledge is a general feature of contemporary relations of ruling. The production of factual accounts in the texts of ruling is organized in a wide variety of ways specialized to the relational contexts of their use. We know them ordinarily as records, statistics, news, data, data bases, files, and so forth. Though some are the product of specialized agencies (the Census Bureau or the Registrar of Births, Deaths, and Marriages, for example), others are integral to the ongoing organization of large-scale institutions of state and business or of the varieties of academic, professional, and cultural discourse. For the most part the production of factual accounts in one form or another is essential to the operation and regulation of such organizations.[9]

Karl Marx's political economy is a critical analysis of relations of interdependence between people that have become differentiated and specialized as the relations of the economy. As described in chapter 2, these relations appear as interchanges between *things*—commodities and money. Though they exist only in the activities of actual people,

people do not appear in them as subjects or agents. The commodity is the point of intersection between the local actualities of people's work, the concrete sites and organization of production, and how the things produced are actually used on the one hand, and the impersonal and abstracted relations of exchange on the other. A commodity is an actual product with a definite use value; it is produced to be exchanged for money. Entering the relations of exchange, it takes on the abstract property of exchange value. Its relationship to its actual makers disappears from its abstract state; its exchange value is expressed in the objective and standardized medium of money. Knowledge externalized in the social relations of ruling is analogous. The "fact" corresponds to the commodity. Facts mediate relations among persons in ways analogous to how Marx saw commodities mediate relations among individuals. We might indeed rewrite parts of his account to do some work for us. He tells us that "a commodity is a mysterious thing, simply because in it the social character of men's labor appears to them as an objective character stamped upon the product of that labor."[10] Rewrite that passage, substituting "fact" for "commodity" and making other appropriate changes, and we get: "a fact is . . . a mysterious thing, simply because in it the social character of men's consciousness appears to them as an objective character stamped upon the product of that consciousness."

People's actual work is objectified in the commodity. Relations between people are mediated by (and appear as) relations between commodities and money. Similarly, relations between individual knowers appear as facts and are mediated by relations between facts. Subjects are necessarily implicated in the accomplishment of facts, but disappear in their product. Through the fact we are related to that other or those others whose observation, investigation, or other experience was its source. But that does not appear. Through the fact *they* are related to *us*. But that does not appear. Through the fact we are related also to other knowers who have known it and who may know it, since in the social organization of fact we enter a relation of knowing in which it does not matter who we are or where we stand, for we constitute it as known the same. Fact exists both at the level of statements and also as events or states of affairs "in the world" that such statements refer to. Like the commodity, their essential character lies in this dual mode of being.

Facts as a distinctive social practice may well be characteristic of the forms of knowledge, vested in texts, that have become general since the invention of printing.[11] The socially organized practices of fact and the relations in which they are embedded go beyond the intersubjective world known tacitly among those sharing a here and now. Rather, subjective experience is opposed to the objectively known. The two are separated from each other by the social act that creates an externalized object of knowledge—the fact. This social organization of knowledge depends upon but transcends the primary intersubjective participation in and constitution of a world known in common. Relations among knowers are organized in determinate ways. Facts mediate relations not only between knower and known but among knowers and the object known in common. Notice, next time you see that movie of wolves hunting caribou, how they attend to one another through the medium of their object. Each is oriented to that caribou and through that to each other. Thus they coordinate the hunt. A fact is such an object; it is the caribou that coordinates the activities of members of a discourse, a bureaucracy, a management, a profession. A fact is construed to be external to the particular subjectivities of the knowers. It is the same for anyone, external to anyone, and, unlike the real caribou and the real wolves, is fixed, devoid of perspective, in the same relation to anyone. It coordinates the activities of anyone who is positioned to read and has mastered the interpretive procedures it intends and relies on.

The textual externalization of the object creates a complementary organization of knowers. A factual organization aims not precisely at a plurality but at an open-ended more-than-one. Although a fact may be restricted in its circulation to a specific group or status,[12] it is the same on each occasion of its telling or reading, no matter who hears or reads it—which is, of course, the grounds for restricting in some cases who it may reach. This "sameness" is of course a product of a social organization in which knowers may treat their knowledge as that which is or could be known by anyone else. For example, an account of a young woman, K, shows how, one by one, K's friends and others connected with her come to "recognize" that she is mentally ill. The account of K's "symptoms" draws the reader into the relations in which K's mental illness is established as a fact independent of any particular subjectivity.[13] Similarly, the facticity of the mayor's account of the encounter between street people and police described above is sustained by detaching the account from the subjectivity of particular individuals.

Factual organization implicates the knower in an act that reaches through the object to a knower "on the other side" for whom that object is identical. It thus sets up relations of equivalence among knowers, making them formally interchangeable. This is the "power" of facticity, of the objectification of knowledge as a social-textual accomplishment.

Michel Foucault's concept of "power/knowledge"[14] is an ideological practice in the terms identified in the previous chapter. The concept is ascribed agency in the absence of reference to how actual individuals are active in the underlying social relations that make sense of it. Both "power" and "knowledge" are mystified; they capture a sense of something significant about contemporary society that they are incapable of explicating. Power has no ontology, no form of existence.

Here power is understood as arising as people's actual activities are coordinated to give the multiplied effects of cooperation. The power of objectified knowledge arises in the distinctive organization it imparts to social relations. Knowing how to read, and reading, a given factual text is to enter a coordinated set of relations subordinating individual consciousness to its objectification; subjects subdue their particularized experience to the superordinate virtual reality of the text. The factual text has power at this point of conjuncture between a reader knowing how to read it as factual and the relations of which it is a constituent. This form of power is not necessarily integrated with relations of ruling; during the Enlightenment it was a weapon against authority and oppression. Its authority, however, may be integrated fully with the relations of ruling, as we shall see in the following chapter. Its capacity to coordinate consciousnesses and to displace individuated experience arises, of course, as people participate actively in the socially organized practices accomplishing an objectified knowledge.

Textual Reality

The social organization of facticity is not discoverable at the level of statements. Propositions stating that something or other is the case are not of themselves factual. The social organization of facticity is a distinctive social form binding actualities and statements about those actualities. Facticity in this view is an organization of practices accomplishing as a virtual reality "what is" or "what actually happened" or some other statement of what is the case. Facts are neither the statements themselves, nor the actualities those statements refer to.[15] They are an organization of practices of inscribing an actuality into a text, of reading, hearing, or talking about what is there, what actually happened, and so forth. They are, as E. H. Carr has emphasized in his discussion of the facts of history,[16] properties of a discourse or other organization mediated by texts. They are its virtual realities, the givens-in-the-text that participants know how to read as present in the same way for them as for any other member of the discourse. They are established, as Bruno Latour and Steve Woolgar have described, in practices of securing a stable relationship between a given event or state of affairs and statements that can be made about it, such that any such statements can be treated as stand-ins for the event or state of affairs. In scientific contexts, the facticity of statements is guaranteed by generally highly technical procedures that can reliably and precisely produce the state of affairs or events expressed in factual statements. The facticity of statements thus arises from their embedding in distinctive socially organized processes.

As with the commodity, facts and factual accounts have a distinctive social organization. As a preliminary simplification, this can be analyzed as made up of two distinct sequences: the social organization of the production of the account and the social organization of its reading and interpretation (see figure 3.1).

Lived Actuality

We begin in and with the lived actuality, before the moment when the organization introduced by the social organization of the production of the account takes up its work. Boxing in "lived actuality" as in figure 3.1 is, of course, an ontological and epistemological error, for indeed "living" encompasses the totality of the processes the diagram describes. Here the box enclosing "lived actuality" marks the point of entry into the textual, the point of transition of the subject from engagement in "living" to reflecting on the lived from the standpoint of the text. The box identifies the lived moment that becomes an event or state of affairs as it is worked up into a factual account. There is no event, no "what actually happened," prior to the moment that the observer enters with an interest in making a record, a report, a story. Between lived actuality and the factual account are

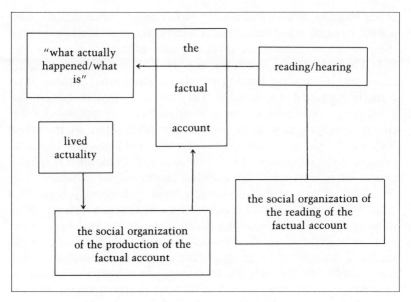

Figure 3.1   The social organization of textual reality

the socially organized practices producing the account. At some point, after various drafts, the account is fixed in textual time and enters the social organization of its reading as factual.

Factual Methods of Reading

A factual method of reading reads *through* the account to what is taken to exist "on the other side," in the reality the account intends. This is represented in the diagram as an arrow passing from the social organization of reading, through the factual account, to a "what actually happened/what is" on the other side. "What actually happened/what is" is not, of course, the equivalent of the "lived actuality"; it is rather the virtual reality intended and organized by the text of the factual account.

Warranting the Relation between the Account and Actuality

The social organization producing the account (sometimes relying heavily on advanced technology, as in television news reporting and in the physical sciences) is integral to the facticity of the account as read. It creates the warranted determination between actuality and its representation. Indeed, the problem of whether facts are statements *about* the real world or pieces *of* it is resolved as we examine facticity as social organization.[17] Then we see facticity to reside in an organization setting up a warranted relation between account and actuality through determinate processes of production and reading. Ludwik Fleck's *Genesis and development of a scientific fact* explores the development of the fact "that the so-called Wasserman reaction is related to syphilis" over a period of four centuries.[18] In his account we see the dialectic of changing conceptual structures, research practices, and research findings. Techniques and technologies of research are integral to the accomplishment of this fact. Factual statements have and must have a distinctive history of reporting from the actualities to which they refer; the particular procedures through which this referential function is established are integral to the status of a factual account.

Statements of what actually happened or what is actually the case must be formulated; they must be established as capable of standing independently of the perceptions and perspectives of particular individuals. Procedures differ in different contexts but must be adequate within a given institutional form to warrant the treatment of given statements not merely as true but as factual, entitling the reader to read the account as such. Don Zimmerman's study of facts as practical accomplishment shows how workers in a welfare agency establish the facticity or otherwise of clients' statements by investigating the relation between statements and the "real world," using institutionally approved procedures that will warrant the facticity of their report.[19] The methodical history of the production of the account is essential in warranting its claim to facticity.

The Mediation of the Account by the Social
Organization of Its Production

Claims for the admission of accounts to membership in a textual reality depend upon establishing the proper relations between the original that it claims to represent and the account that has been produced. These relations are methodical, enforced, and specific to the discourse or organization of which the textual reality is or will be a constituent. The moment of inscription, when what is lived is entered into the record as an event or a state of affairs, must be governed in accordance with the relevant conventions and technologies if it is to be admissible. Inscriptive practices may be various kinds of interviewing, investigation, inspection, observation, and so forth. They involve techniques and technologies of keeping records, asking questions, taking notes, measuring, tape recording, filming, and so forth. These are the primary steps in the making of the "what happened/what is."[20] In social scientific and administrative contexts where people are the objects of the inscriptive work, the major techniques are those of eliciting information or data by questions, or by establishing categories or codes for observation and recording. These structure the account in definite ways. Methods of inscription are not treated as features of the textual reality once an account has been admitted. Yet their effects remain. For example, in sociological inquiries we routinely treat only what the respondent says as data. Though the forms of questions are indeed included somewhere in the report, for the purposes of analysis and interpretation the data are not treated as elicited by the questions. The questions become an issue only if a candidate for admission to textual reality is challenged because its inscriptive practices fail to warrant its proper relation to the original.

Entering Textual Time

At some point the account is fully worked up; at some point it drops away the traces of its making (references to evidence, research, researchers, the technical processes involved, and so forth) and stands forth as an autonomous statement representing the actuality of which it speaks. Indeed, at this point, as it enters "textual time," it can generate statements using different terms, provided that the original conceptual structure, temporal and spatial order (chronotopy),[21] and so forth are preserved. Traces of how it came about that may have been in textual form, such as its previous drafts, corrections, alternative wordings, and so forth, which provide for scholars of literature an inexhaustible mine of indeterminacies—all are obliterated.[22] In textual time, the processes of working up the formulation become invisible. The account comes to stand in for the actuality it claims to represent. In the contexts of the social organization of its reading, it becomes a virtual reality. The text is stabilized. It has no apparent history other than that incorporated in it and does not acquire one as a product of the various occasions of its use. Fixed in an official form (for instance, by publication), it is the same on each occasion of its reading. Readers reading the final version are held to be reading the same text. Upon this depend the forms of organizational consciousness typical of contemporary bureaucratic and professional practice.

Reading the Structure of the Account into "What Actually Happened/What Is"

At the point at which textual time is entered, the account has been given a determinate structure. Lived actuality has been worked up as "what actually happened/what is." The completed textual reality, both production and reading, has a circular structure by which the conceptual structure built into the account becomes the reader's interpretation of the actuality it represents. The conceptual structure has operated on a lived actuality to produce "what actually happened/what is," incorporating, for example, a temporal organization that selects from actuality and establishes the temporal boundaries, thus giving "what actually happened/what is" the form of an "event," "episode," "state of affairs," and so forth. An internal temporal structure is accorded in analogous ways. The factual account from the mayor's office described above sets the confrontation between street people and police in sequences of action beyond the moment that is directly witnessed. Those involved may be already known to the police, have been charged and found or pleaded guilty. The temporal structure of such institutional practices and procedures is built into the factual account, but its institutional ground is invisible. At the point at which textual time is entered, the account is detached from its past and stands as if it had a direct and simple relationship to the events it tells.

The procedure of "reading through" the factual account to a "what is" or "what actually happened" means that the structure, syntax, and conceptual organization of the account is read into the "what actually happened/what is" it evokes. Hence concepts organizing the inscriptive procedure are transposed, via the account, into the representation of what is out there beyond it, the "what actually happened/what is" that arises at the moment of reading. The way in which questions are framed, for example, may be a powerful organizer of the version of the world that is built from the responses. In one instance, a sociologist interviewed school children to find out what

---

Hippie = someone who is dirty + doesn't like money + doesn't like work.

Figure 3.2   Images of hippies 1

their images of "deviants" were.[23] She assumed that images were there prior to and independent of her inquiry. Her preliminary work showed that different kinds of questions produced answers with distinctively different structures. She had experimented with questions in alternative forms to find out which one gave "the best results." These were "What would you say a hippie was?" and "Do you know any hippies?"

The first question elicited a simple additive structure represented in figure 3.2. The second question elicited a very different procedure, expressed in figure 3.3 as an algorithm, matching experience against the criteria of "hippieness." While either question could be taken to explore the children's images of hippies, they generated very differently structured responses. The children's responses are the data on which a factual account could be based. In such an account, the "images" would be attributed to the children as theirs. They would be read as an aspect of "what is." Yet, depending on which procedure for questioning was used, the properties of "image" could be quite different.

Such effects both depend on and are complemented by the social organization of reading factual accounts. Methods of reading factually are distinctive. They differ from methods of reading fictional accounts, for example. In reading fiction, readers use methods that do not refer back to an actuality existing independently of the work of fiction; details in the fictional account cannot be checked out, or if they were to be checked out, the implication for the fictional account would be indeterminate; readers don't expect, though they might like, to know what happened to the people in the story after it has ended.[24] By contrast, factual methods of reading "read through" the account to the actuality beyond it; it is always supposed that there is more to be known than the account contains and that the account can (in principle at least) be checked against the actuality to which it refers. This "reading through" the account to the actuality posited as its origin is represented in figure 3.1 by the arrow traveling from the social organization of reading through the account to "what actually happened/what is."

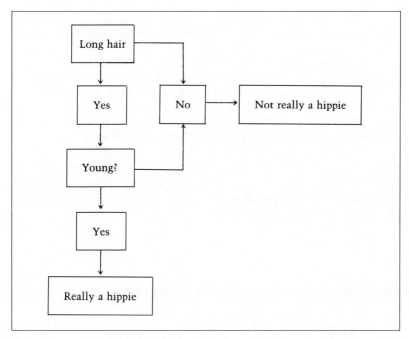

Figure 3.3   Images of hippies 2

An actual account has a "dynamic" relation to "what actually happened/what is"; it is open to elaboration. When an actuality is posited "on the other side" of the account, more and other questions can be asked about it; it is assumed that there is more to be known. Indeed, it is in relation to the working up of factual accounts that actuality is constituted as an inexhaustible and indefinitely open resource for elaboration of detail, modification, and correction. In his reflections on mundane reasoning in the context of traffic court proceedings, Melvin Pollner writes of this property of factual methods of reading:

In court, "what really happened" is typically made available through verbal accounts. Obviously, to describe what really happened requires more than simply stating "This is what really happened." It is necessary to provide the details, the properties, the features of "what really happened" in order to realize or make observable the state of affairs, which is the intended object of analysis. For example, "what really happened" may be realized by reference to a specification of the vehicles, their speed, inferred intentions of the driver and a virtual infinitude of other possible details. The descriptions may be extended indefinitely by a progressive explication of its details and/or by explication of the encompassing context in which it takes place. The event proper may be elaborated by reference to the make of the car, the number of scratches upon it, their size and so on, as well as by an elaboration of the prevailing world situation. Because the scene is available for infinite explication, the specifically noted aspects do not exhaust or fully comprehend the scene of which they are details.[25]

It is, however, a process controlled by the conceptual structure already in place—in this case, determining the defendant's guilt or innocence. Structures such as these determine the relevances selecting and assembling further detail.

◖ The Social Organization

of Facticity

A fact's organization of actuality is not simply the explication of an order already perceived. A fact is constructed in a definite institutional context, and its organization reflects that context. An inner coherence is established between the actuality thus represented and the statements that can be made about it, such that the actuality, produced as "what actually happened/what is," can be seen to require its own descriptive categories and conceptual procedures.[26]

Questions of accuracy about descriptions that have already been made take for granted the organization already built into the descriptions. This is apparent in Pollner's account. Though the description may be extended indefinitely, its extensions are elaborated within the structure of the account—the make of the car, the number of scratches, and so forth—and the account is structured by the relevances of the traffic court. The social organization of reading factual accounts "inserts" categorical, conceptual, and syntactic procedures into the actuality. The interpretive schema established by the account governs the procedures used to select, assemble, and attend to the actuality. It appears not as an imposition upon the latter but rather as a revelation of how it is.

The two phases of the social organization of textual reality "break" at the point at which the account enters textual time. Though the social organization of the account's production incorporates attention to the interpretive methods that will read it (including that it will be read factually), the productive process isn't visible in the account. It appears in textual time as a mere representation of actuality. Hence the moment of entering textual time is that crucial point at which much if not every trace of what has gone into the making of that account is obliterated and what remains is only the text, which aims at being read as "what actually happened/what is." In reading back from the account to the actuality, therefore, the interpretive procedure bypasses the processes producing the account and lodges directly in the actuality thus constituted as "what actually happened/what is." In figure 3.1 the arrow that returns the reader to "what actually happened/what is" passes through the account as if it were transparent. This is a visual metaphor for reading factually. The relation between the account and what it speaks of is treated as unmediated. For example, arriving at a verdict of suicide is a complex organization of legal, medical, and police practice. Yet once it is achieved, the category appears as directly descriptive of the "event" of someone's death. The factual account appears as a mere representation of "what happened/what is" without a trace of the social organization that produced it and that intervenes between it and the original lived actuality.[27]

A textual reality is a product of this total process. It is fully constituted only in the dynamic interrelation of *both* phases. The social organization has something like a grammatical form that is incomplete in the absence of one or the other part. The history of the making of the factual account is also a guarantee of its facticity; the social organization of its production structures "what actually happened/what is" so that it will intend the schemata, concepts, and categories that both describe and interpret it. The proper organization of the relation between statements that can be made on the basis of a textual reality so constituted and the actuality it stands for *is facticity*. Facticity is essentially a property of an institutional order mediated by texts.

Power and knowledge are not linked in some mystical conjunction such as that enunciated by Michel Foucault.[28] What we call "power" is always a mobilization of people's concerted activities. If facticity, if objective knowledge, is a form of power, it arises in the distinctive concerting of people's activities that breaks knowledge from the active experiencing of subjects and from the dialogic of activity or talk that brings before us a known-in-common object. Objectified knowledge stands as a product of an institutional order mediated by texts; what it knows can be known in no other way, as we've seen in the police account of the street confrontation cited above. The knowing of participants is captured in the objectified knowledge mediating ruling. Objectified knowledge, as we engage with it, subdues, discounts, and disqualifies our various interests, perspectives, angles, and experience, and what we might have to say speaking from them.

CHAPTER

4

TEXTUAL REALITIES, RULING, AND THE SUPPRESSION OF DISJUNCTURE

❚

◨ Textual Realities

as Relations of Ruling

Textual realities are the ground of our contemporary consciousness of the world beyond the immediately known. As such they are integral to the coordination of activities among different levels of organization, within organizations, and in the society at large. At the surfaces where social scientists read or where we read or watch news, such realities may appear simply as informative data speaking of the world beyond. This is misleading. Depths and complexities of the social organization of ruling interpose between local actualities and textual surfaces. Still, textual realities are not fictions or falsehoods; they are normal, integral, and indeed essential features of the relations and apparatuses of ruling—state administrative apparatuses, management, professional organizations, the discourses of social science and other academic discourses, the mass media, and so forth. Such methodologies of organization are enforced: the registration of a birth is legally required; a kid in trouble is subject to the law governing juvenile offenders; trade unions have no voice in the frameworks governing how strikes are reported; the lives of the Vietnamese people were in pawn to the production of the textual realities of the U.S. military; the relations between psychiatrist, social worker, and patient are organized by the patient's case history. These relations underlie the textual surfaces that present themselves for social scientists' reading. Such textual surfaces presuppose an organization of power as the concerting of people's activities and the uses of organization to enforce processes producing a version of the world that is peculiarly one-sided, that is known only from within the modes of ruling, and that defines the objects of its power. The subjects entered into these virtual realities are displaced as speakers both at the point of inscription, where lived actualities are entered "into the record," and as the characteristic hierarchies of organization set up a self-sealing division of labor in the making of objectified knowledge.

Factual social organization is foundational to the relations of ruling. Characteristically, whether as "bodies of knowledge" vested in professions or as "corporations" (inserting via the Latin origin of the term a metaphor also of bodies), government "agencies," or "bodies of law," the relations of ruling are organized as supra- or extrapersonal. Corporations and agencies act through their employees; their employees' concerted actions become the acts of the corporation or agency. Objectified bodies of knowledge embedded in discursive organization are *known* by the members of the relevant discourse; through processes of controlled training, those members bear a body of knowledge externalized in texts; they become its knowers. Textual realities are essential constituents of these social relations and their organization, which depend upon objectified forms of knowledge independent of particular subjectivities, appearing in rationally standardized forms invariant as to time, place, and the particular perspectives, interests, and will of participants. Textual realities constitute shared, identical, and perspectiveless objects and environments, locked into decision processes through the schemata, categories, and concepts that organize them.

This chapter examines how the underlying relations of ruling determine the factual surfaces of textual realities. It focuses on the mediation of demographic data by the organized practices of state, medicine, and hospitals; the institution of the case history; the ideological circle generated by the hierarchical structuring of official information; and, finally, the discounting of women as authoritative speakers in public, textually mediated discourse.

◗ The Mediations of Textual Reality

by the Relations of Ruling

Sociological discourse, like other social scientific discourses that provide a systematically developed consciousness of society, characteristically relies on the data generated by the state in the course of its practices of governing. We incorporate this information into the texts of our discourse with a certain brash confidence in the determinacy of its representation of reality; it is *hard* data. In recent years, ethnomethodologists have questioned the capacity of such data to stand in for the actuality they seem to represent. Don Zimmerman and Melvin Pollner in an influential paper propose that data, including the kinds that sociologists themselves create, cannot be treated as if they were independent of people's everyday activities. They propose indeed that in interpreting such data sociologists rely and must rely on their and others' everyday practices as "an unexplicated and invisible resource." Using demography as an example, they write as follows of this relation:

> Though the investigator relies upon the work whereby members, including the investigator, do *sex* and *age,* and *do* recording of such properties, and *do* the demonstration that such recording was done in accord with the ideals governing the procedures of counting and categorizing, the *doings* are specifically severed from the subsequently produced distributions and interpretations of them. For the demographer, as for the members he counts, sexness is not a matter for speculation.[1]

Zimmerman and Pollner, however, posit a direct relationship between the phenomenal order sociology constructs and the actualities it intends. They want to fill in what is missing, namely (for example) that demographic data involving gender presuppose a world of actual everyday practices in which gender differences are ongoingly generated as a feature of social organization. The observables of social science originate in members' practices, and hence the work of the demographers no less than others depends upon a social organization prior to their abstract symbolic work. For Zimmerman and Pollner, there is a *direct* relationship between the demographer's categories and the normative order: "The demographer presupposes the operation of a normative order local to the society in question. The normative order is presupposed by the demographer as an enforceable schema of interpretation and guide to action used by members to present themselves in a particular fashion and to recognize the presentation of others in stable ways."[2]

The normative order is treated as unitary, and it appears that members' practices constitute the phenomenon just as the demographer knows it. Recording, counting, and so on are included among members' practices, but they are not assigned a distinctive constitutive role. Nor is "the operation of a normative order" made problematic.

Zimmerman's and Pollner's observations are from within the sociological discourse; their standpoint is given by the textual realities of demography; they, and we, their readers, are situated by their text at the point of entry to textual time where the social organization of the production of facts is already forgotten, invisible. Their problem begins at the point where the social organization of the production of the demographic text is already done, its categories established. They presuppose and leave unexplicated the massive organization of state data collection; the census bureau; the reporting procedures of various government agencies; the legally enforced registration of births, deaths, and marriages; and the institutions of death certificates, coroners' courts, and the like. To complicate things, sociological discourse itself intersects with the state at the juncture provided by the surface of demographic texts. Demographers (social scientists, often sociologists) have participated as experts in the making of the systems of state data collection. The textual realities structure the same standpoint for state as for even the critical sociologist. Here we attend to the power of this organization to situate reading sociologists in a site that divorces them from the lived actualities of those who were there at the origin of the records.

How it is that the phenomenon, say, of birth can appear as "mere" birth, as a birth simply to be counted. The demographer's stripped version, a "mere birth," is not birth as it is in the experience and practices of the child's mother, father, kinfolk, and friends. The construction of a birth as merely a birth is the product of a specialized organizational practice of reporting. A fact such as "Jessie Frank was born on 9 July 1963" appears maximally unequivocal in this respect. But as we examine how it has been fabricated it becomes apparent that its character as *merely* a record is a product of a further institutional process. Her mother's experience of labor and delivery (was it easy and joyful? hard, long, and painful?), her father's experience of her mother's labor and delivery (was he present and supportive? was he excluded and anxiously waiting? was he there at all?)—these experiences of birth as a lived process are specifically discarded. They are not relevant. The recording agency is concerned only to set up a certified and permanent link between the birth of a particular individual (an actual event), a name, and certain social coordinates essential to locating that individual—the names of her parents, where she was born, and so forth. The official processes of registration that are the business of the registering agency of the state rely on medical and hospital organization. A legal responsibility is imposed on hospital and physician. Birth, for the purposes of legal registration, must be verified in some way, such as by the signature of the physician or of a representative of the hospital in which the child was born.

The form will also be stamped or will carry in some way a mark that establishes a proper connection between this written form and the actual event of birth and its parental coordinates by warranting it as an act of the appropriate agency. It is the first moment in a lifetime's documentation of an individual citizen's identity. This guaranteed relation between written form and actuality makes the certificate of birth dependable as knowledge for other bureaucratic agencies—for example, when the child's age must be established for school purposes, when secondary identification such as a passport is needed, or for various legal purposes. And the same agency that constitutes that birth as merely a birth also counts it for the purposes of compiling government statistics.

That reporting procedure is further mediated by the routine practices of the hospital and of the medical profession. The practice of obstetrics, the organization of delivery and labor rooms, the ward, nursing practice, and so forth, all provide the settings, contingencies, and administrative procedures that are taken for granted and made use of by the official registrar of births. Hospital procedures must provide for and guarantee that *this* baby is the child of *these* parents. The prospective mother is given an identifying label when she enters hospital; the baby is labeled at birth. Even though for the hospital each birth differs, it responds with a standardized record-keeping routine. This is integral to its organization. Thus hospital and medical practices anticipate and provide for the conceptual structure of the birth certificate and the demographer's count; their routine practices also constitute birth as merely birth.

By contrast, we can imagine the living of a birth for a child's mother and father. For them it is a profound physical and emotional experience. As it is lived, it does not yield the stripped-down categories of the demographer. The emotions of the birth itself are tied not simply to the immediate event but also to relationships built up in the past and continuing into the future. For the parents, birth is the beginning of something not fully complete at that moment. Their child's birth is not a unitary event that can be conceptually detached from the full context of their lives. By contrast, the administrative and technical organization of the hospital and of medical practice constitutes a birth as a single episode in a work routine of many such episodes, and thus as merely a birth. Hilary Graham and Ann Oakley describe these differences in knowing a birth as a disagreement about whether "pregnancy should be abstracted from the woman's life-experiences and treated as an isolated medical event."[3] Certifying the birth is a routine of the bureaucratic process in which the isolated medical event is embedded. It is a routine of the hospital's everyday/everynight work, involving physician, nurse, and administrative workers.

Thus the "mere birthness" of the demographer's reading is mediated by a complex organization of power mediated by texts. These mediating relations of ruling place the sociologist in relation to the experienced worlds of those in whose lives the facts originated. Between the sociologist and the lived actualities of the original that the demographic fact stands in for lies a complex of legally enforced practices coordinating the reporting of local events into a state system of information collection. Demographic data are straightforward. The significance of the invisible presence of their prehistory in the ruling relations may not seem consequential for such textual realities; nonetheless, the social scientist must grasp these mediating processes, how they generate properties and structures of data, and how they express the policies and ideologies of government. While demographics have a kind of innocence, the textual realities of labor statistics and the like are integral to state management of a labor force. The latter are entered into what in a later section is analyzed as the circuits of ideological organization.

◖ Cases and

Case Histories

Textual realities create a specific relationship between the reader and "what actually happened/what is." This relationship is organized not merely by choices of language and syntax: properties of the relations of ruling built into the text enter and determine the reader's relation to the realities constituted therein.

A distinctive organization of ruling is entered into a specific textual form, the case history or case record. In organizations concerned with processing people, there are characteristic forms of coordinating work processes focused on the individuals who are their objects. In welfare and psychiatric contexts, *cases* as organizational elements exist as continuous (locally accomplished) relations between individuals and their records. Individuals are known as *cases* under the interpretive aegis of their records. When decisions are to be made, their current status is located in the documentary traces of their past contained in them. The phrase *current status* itself refers to this documentary order.[4] Case records and case histories provide material that is entered into professional and academic discourses, usually in a specific narrative form, as representations of the object of their knowledge.

Case histories and case records evolved as what Bryan Green calls "knowledge devices" when government welfare agencies or charitable organizations were confronted with the numbers and anonymities of the late nineteenth-century city,[5] when the particularized knowledge of people and their histories characterizing smaller communities no longer served. They were part of a larger development of administrative technologies characterizing the latter part of the nineteenth century, which initiated contemporary forms. Case histories and records are typically embedded in and integral to forms of organization where the immediate and day-to-day contact with the people to be processed is at the front line and involves subordinates, whereas decisions about those people are made by persons in designated positions of responsibility who lack such ongoing direct contact.

As professions and professional discourses have been established, case histories and case records have become part of the knowledge basis of the professional discourse, as well as of professional administrative practice. Methodical procedures for writing them are developed, ensuring that records are collected in standardized ways and not as idiosyncrasies of individuals or particular hospitals or clinics. Standardized methods of observation and investigation, categories, interpretative schemata and practices, and the like have evolved in related professional discourses. They are typically structured so that all major items of information appear as predicates of the subject of the report. Here is an example from Aaron Cicourel.[6] This is a probation officer's report:

> Talked to Mr. J. at Jr. Hi. re Audrey—he says Audrey jumped into the fight to pull white girl off Jane Johnson—(negro[sic]) who was beating up the girl's younger sister. Audrey hit the oldest Penn girl a couple of times and then Candy Noland took over and Audrey withdrew. Audrey was suspended the rest of that day. A couple of minor incidents since—yesterday she and some other girls jumped on a laundry truck at school and Audrey didn't obey bus driver on bus. However, Mr. J. reports that Audrey's attitude was good—admitted everything and promised she wouldn't anymore.
> Talked to Audrey at school—lectured her re any fighting or disobedience. Told her if she hadn't done so well up to now she would be in serious trouble. Audrey promised not to get involved in anything and "to walk away" if trouble started around her.[7]

As Cicourel points out, "The P.O.'s remarks . . . constitute the 'facts' of the cases." These facts have been abstracted from the events as they actually happened. Clearly the original events involved a number of other people, some of whom are mentioned by name, but in this report they are organized in relation to Audrey. Thus, "Audrey jumped into the fight. . . . Audrey hit the oldest Penn girl . . . Audrey withdrew. . . . Audrey was suspended. . . . [Audrey] and some other girls jumped . . . Audrey didn't obey bus driver. . . . Audrey's attitude was good. . . . Audrey promised. . . ."

The account reorganizes the original events so that Audrey stands in relief. The events become assigned to her as *her* trouble. It doesn't make any difference who started it, "if you hit her back you're in trouble too."[8] It is *her* record that is being thus compiled. The focus on Audrey is a product of the structuring procedures involved in making a report in the context of probation work.

The collection of specific times that make up Audrey's misconduct, as well as how those items are recognized as a reportable matter, presupposes not only the primary work of members who participated in the events but also the secondary work of school administrators. The break between Audrey's own experience in living the events and the record has already been made. The power relations within which the incidents and the report arise are built into its making; they are indeed necessary to and implicit in its distinctive structure, representing as it does the disciplinary order of school and juvenile justice. That Audrey participated in a fight, that she jumped on a laundry truck, that she failed to obey the bus driver, these become a collection that makes sense only in the context of the school's disciplinary jurisdiction over the settings in which they occurred. What she did or what happened becomes her misconduct only in that context. The reporting procedures are part of the administrative practice of the school. What she did was not reported as *merely* what she did, but as how what she did was a reportable matter. The mediating procedures directly enter into the constitution of the object as it becomes known.

The structuring of the case history in this characteristic form is articulated to an organization of power and position in which some have authority to contribute to the making of the textual realities and others do not. Those who are the objects of case histories are normally distinctively deprived. The psychiatric setting is strikingly exclusive of the patient's voice other than as a symptomatic expression. The division of psychiatric labor ensures that those who have most direct knowledge of the patient's life outside the hospital or of her daily routines in the hospital are least privileged to speak and be heard. The patient herself does not define the terms of her interrogation:

> The psychiatrist started asking me how long I'd felt the way I did, which puzzled me. I felt pretty much as I had all my life. I still don't know why I was there or what I was supposed to say. I didn't feel like telling her how I felt about my father and step-mother; there wasn't much else to tell. Then she said my problems were so deep I'd need some serious therapy. They said, "Well, wouldn't you like to go into the hospital for a rest."[9]

Where the patient is privileged to speak of her experience her statements are treated not as information but as indications of what is wrong with her. She is a resource but not an agent in the making of accounts of her behavior; reports may make use of what she says, but she has no say in their making: "Once I was in hospital, it was useless to ask to get out. They just marked down that I asked to go home and it was a black mark against me. I refused to take their pills and that was a black mark."[10]

A deep disjuncture is created between the lived experience of the objects of psychiatric work and the social organization producing their representation within the order of textual reality. Whatever has been happening to and with that individual who becomes defined as mentally ill happens where she lives, in the concrete, actual conditions of her experience and in her relations with others—not as these become specialized into the relations of talk in clinical settings, but as they are lived. In this context also there are others whose worlds and experiences intersect with hers as hers with theirs. The organization of psychiatric care serves to separate an individual from the contexts in which her actions arise as part of a situation in which others also act. She is taken from that context (for the purposes of treatment, if not for custody) into a process that progressively cleans her up and detaches her from the actualities and the particular contexts of her living. The reports made of her are, like the probation officer's report of Audrey's misconduct, organized around her as subject.[11] The organization of psychiatric care structures that procedure as well. *She* is taken from her situation and relationships. *They* are left behind. She is placed in a context appropriated by the agency. The setting is not her business. Nothing there is her business. She is *their* business. The organization is set up to ensure that what she does there is not consequential for it, is not productive or meaningful, and does not contribute to it as an enterprise. She is constituted as the object of its work, not as participant to it. Therefore what she does appears as a behavior attached to her and detached from her situation.

Everything that contextualizes her has been rendered invisible or has been packaged into reports that use the observer's experience to replicate an organizational form, and that practice structuring procedures of the type described above. What can we know about whatever it was that lay back there and that we talk of as mental illness? As we shall see in the following chapters, this work of abstraction as an organizational practice is a condition to the ideological structuring of psychiatry. When the patient reaches the point where a decision is to be made, she is abstracted into a merely talking presence and a bundle of reports. But this effect is, of course, invisible in textual time.

Case histories and records are a major datum for the theorizing of the professions concerned with these areas, notably of psychiatry and social work. The typical organization of case records or histories or texts is taken for granted. The typical constructions organize the account around the individual, obliterating the local contexts of her life and in particular the local contexts of the production of the account. The power relations, division of labor, and work organization of the settings in which the record is produced are integral yet invisible in its forms. Hence the detritus of power enters unseen into the theoretical formulations of professional discourse.

🔰 Hierarchy and
Ideological Circles

By *hierarchy* I mean differentiations of policy- and decision-making capacities ascribed to positions in an apparatus of ruling or in organizing relations of ruling. Hierarchy isn't just internal to an organization: relations among professions in the same field are ordered hierarchically, and particular local sites of administrative, professional, or managerial activity are tied in hierarchically to relations operating at extralocal levels. The policy- and decision-making process at the central levels of organization depend on the socially organized work of producing accounts at the periphery.

In this chapter, the circularity of the ideological process is examined as a property of apparatuses and relations of ruling. Ideology (in the sense specified in chapter 2) is addressed as a feature of organization itself rather than simply of the intellectual practices of individual participants in a discourse. In chapter 2 ideological practices were identified in part with methods of creating accounts of the world that treat it selectively in terms of a predetermined conceptual framework. The categories structuring data collection are already organized by a predetermined schema; the data produced becomes the reality intended by the schema; the schema interprets the data. Any questions bearing on the facticity of statements based on the intersection of data and interpretive schema (such as issues of ac-

THE CONCEPTUAL PRACTICES OF POWER

curacy, reliability, and the like) may be raised without breaking the ideological circularity of the procedure. For though it is perfectly possible to prove or disprove statements, issues of objectivity must be framed within the established structure. Issues, questions, and experiences that do not fit the framework and the intercalated relation of categories and schemata simply do not get entry to the process, do not become part of the textual realities governing decision-making processes.

A collective of British government statisticians has described how official statistics are produced as a hierarchical division of labor organizing what I am calling an *ideological circle* (see chapter 2). The mandarins at the top set policy in relation to the relevances of ministers of the crown; policies establish schemata in terms of which statisticians develop the categories of data to be collected; these are embodied in forms that are sent out to be "administered" by low-level staff. The completed forms return to the statistician as data to be analyzed and interpreted in terms of the policy concerns of the department; finally, the product is interpreted at the top level by the mandarins whose policy formulations have governed the production, analysis, and interpretation of the data.[12] Another paper in the same book describes an analogous circularity in an analysis of the sexism built into the conceptual frameworks and categories of state census and labor data collection.[13]

The organizational impregnability of this circularity identifies its distinctively ideological character. By contrast, scientific facticity is always subject to erosion. Though analogous circularities can certainly be detected, they are relatively fragile and exposed to the continual and open-ended work of exploring the actual and exposing concepts and theories to its constraining effects. Facticity accomplished according to scientific conventions is a quarrelsome process; the stabilization of the relation between "what is there" and the schemata structuring and expressing it is established over time and disagreement and is always subject to disruption.

For example, in the legal context, the police account of what happened is structured as the "particulars." The particulars mediate lived actualities and the legal determination of a crime. They are the product of procedures used by police investigating what is to be alleged as a crime to construct from the accounts of witnesses, the account given by the person charged with the offense (if any), observations by police, written or printed materials, and so forth, a set of "items" that will intend and can be read as the category of crime with which the person is charged.[14] Patricia Groves describes how defense lawyers, in preparing their clients, elicit their clients' stories by confronting them with the particulars of the police case against them: "Having to tell his story in comparison with and up against the particulars structures in obvious and subtle ways what the client will say; for instance, he is likely, as a naturally influenced effect, to speak to events in the order in which they are laid out in the particulars (or in the order in which he recalls the just read particulars to have laid them out)." The alternative version is further constrained because it must account for how the particulars could have appeared as they did in the police record. Thus a client "constructs a story that shows us how one set of appearances (as laid out in the particulars) can be seen to be generated by an alternative course of action that is not a criminal course of action."[15]

Clients' stories are structured by the particulars, a product of police practices of observation and reporting. Clients' stories mediated in this way may correspond not at all to what happened as it was lived and experienced. They must draw upon what happened as they experienced and can remember it and upon any other resources they command (of invention, elaboration, the talk of friends who were witnesses, and so forth) to construct jointly with the lawyer stories responding to the particulars and having some chance of standing up in court. This complex fabrication (not necessarily, of course, a falsehood) then becomes their own, for them to tell and take responsibility for.

Characteristically such ideological circles are laid down in and inhabit organizational forms separating those who theorize, formulate, conceptualize, and make policy from the front-line workers who experience the actual ways in which the organization interrelates with its objects. Those in actual contact with those who are the objects of action are not those who frame the policies, categories, and concepts that govern their work. Sociological interviewers do not adapt the interview schedule because individuals find the questions meaningless; social workers investigating welfare claims do not make the categories and criteria that govern success or failure; police at the front line do not determine the categories or criteria of crime. Hierarchy, power, and domination sustain the circularity of schema and data. Factual accounts do not aim at contexts of reading uncontrolled by the purposes and policies structuring their relevance. Rules of confidentiality, corporate ownership of information, corporate systems of data storage, and so forth provide specifically for the exclusive control of texts, keeping them within the scope of specific interpretive contexts of reading and use. We saw, in the 1960s and since, how organizational records can read quite differently when exposed to interpretive practices not controlled by the organization. Sit-ins in the offices of university presidents, for example, yielded files that implicated universities as slum landlords, as supporters of tyrannical regimes, and the like. Texts read in contexts outside and uncontrolled by a given jurisdiction of reading and controlled schemata of interpretation will not necessarily construct the same virtual reality. Challenges to such organizationally produced virtual realities by the voices of those outside and suppressed by them are made, if at all, as a political process and not as a process of "scientific" reasoning. As we have learned in the women's movement.

Ideological organization insulates governing schemata from encounter with the givens of local historical experience. The categories, coding procedures, and conceptual order sanctioned for use in the context of formal organization are a linguistic and methodological specification of organizational (or professional) structures of relevance. The objects, environment, persons, states of affairs, and events thus given reportable status are themselves constructed in the everyday organizational practices realizing the enterprise. The categories and conceptual procedures forming the enforced linguistic resources of a given organization (or profession) assign determinate properties and order to "what actually happened/what is" in its account. Terminologies depend upon and bear implicitly properties of organization that remain unexplicated and yet are an essential resource in any sense they can make. An organization may virtually invent the environment and objects corresponding to its accounting terminologies and practices.

Ideological organization creates a disjuncture between the world as it is known within the relations of ruling and the lived and experienced actualities its textual realities represent as "what actually happened/what is." This chapter explores that disjuncture as an essential property of the social organization of textual reality. Taking the standpoint of women situates us, I've argued, where our lives are lived, where we act and experience. The sequence mapped in figure 3.1, "The Social Organization of Textual Reality," describes the course of production of an objectified knowledge of happenings and states of affairs that have been or are lived by actual individuals. The parameters of the factual account as it has been shaped by its process of production, including the interpretive schemata of the social organization of its reading that structure how the account is organized, and, as we shall see, the categories under which the account of the original has been made, are then read into, or more correctly, read as, the world. In the context of relations of ruling, the peculiar power of social organization of facticity to subdue and displace the perspectives of particular subjects is a constituent of ideological organization. The latter has, as we shall see, a distinctive circularity that insulates the organization of ruling from the effects of disjunctures between the lived actualities as people know them in their everyday/everynight lives and the representation of the world as actionable in the textual realities of administration, management, professional discourse, and the like.

The categories set by formal organization are enforced. When they do not correspond to how the actuality they address is put together, organizational hierarchy and systems of enforcing accountability inhibit the development of alternative terminologies and schemata. The enforced terms and procedures describe environment and object in terms relevant to organizational policies and objectives. Characteristically, as in the example of "official statistics," policies are made at the center of formal organization whereas what must be reported and where the work of the enterprise is concretely done is in large part at the periphery. In his critique of the official versions of American military functioning in the Vietnam War, Daniel Ellsberg describes a characteristic inability of ideological organization to "learn":

> The urgent need to circumvent the lying and the self-deception was, for me, one of the "lessons of Vietnam"; a broader one was that there were situations—Vietnam was one example—in which the U.S. Government, starting ignorant, did not, would not, *learn*. There was a whole set of what amounted to institutional "anti-learning" mechanisms working to preserve and guarantee unadaptive and unsuccessful behavior: the fast turnover in personnel; the lack of institutional memory at any level; the failure to study history, to analyze or even record operational experience or mistakes; the effective pressures for optimistically false reporting at every level, for describing "progress" rather than problems or failure, thus concealing the very need for change in approach or for learning.[16]

Ellsberg ascribes the problem to defects in the flow of information or of feedback. Our analysis suggests that such problems arise within ideologically organized hierarchies that effectively repress the working experience of people at the periphery and preclude its admission to the textual realities operative for the organization.

Examination of descriptive accounts such as those of Jonathan Schell[17] suggests this a fundamental difficulty: the world in which the American military fought, in which personnel had to report, and for the effects of their activities on which they were held accountable, did not correspond to the categories in which they had to make it accountable. Disjuncture between the enforced categories of reporting and their experience was repaired at the periphery by those doing the actual work of fighting and reporting. Military personnel at the front line had to find ways of acting so that what they did could be described in the terms they had to report it in. As described by Schell, the methods used were various and, in many cases, highly ingenious. Here is one:

> *Most of the terms used in the Bomb Damage Assessment Reports seemed to have been devised for something like a bombing raid on a large, clearly visible, stationary military base, and not for the bombing of guerrillas in the setting of fields, villages, and jungle* which the FAC pilots actually guided [italics added]. Finding himself having to guide air strikes with the aid of a set of instructions that had little relevance to his actual task, each FAC pilot had to improvise his own ways of trying to tell where the enemy was operating. This was how Captain Reese came to think that he could spot, on the trails, grass that had been freshly bent by the passage of enemy troops, and that he could distinguish enemy houses from civilian houses by whether they were in the tree lines or not; how Lieutenant Moore came to think that he could tell a farmer from a soldier by the way he walked; and how Major Billings came to believe that he could tell enemy soldiers from civilians by making a low pass over the fields and seeing who ran for cover, and that he could judge whether a wisp of smoke hanging over the woods was rising from the fire of a Montagnard or from the fire of a Vietcong soldier.[18]

This work was done at the front line prior to the making of any written account or tally sheet, but directed toward such texts. The men at the front line evolved practices of knowing and acting in the world that overcame the disjuncture between the sanctioned and enforced terms of military reporting and their actualities. They reproduced the world as those at the top said it had to be. This is not a matter of accuracy, nor of how "scores" might be exaggerated, nor of communication. Rather, the policies and hence the conceptual frameworks conceived at the top determined their specification as reporting categories (done, presumably, by specialists at middle levels of military organization) to be used by those at the bottom reporting back. The awful ingenuity of Major Billings and Lieutenant Moore repaired the disjuncture between the categories and the world so that the cogency of the policies and the schemata embedded in them were confirmed continually at the top in their capacity to make sense of the information received. The "actuality" on which they were based was one *produced* by the enforcement of the accounting procedures as actual military action. The circularity of ideological organization detached the textual realities operative within the military from actualities experienced at ground level. We do not have to read accounts of this war from the standpoint of the Vietnamese to discern this gap; accounts of or based on the experiences of the American soldiers who had to fight this war exhibit plainly its failure to make sense at ground level.[19]

Hierarchical structures of this kind are, of course, familiar from sociological analyses of bureaucracy from Max Weber on. Less well developed is the study of relations among professions as hierarchies built into professional organization, but not attributable to a particular corporate form of organization. There are, of course, internal hierarchies within the formally collegial relations of professional discourse based on the positional structures of universities, hospitals, research institutes, and so forth, and on their relative status. I am concerned here with the social organization of relations among professions that are reproduced in the multiple sites of professional organization: the relationships of nurses and physicians, of social workers and psychiatrists, and so forth. Typically the relationships of super- and subordination in these relations both recapitulate and perpetuate historically established gender relationships.

This is the context of the making of case records and, ultimately, case histories. Normally, the only authorized contributor to the making of the case record who has any kind of direct access to the situation and people involved in the events leading to a patient's hospitalization is the social worker. The patient herself and her friends, family, or coworkers appear only in "reported" speech. Similarly, nurses are the only authorized contributors to the making of the case record who are directly part of the patient's experience on the ward. These professions are subordinate to psychiatry. Their modes of reporting are technically developed; learning how to make reports or to write up ward notes is part of their professional training; the modes of reporting are determined by what will enable the psychiatrist to make decisions. The controlling schemata of the psychiatric discourse and of the subordinate discourses of social work and psychiatric nursing are built into the categories and concepts used for reporting, sharply restricting what may be incorporated into the textual realities that ground the psychiatric decision-making process. Out of the totality of a woman's actual living, at home, at work, and on the ward, a particular selection is made, assembled according to certain rules and conventions, and deploying categories and concepts expressing discursive schemata (more fully examined below in chapters 5 and 6). The procedures for constructing the case record, as we've seen, organize events around the patient, produce her actions and utterances as "symptoms," ignore the contexts in which events, actions, and utterances occurred, and conceal the observational and other work of those reporting as components in the making of the report.

In articulating the local actualities of people's life and work to the psychiatric decision process, such inscriptive practices produce as a textual reality only what can be admitted through them. It is the business of the social worker to know of the patient's circumstances outside the psychiatric setting; she may have visited and talked to members of her family; she has informed herself about the patient's problems of money, jobs, presence or absence of spouse, children, and so forth. What she learns is worked up into reports to the psychiatrist. These reports are structured by the professionally sanctioned concepts and categories of a profession subordinate to psychiatry. Everything going on in the everyday settings to which a social worker (or nurse) has had access that does not fit the prescribed frameworks of reporting is left unsaid; there is, organizationally, no way of saying it. To step outside the professional role, to use a language that is not already fitted to the circular frameworks established by the professional division of labor, ensures that what is said will have at best an uncertain place, lacking authority. If it cannot be resolved into the appropriate terminology, it cannot gain currency within the system. This closure is reinforced by the subordinate status of those with direct access to the patient's ongoing lived situation; they lack entitlement to redefine the terms in which what is happening to or going on with a patient may be discussed.[20]

◨   Women as Discounted Speakers

in Public Discourse

That women have been silenced and excluded is not news. I want to
attend here to how this may be consequential in determining the
textual surfaces of objective knowledge in public contexts. Authority
in the public discourse is not defined by position in a determinate
system of positions, as it is in organizational hierarchies. It appears
instead as the difference between the credibility granted to some
sources and the treatment of others as mere opinion or as lacking
credibility in some way.[21] Authority bleeds from the institutional
relations of ruling to the relations of authority at the surface of media. There are also specific social forms that have been developed by
the state on the terrain of public discourse: investigatory committees, task forces, royal commissions. The purpose of these is to arrive
at a decisive public version of events or a decisive basis for the introduction of government policy. The differential authority of participants in these processes is highly consequential for the textual reality formed in the media. There are the distinctive effects for women,
including the repression of their local experience. These may be examined in the workings of a royal commission of inquiry into a series
of unexplained deaths on a cardiology ward for infants in the Toronto
Hospital for Sick Children in 1983.

Postmortem blood tests had shown abnormally high levels of digoxin in the dead infants. A police investigation was begun. The
framework organizing their accounts as presented in the media con-
formed to notorious, though dubiously substantiated, stories of multiple hospital killings by nurses. The police worked from the outset
from the assumption that it was a case of multiple murder and that
the culprit was a nurse. They also worked with a very limited understanding of hospital practice and on this basis arrested a nurse who
had later to be released for want of evidence. The story, along with
the police's progress or lack thereof, was a focus of intense media
coverage. "Public outcry" was organized by the media through interviews with persons having public authority (such as members of
opposing parties in the provincial legislature) and with the parents of
the dead children. A royal commission of inquiry under Mr. Justice
Samuel Grange was set up to provide a public determination of how
the children met their deaths and to review the much criticized

performance of the police in arresting a person without adequate evidence for a charge. The sessions of the commission were intensively reported and televised. Its participants were onstage to the public throughout the process.

In the course of the inquiry, physicians and nurses connected with the infant cardiology unit were treated in strikingly different ways. "The proceedings began by hearing testimony from doctors who presented evidence in the capacity of expert witnesses. This was the manner in which their credentials were submitted before the Inquiry, and the spirit in which they were questioned. The nurses were called as witnesses because some of them had been present when infant deaths occurred, not because they were regarded as having any expertise."[22]

Throughout, physicians were treated as professionals, equals of the judge and lawyers. They were consulted; they were treated as authorities; they were never treated as suspects in the imputed murder. By contrast, the nurses were asked questions about their personal and social lives; they were interrupted and badgered. "At one stage even Mr. Justice Grange was finally moved to comment on lawyer Barry Percival's constant badgering of witnesses, 'If I could just ask you, perhaps, to pause an instant before you got at her.' "[23] The evidence of physicians and police witnesses was treated as a credible source of information. Not so that of nurses: one was asked if she were willing to submit to hypnosis, another if she would take a lie-detector test, and yet another if she were willing to take "truth serum." Because nurses, including nursing administrators, had gotten together to discuss how they should respond to the events, they were treated as if they were involved in a conspiracy to obstruct the inquiry. They were never treated in any way as professional authorities whose observations of the situation on the ward, of the children's conditions, or of the actual routines of the work organization of care would be of equal relevance to the inquiry as the observations of physicians. Their knowledge was never made use of. It was not recognized as knowledge.

Throughout the framework of the nurse or nurses committing multiple murders was an implicit organizer of the proceedings. If there was insufficient evidence to charge the nurse first arrested, it could have been because she was working with another nurse, or because she was not the murderer, in which case another must have been. Perhaps the implicit operation of this frame entered into the refusal of Mr. Justice Grange to take seriously suggestions by some experts that the tests used to determine an excess of digoxin in the blood of the dead children were not reliable. At all events, the inquiry focused exclusively on nurses as possible culprits and on how to determine which among them might have been positioned to supply extremely sick children with excess or unprescribed doses of digoxin. The discounting of nurses' professional knowledge and their status as credible witnesses sealed in this effect by depriving the course of inquiry of a source of specialized knowledge, one particularly capable of speaking of the actual, local sequences of events leading to the deaths of the children, of the technical practices of how medications are approved and administered, and of the working order of the cardiac ward that must have been relevant to a consideration of who might have killed the children.

Subsequent criticism has questioned whether any of the deaths were murder, but the commission's report has entered textual time, is warranted as the textual reality, and is part of the public currency on which news accounts, books, and articles can rely. As soon as the report was published, the media's endless speculations about who and how were silenced. Furthermore, the case is now enshrined textually where it can be referred to when there is again suspicion of multiple killings in a hospital setting. The social relations of dominant and subordinate professions and their gender subtext has been carried forward into the virtual realities of public, textually mediated discourse.

These explorations locate the ideological rupture between the world known in experience and the textual realities representing it in relations and apparatuses of power. The latter are integral to the social organization of the production of the account, determining who are the authorized speakers of "what actually happened/what is" and how and where the categories and concepts of reporting are decided. Accounts are shaped to fit the textual realities called for within the relations and apparatuses of ruling. Distinctive narrative forms with powerfully jural features, such as case histories, transpose the actualities of people's lives into the organizational and professional contexts that govern them. Ideological circles built into hierarchies are more than circular practices of reasoning about the world. They are a property, perhaps essential, of large-scale organization and of the institutionalized relationships among professional discourse and the local sites of professional activity. They are also a property of the organization of public textual discourse—and here we've seen an instance of the actual organized practices silencing women and the implications of that for the accomplishment of a piece of public virtual reality.

The presence of relations of ruling as determinants disappears, of course, at the surface of the text, from which, in the social organization of reading that concludes and completes the textual reality, a "what actually happened/what is" is read off. And where gaps and disjunctures appear between the actualities of people's lives and the categories and concepts laid down for the bureaucratic and professional textual realities that make the world bureaucratically and professionally actionable, those in direct contact with those actualities work hard to reproduce the sense of the enforced and enforceable categories in which they are to be made accountable.

CHAPTER

5

THE
STATISTICS
ON WOMEN
AND
MENTAL
ILLNESS

❏

THE RELATIONS
OF RULING
THEY CONCEAL

◧   Women and the "Facts"

about Mental Illness

The previous chapters have developed an analysis of the social organization of objectified forms of knowledge as integral to the relations of ruling of contemporary societies. This chapter investigates the statistics on gender differences in rates of mental illness as an instance of this form. It questions procedures that read from the statistics to gender differences in mental illness and explores the social relations underlying the production of such statistics, examining these in terms of the institutional relations of power implicit but unspoken in them.

We start where we do as readers, encountering the statistics on differential rates of mental illness among women and men as they come before us as texts to be read factually. We are positioned then at that point of rupture in the social organization of knowledge identified in the previous chapter as the point of entry into textual time. In this relationship of reader to text and using factual methods of reading, the text comes before us as speaking of an actuality beyond and outside it. We do not attend to what has gone into its making, which is, in any case, not available to us in the text. Rather we read and interpret the statistical tables and the commentary accompanying them as evidences of a reality "in back of" the text. We read back "through" the text to what it speaks of, real differences in women's and men's rates and types of psychic illness.

Of course, the critical reader will attend to methodological problems in counting cases of mental illness and in making inferences from the statistics, but this is a problem of uncertainties about the accuracy of the textual image of a reality beyond and behind the text; it does not call into question or make visible the organization of the production of the figures, what they arise out of, what institutional forms of power they trace or the part played in the production of the figures by the processes of recording. It does not see, as we shall try to do, this surface, the text, as a moment in the organization of a social relation that transforms the local experiences of actual people and works them up into this stripped-down representation of them. These texts are products of the peculiar ways of counting and accounting for moments in the institutional life of people who are at some time, and sometimes more than once, psychiatric patients.

Texts showing gender differences in rates of mental illness have been entered into the political discourses of the women's movement. They have been read by feminists, notably by Phyllis Chesler in her early and ground-breaking *Women and madness*, as an indicator of the distinctive forms of women's oppression. My analysis here continues that interest and that debate, shifting the ground to a focus on the texts themselves as implicated in the oppression of which they are evidences. While Michel Foucault has theorized the "power/knowledge" of institutional processes such as those of the prison and asylum,[1] feminists have brought forward a much more specific political critique in which the psychiatric institutions are understood as extensions of patriarchy, modes of either regulating the lonely and inchoate resistances of individual women trapped in oppressive personal situations vis à vis men, or caretaking the end products of such solitary struggles.

Here I am not concerned with gender differences in mental illness as such. In fact, the Canadian data from the same period show much less marked differences than the U.S. data used by Chesler. My focus here is not on whether statistics can tell us that patriarchal and capitalist society creates greater mental distress and disturbance for women than it does for men. Rather, I am interested in exploring how these statistics are put together and in the patriarchal political relations and organization underlying the production of the textual realities of the statistics.

I begin by raising some questions about the findings at the level of the statistical material because I want to undermine first of all a familiar and "normal" practice in the reading of such statistical material. If those who read are not "expert" readers, we depend upon statements telling us how to read such materials, thus "interpreting" them for us. They may be statements such as "the figures show a consistently larger female than male involvement in psychiatry." Backed up with a dense array of numerical description, the statement is read as weighty and authoritative. We read it factually, that is, we read through the text to an actual state of affairs that will allow us in our turn to talk or write as if "So and so *has shown* that more women than men are mentally ill." We think we are talking about the real world, for the text itself, in textual time, conceals the depth of the institutional order and organization that accomplishes it. In our factual reading it has come to have a simple and representational relation to that of which it speaks.

◻ Gender in the Rates of Mental Illness:

Is There a Difference?

The Canadian figures don't show us the same kinds of relations between being a woman or a man and being mentally ill as studies in the States have shown. Phyllis Chesler, in her powerful political interpretation of mental illness among women,[2] has taught us to interpret the statistical information on mental illness as indicating the effect of oppression on women and to expect to find that the rates of mental illness among women are higher than among men. Proportionate to their numbers in the population (which at the ages we're concerned with is more or less equal), more women than men should be showing up for treatment or other kinds of psychiatric care because of this effect and hence get counted and show up in official statistics—the social bookkeeping of nations.

Chesler reports a number of surveys questioning people about themselves that show higher rates of mental disturbance or mental disorder among the women than among the men who respond. In addition she cites official U.S. statistics that show

a consistently large female involvement with psychiatry in America, an involvement that has been increasing rather dramatically since

1964. The total number of women in psychiatric facilities (including the predominantly all-male Veterans Administration psychiatric facilities) increased from 479,167 in 1964 to 615,112 in 1968. In 1964, there were 1079 more women than men in psychiatric facilities. By 1968, 50,363 more women than men were psychiatrically hospitalized and publicly treated. . . . During the 1960s, adult women, far more than adult men, constituted the majority of patients in general psychiatric wards, private hospitals, public outpatient clinics, and community mental health centers. In 1968, for example, adult women comprised 60 per cent of the patients in general psychiatric wards, 61 per cent of the population in private hospitals, and 62 per cent of the population in out-patient clinics. In 1968, women of all ages comprised 50 per cent of the population in state and county hospitals. From 1964 through 1968, 125,351 more women than men were patients in all psychiatric institutions. Between 1950 and 1968, 223,268 more women than men (many of them "old" women), were confined in state and county hospitals.[3]

This adds up to a pretty powerful picture. However, when we look at the Canadian statistics from approximately the same period (1970) we don't find quite the same relationship. Table 5.1, based on data from Statistics Canada, brings to the surface of this text a textual reality that is generated in processes of the kind described in the previous chapter and to be further analyzed in this. It shows considerable differences between women and men admitted to some types of public psychiatric facilities, *but little difference overall.*

When the numbers of women and men at different ages admitted to public psychiatric facilities in Canada are related to the female and male populations at those ages, again the differences are minor. Out of every 100,000 women between fifteen and nineteen living in Canada in 1970, 300 were admitted to a public psychiatric facility of some kind. The rate for men of that age is about the same. Between the ages of twenty and twenty-nine, 344 women out of every 100,000 were admitted for the first time to a public psychiatric facility. The rate of men in that age group is somewhat higher—356 in every 100,000. In only one age group are the rates for women significantly higher than the rates for men: out of every 100,000 women between the ages of thirty and thirty-nine, 373 were hospitalized for the first time as mentally ill. The rate for men at this age is a little lower, only 369 out of every 100,000. At later ages, however, the rates for men exceed those for women.[4]

The figures we're looking at so far don't give us quite the same

Table 5.1 Type of Institution, First Admission, 1970, Percentage of Women and Men ages 15–59 (Statistics Canada)[5]

Type of Institution	Percentage Women	Percentage Men	Total
PUBLIC MENTAL HOSPITALS	39 (4,608)	61 (7,223)	100 (11,831)
PUBLIC PSYCHIATRIC HOSPITALS	60 (11,948)	40 (7,815)	100 (19,763)
PSYCHIATRIC HOSPITALS	47 (2,485)	53 (2,752)	100 (5,237)
FEDERAL PSYCHIATRIC HOSPITALS	0.3 (19)	99.7 (709)	100 (728)
HOSPITALS FOR ADDICTS	21 (846)	79 (3,164)	100 (4,010)
ALL FACILITIES	48 (19,906)	52 (21,663)	100 (41,569)

picture as Chesler's. As compared with men, we don't find a consistently large female involvement. Is this because we're looking at a different society with different problems for women and for men? They certainly don't show women experiencing more mental illness than men overall—if anything, the opposite is true. Or are there problems in how Chesler has presented the state of affairs in the U.S.? Has she in fact described it properly?

Here are some possible reasons for the difference in what the official Canadian and U.S. figures say:

1 The picture could be different because the statistics used are put together differently. For example, Chesler is using numbers of people "in treatment" whereas Statistics Canada gives us "first admissions." The latter can give you for any year an idea of how many people are becoming mentally ill but it doesn't tell you how many people are in treatment at any one time. Chesler suggests that women are more likely to stay and more likely to be readmitted.[6] If this is so, similar figures for women and men on first admissions would show up as more women than men on the institutional books at bookkeeping time.

2 I've cut the cake differently because I have left out the statistics on persons over sixty. For these you must compare rates rather than, as Chesler does, the overall numbers. We don't know from Chesler's data how far the differences she finds between women and men result from factors of this sort. We can't take for granted as we can for the ages between fifteen and fifty-nine that the numbers of men and women at all ages are more or less the same. We know that women tend to live longer

than men, and that there are therefore more women than men in the over-sixty group. There are likely to be more women in treatment in this age group simply because there are more women than men in it. We can't wash out this possibility without comparing the rates.

3   Perhaps Chesler's descriptions focus on figures that show more mental illness among women than men and neglect those that don't show this or show the opposite. Her account of the increase in numbers of women overall and relative to men from 1964 to 1968 sounds pretty impressive in absolute numbers. But if we compare the shares women and men have in a total figure that increases year by year, then the increase of women over men becomes much less dramatic—over the five-year period women's share has increased by only two percentage points, from 50 percent to 52 percent.[7]

4   The Canadian figures show more men than women in public mental hospitals, federal psychiatric hospitals, and hospitals for addicts, and more women than men in public psychiatric hospitals. Chesler, however, doesn't examine such variations. Notably, she doesn't mention the much greater numbers of men in Veterans Administration hospitals and outpatient services. In 1968 there were 61,493 men in VA in- and outpatient care and only 2,220 women. Women of course are less likely to have been in the armed services and thus less likely to be entitled to use VA facilities. Why doesn't Chesler include them in her discussion? (They are included in her overall figures.) Perhaps because this explanation for a difference between the sexes doesn't fit into the framework she (and we) are working with. It tells us something about administrative practices in the U.S. government. If we don't think of war as a cause of emotional disturbance, the Veterans Administration figures don't seem to tell us anything about how social contexts may contribute to rates of mental illness. So it gets left out. But since much mental illness among men is being treated in these facilities, that omission introduces a bias into the discussion.

Perhaps after all there isn't much difference between the Canadian figures and the U.S. ones. Certainly Chesler's formidable description is beginning to seem much less grounded. The differences, which seem so clear and strong on first reading, become ambiguous when we look at them closely.

Another American study done by W. R. Gove and J. F. Tudor[8] comes up with findings similar to Chesler's but based on different types of statistical information. They believe that women's role in modern industrial societies has characteristics that are likely to produce higher rates of mental illness among women than men. They bring together a lot of information, including studies on the use of outpatient facilities. They conclude, "The information on the first admissions to mental hospitals, psychiatric treatment in general hospitals, psychiatric out-patient clinics, private out-patient care, the practices of general physicians, and community surveys all indicate that more women than men are mentally ill."[9]

Of course, Gove and Tudor are using some information from sources not used in the Canadian data—from private outpatient care, practices of general physicians and community surveys—and their study is very useful in that it brings together a lot of material. But they are using first admissions, and insofar as their information overlaps with the statistics we've looked at already, the Canadian figures don't show that more women than men are mentally ill. On the basis of these figures, their generalizations aren't confirmed for Canada. Why this difference?

Gove and Tudor treat mental illness in a special way. They define it so as to exclude some of the kinds of problems that bring people into psychiatric treatment or care and that therefore get counted in the overall figures. Mental illness is a very loose category, which covers almost anything that can turn up in treatment or care in a psychiatric agency. Gove and Tudor refine it and narrow it down so that the term applies to a single range of problems only. In their view mental illness is "a disorder which involves personal discomfort (as indicated by distress, anxiety, etc.) and/or mental disorganization (as indicated by confusion, thought blockage, motor retardation, and, in the more extreme cases, by hallucinations and delusions) that is not caused by an organic or toxic condition."[10] They define mental illness in terms of states of feeling, or emotion, and mental states. In their view it is a disorder of mental or emotional processes that is not part of an organic disease and doesn't result from using drugs or alcohol.

When patients are admitted to psychiatric facilities of the kind we are concerned with here, they are given a diagnosis. The systems of diagnosis used in the U.S. and Canada are more or less the same. Some diagnostic categories fit with their definition and others don't. In looking for evidence in the kinds of statistical material we've used here Gove and Tudor focus on four diagnostic categories, two major (neurotic disorders and functional psychoses) and two minor (transient situational disorders and somatic disorders of psychic origin). Proportionately very few are diagnosed in the last category, and for the purposes of our discussion I'm going to leave it out.

Neurotic disorder is defined by Gove and Tudor as "anxiety in the absence of psychotic disorganization."[11] The difference between neurosis and psychosis is mainly that in the latter there are problems with processes of thinking or with how the patient perceives and understands what is happening, whereas neuroses are mainly emotional difficulties.

Gove and Tudor exclude, as I have, all forms of mental illness arising from organic causes.[12] They also apparently exclude mental illness originating in or identified with toxic conditions such as alcoholism. They exclude as well a diagnostic category called "personality disorders" because, they argue, people identified in this way are nonconforming in ways that are disruptive to others, but they don't themselves experience mental distress. Therefore they don't fit their definition of mental illness.

This all makes perfectly good sense. Their conclusion—that more women than men are mentally ill—works because it applies to this definition of mental illness only and does not apply to mental illness as it's generally and casually used by all of us to talk about almost anything that gets you into a psychiatric facility as an inpatient. But we have not yet fully accounted for the discrepancy between Gove and Tudor's U.S. figures and our Canadian figures.

There is still another problem to consider. When we look at how women and men are distributed in the various diagnostic categories in the Canadian figures, we find a quite unequal distribution. It is described as follows by Statistics Canada: "Mental disorders such as alcoholism, alcoholic psychosis, personality disorders, sexual deviations, and drug dependence continued to be predominantly male disorders, while neuroses and affective psychoses continued to be predominantly female disorders."[13] Gove and Tudor's definition of mental illness excludes at the outset all those categories in which men predominate—at least in the Canadian statistics. If we assemble the categories, men are three-quarters (76 percent) of the resulting group; if this group were removed from the total of admissions to public psychiatric facilities, almost half the men (48 percent) would be eliminated.[14]

This is troublesome. Have Gove and Tudor selected a definition that eliminates all the diagnostic categories in which men predominate over women, with the exception of schizophrenia, where the difference is not great? Certainly this is what it looks like when we use the same procedure on Canadian data. Following the Gove and Tudor procedure, women in Canada do have a larger share (60 percent) of the total who are admitted to psychiatric facilities as mentally ill. But when we include those categories that Gove and Tudor exclude, this difference disappears. In fact, women, with 48 percent, have a slightly lower share of that total than men, with 52 percent. We must be suspicious of so neat an outcome as this.[15]

In arguing with Chesler and with Gove and Tudor, we've begun to find out something about the picture provided by the official Canadian statistics. These show us that the shares of women and men in the overall numbers first admitted to treatment in various psychiatric agencies named are about equal. If anything, rather fewer women than men come into treatment or care. But the overall figures hide some pretty wide variations. The main ones are these:

1   Different kinds of agencies seem to specialize to some degree in one sex or the other. More men than women are admitted for the first time to public mental hospitals for addicts. On the other hand, more women than men are admitted to public psychiatric units (see table 5.1). Both Chesler and Gove and Tudor report studies showing that women have a bigger share than men in the use of psychiatric outpatient facilities.

2   Rates of mental illness also vary with age, and women and men differ here also. For most ages, according to Canadian statistics, fewer women than men in proportion to their numbers in the population at that age are admitted to one of the named psychiatric agencies. There is one age group in which the rates for women are higher than for men. Out of every 100,000 women in Canada between the ages of thirty and thirty-nine, 373 are admitted, as compared with 369 men per 100,000.

3   Finally, when we looked at the Gove and Tudor information in relation to what we found in Statistics Canada, another source of variation concealed by the overall figures emerged. There are what Statistics Canada call "female and male disorders." This means simply that women predominate markedly over men in some types of psychiatric diagnosis (notably in affective psychoses and to a lesser extent in paranoid states) whereas men predominate (very markedly) in the diagnostic categories of alcoholism, drug dependence, and personality disorders.

Chesler and Gove and Tudor have attempted to "read through" the data produced from the records of the various types of psychiatric agency to states of psychic disturbance among women, tacitly assuming that the construction of the individual's illness in the figures has an unmediated relationship to the "real world." This is a method of reading already familiar to us from the previous chapters.

We'd like to be able to do the same thing with the Canadian statistics—to read back through the statistical information to actual states of mental illness, relating them to the oppression women experience in contemporary society. But when we try to do this we run into difficulties. Social scientists reading from such statistics are reading from texts that are the product of complex government accounting practices applied to the variety of institutional forms of psychiatric care. The points we have criticized in how Chesler and Gove and Tudor have interpreted the information available are problems that people working in this area run into again and again.

People have had to make do with the official statistical information or with statistical data specifically created for the purpose. In both cases, special kinds of operations have to be done on the data to strip it down and purify it so that somehow it will speak only of mental illness and can be treated as representing where mental illness is located and how it is distributed in a given population. This always involves the ditching of some kind of administrative or professional detritus that introduces an arbitrary source of variation into the data (that is, one that doesn't have anything to do with the main focus on mental illness as a state of the individual existing independently of how psychiatric agencies work). This is what Chesler does with the Veterans Administration figures, where the bias toward men is clearly administrative.[16] Each cleanup job makes perfectly good sense on its own; but each time we leave something out in order to make it possible to read from the statistics to actual states of mental illness in a population we must ask whether any conceivable cleanup could do the job. The analyses of the previous two chapters indicate that the statistical information cannot be decontaminated because the relations and apparatuses of ruling that generate it are profoundly implicated in how it appears. The remainder of the chapter explores these relations and apparatuses.

◖ Ways of Thinking

about Mental Illness

Throwing out this or that in order to penetrate to the actuality we suppose to be there in back of the statistics implies a particular way of thinking about mental illness. This assumes that it is a state of the individual that can be separated from what is happening to that individual in the psychiatric context. A number of recent thinkers in this field have argued that becoming mentally ill is a process in which psychiatric agencies participate. Put simply, in terms of the statistical information, this means that when you seem to be counting people becoming mentally ill you are in fact also counting what psychiatric agencies do. The two aspects can't be taken apart. *The figures can't be decontaminated.*

In interpreting any kind of factual information, we have to use some kind of method of thinking that shapes what is there into categories of objects and decides what kinds of connections we are going to make between them. Gove and Tudor use a very general method. Chesler's approach is harder to pin down, but belongs to the same general type.[17] I describe it here in very simplified terms and, using the work of Thomas Szasz, Thomas Scheff, and R. D. Laing,[18] suggest an alternative method of thinking about mental illness.

The method of thinking that requires us to clean up the data begins with mental illness as a distinct state of the individual which is recognizable in symptoms. You can tell when this state exists and what its nature is by examining, observing, or being told about the individual's symptoms. The symptoms are definite types of behavior, which can be identified and named.

This state may have serious causes. One type of cause is believed to be social situations that causes stress. In such situations and over a period of time individuals experiencing stress may become emotionally disturbed. As the underlying state of mental illness develops it becomes observable to the individual or others as symptoms. At some point she or her relatives or friends put her in touch with a psychiatric agency. Her illness is diagnosed and she is counted (thereby producing the statistical information through which we can reach back to the original state of mental illness).

Briefly the story goes like this: There is first a situation that causes stress. This leads to mental illness. The mental illness is treated professionally—hence the statistical information. This method of thinking about mental illness is diagramed as four stages in figure 5.1.

To bring it round to where we are, on this side of the text, we could add a fifth stage, the statistics. The different stages are distinct. The connections represented by arrows are simple (causal-type) connections, and they all go in the same direction. It is this method of thinking that makes it possible to begin with statistical information created at stage 4 and use it to learn about relations between stages 1

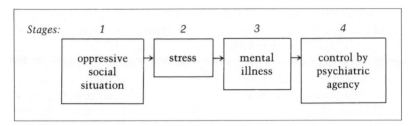

Figure 5.1   Thinking mental illness 1

and 3. The key elements—social situation, mental illness, and psychiatric agency—are all distinct and fully separated from one another. Mental illness is out there as a distinct state. It comes into being before an individual goes for treatment. It may be caused by social situations, but it is separable from them. There may be some slippage between becoming mentally ill and going for treatment because of such things as lack of facilities, inadequate knowledge about mental illness, prejudice, and so on. There may be inadequacies in the bookkeeping procedures used by psychiatric agencies. But there is no doubt that in principle you can, just as with other diseases, go from the bookkeeping procedures of the treatment agency to talking about distribution of the problem in the population. That's what is generally attempted. It's because this model is used that cleaning up things that muddle the clarity of the connections (as Gove and Tudor do with the category of mental illness) makes sense.

The alternative says that mental illness can't be separated as a thing, object, state, disease, entity, or what have you, from the social operations of psychiatry. Szasz and Scheff have suggested that there is no such thing as mental illness, that the statistics point back to no definite entity.

Szasz's view is that people come to psychiatric agencies for many kinds of problems. People experience despair and misery. There are many forms of suffering and of psychological malfunctioning of various depths and degrees. Most of these, in his view, arise out of facets of the human social condition. They are packaged as mental illness by the psychiatric agencies. These agencies sort them out, put them in categories, work their technical work upon them, and if necessary, shut people up in places apart. The mentally ill are the people upon whom this work is done, and that is all they have in common.[19]

Scheff takes a rather similar view. He suggests that becoming mentally ill begins with various and vague ways in which people's behavior doesn't fit with what other people see as standard ways of doing things. Mental illness is rather like the file marked miscellaneous. After all the other ways in which people break rules have been named, identified, and dealt with by their appropriate agencies of control (the law courts, the schools for the handicapped, and so on), there is a bundle left over that doesn't fit any one of these categories. He calls these *residual* deviations. Most people deviate in these ways. Sometimes these deviations lead to psychiatric treatment. When this happens, that individual begins to play the role of being mentally ill. What we call symptoms are behavior appropriate to the role people have learned to play in the psychiatric context.[20]

A fundamental problem is that unless you are concerned with a kind of mental illness that has a definite physical basis, objective criteria for recognizing behavior as the symptoms of mental illness or otherwise establishing that someone is mentally ill are hard to come by. Mental illness is not out there to be observed like a rock or a buttercup or a planet or even like measles. Nor, as Scheff points out, is there any definite rule or set of rules which people who are identified as mentally ill can be said to have broken or deviated from.

Seeing what people do as symptoms of mental illness is something that comes about between people in interaction with one another. Symptoms are not observable independently of actual settings in which people are relating to one another. There are always two parties to a symptom. We generally don't pay attention to this when one of them is a professional whose position is theoretically one of detachment. But being detached is a special way of relating to people, and examining someone is a special kind of interaction.[21] Therefore it isn't clear how the behavior of people described as mentally ill can be considered "wrong" in a way that separates that judgment from particular individuals (relatives, friends, psychiatrists, psychologists, social workers, nurses) encountering particular people (a friend, a child, a wife, a husband, a patient) in particular settings (at home, in a psychiatrist's office, in a hospital ward, and so on).

Many attempts have been made to locate mental illness in the community before people have made contact with a psychiatric agency, using interview methods rather than the official statistics of admissions and such. But those attempts also are subject to this difficulty—the judgment of whether anything is wrong or what is wrong is always made by people who begin with particular understandings of behavior and with particular ideas about mental illness. Those kinds of background understandings of behavior are built into how we see others. We can't escape that. They are essentially part of *any* relationship, *any* conversation, *any* interaction, *any* understanding of behavior. All of us bring to a situation our understanding of what is going on. What happens there is partly a product of how we understand it.

This means also that psychiatric diagnoses are not like the diagnoses of disease, which depend upon physical symptoms or signs. It is the functioning of the individual in routine situations that becomes the problem. How she behaves depends on the situation, on others present and how they interpret what she does. Knowing who she is, her sex, her background, her age—these considerations enter into the picture that leads to the diagnosis. The psychiatrist already works with an array of typical pictures of the kind of person who is schizophrenic, who is neurotic, who is alcoholic, and so on.

The types include characterizations of sex and age. They include notions of the behavior appropriate for women and for men. They include judgments about people's physical appearance. And so on and so on. Diagnoses, dispositional decisions (decisions about where to place someone), and decisions about treatment include this invisible judgmental work on the part of psychiatric professionals. This same work thus also counts in the bookkeeping operations of psychiatric agencies.

Furthermore, one major dimension of interpretation that enters into the relation of everyone toward someone who has been defined as mentally ill is the definition itself. Once someone has been labeled mentally ill she is related to in those terms. She is not expected to make sense, so people tend not to listen to or respond to her as if she does.

The attitude can be summarized as a set of instructions that tell us how to respond to someone who "is" mentally ill. The first instruction says, "Find out how to see this person's behavior as not making sense."[22] One method of doing this is to separate the person's behavior from the situations in which it belongs. This is done routinely in psychiatric settings, both by the way in which the patient is seen outside her lived settings and by the way in which the psychiatric procedures of making accounts and clinical description lift pieces of behavior out of context (as we'll see in an example given in the following section). In any case, if your instructions tell you to make nonsense of what people do, it's surprisingly easy to do it.

The second instruction says, "Don't relate to this person as if you could look at the world from the same place." People don't relate to people who "are" mentally ill in the same way they relate to others. They don't readily enter into a "we" relation with them in which it is taken for granted that both share the same social and temporal coordinates and experience things from the base of a shared set of conditions.

Finally, the third instruction says, "Don't take what she says seriously. Don't make it into anything you have to act upon or respond to." This is something like a "don't trust her" instruction, but it goes further than that because it means that what she says and does is discredited or discounted as a basis for action. For example, if she who has been labeled mentally ill is angry with you, this instruction tells you not to treat that anger as a reason for getting angry back or asking yourself what you've done or the like. Together these instructions suspend a person's capacity to function as *subject* in creating the intersubjective order of the everyday/everynight world.

Whatever it is that gets called mental illness becomes recognizably and distinctly what it is for the official record in psychiatric offices, admissions suites of mental hospitals, the intake practices of clinics, and so on. It is a whole relation to the world, which the person becoming mentally ill in this sense discovers. When she is being put on record she is already in a relation to the world that is changed for her. This is the relation of mental illness. There is no phenomenon of mental illness that can be separated from the procedures that produce the statistics. The agencies that produce the statistics also produce mental illness. They don't produce the suffering, the despair, the misery, the loss of self that leads in one way or another to someone's entry to the psychiatric process, but they do produce the distinctive behaviors, how they are recorded and understood, and that pattern of relating to others that we call mental illness.

This doesn't mean that individuals who eventually make contact with psychiatry are not experiencing something real. We have to understand that there are experiences that are overwhelmingly fearful, states of total suspension in diffuse anxiety, and conditions of profound despair and grief, and further, that there are also people with whom others cannot live or who make others afraid for themselves (we see here again how troubles are defined interactionally). We begin to call others—or ourselves—mentally ill as a way of organizing these kinds of responses in order to do something definite about them.

All this means that we can't go back through the statistics to find

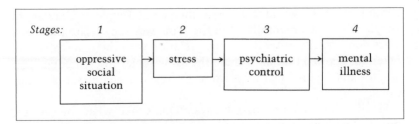

Figure 5.2   *Thinking mental illness 2*

either a definite phenomenon that we can call mental illness or a way of counting it that ensures that we are counting *something* and that it is something we can properly treat as being the same sort of thing (allowing for errors) every time we count it. Nor can we separate what is called mental illness from what we'd like to view as its cause. Nor can we separate the processes by which people come to be counted as mentally ill (by coming into treatment, usually) from the ways in which being under psychiatric jurisdiction changes how others relate to them. This changes how they relate, are seen to relate, are responded to, and are interpreted. To be there (and that happened to me), and under that kind of scrutiny, changes all your relations to the world and to yourself. That special experience can't be separated from the experience of being or becoming mentally ill and can't be separated from the behavior and responses that lead to people being labeled as mentally ill (let alone the sometimes radically stressful and frightening experiences that some experience in mental hospitals).

We could rewrite our model for thinking about mental illness to look like figure 5.2. Most people thinking along these lines don't view mental illness as actually *caused* by psychiatric intervention but rather take the view that wherever it originates it takes on its particular character in the social contexts created by psychiatry. It *becomes* mental illness—rather than something else—in that context. (And that has consequences, then, for what the patient becomes.)

◖ Cleaning Up

We must drop the idea that we can trace back through the statistics on mental illness to find a reality hidden behind them. We can't look through them as if they were a dirty glass through which we could see perfectly if we could only clean it up. Statistics Canada, in the introduction to its statistical information, tells us that we have to be careful in reading and interpreting its data:

> The level and rate of change of first admissions by province should be interpreted against a backdrop of existing services for the mentally ill; the number of psychiatric beds available; the official and unofficial admissions policies of the psychiatric facilities; the extent of health insurance coverage for the various mental disorders; demographic characteristics such as population size, and composition by age and marital status; sociological factors such as degree of urbanization; and attitudes toward psychiatric facilities and the mentally ill. Each province incorporates a unique constellation of these factors which determine the extent of provincial variations in psychiatric in-patient movement.[23]

An alternative to these precautionary measures and to the kind of interpretation we have been criticizing is to turn the problem on its head. How is it that these varieties of relations between psychiatric facilities and community can produce a coherent and *apparently* unproblematic collection of statistical information? How does all this mess get cleaned up so that it can be presented as it is and used as it does so often get used? We have to think about the figures differently and in fact much more straightforwardly. We have to begin by asking questions about how they are produced. How do they come about as we find them on the books? What are the institutional processes that produce them? In what sorts of work context does the routine work of producing the data to be counted get done? How are these varieties of experience, situation, policy, practice, conditions, and exigencies worked up into the forms in which they are made so simply accountable? If we focus on *this* as the reality that lies in back of the statistical information, perhaps we can begin to say something about it in a rather different way. Thus the question this section attempts to answer is: How are these standardized and general forms of statistical information produced out of the varieties of particular local contexts that Statistics Canada describes? I present here a general picture of the processes involved in getting this done.[24]

We begin with the fact that the statistics on mental illness are put together as part of a system of professional and bureaucratic bookkeeping. Governments are necessarily interested in such things as the costs of psychiatric services and the "needs" of the population. They are concerned with how many people come into treatment, how many are in care during particular accounting periods, what types of facilities are being used and by whom, and what are the alternative sources of support (family, lack of family, and so on). Their interest in the statistics are different from ours and from those of researchers into the "causes" of mental illness. We make secondhand use of information that is collected for other purposes.

Furthermore, the character of the statistical information is shaped by the role these reports have traditionally played in the system of governmental control over psychiatric facilities. For example, the statistics on mental hospitalization that are to be found in earlier annual reports of the Mental Health Branch of the British Columbia Department of Health give information organized exclusively around the economics of running mental hospitals. Until 1972 they gave no information about the age or sex of patients: they just counted how many came in, how many were on the books, and how many left either by discharge or death. Statistics Canada's mental health information appears to have been elaborated from a similar base—the ordinary operation of inpatient psychiatric facilities. Various additional pieces of information have been added on. Diagnostic categories and the marital status of patients, as well as their age and sex, are included. There is, however, no information about the occupational, educational, or income levels of patients or where they came from. (Anything that would allow the reader to tie down some of the factors mentioned by Statistics Canada in their preliminary warning is lacking.)

The production of such statistical information is part of an extensive bureaucratic and professional organization. It includes, of course, the work of transforming the raw material of the world into the forms in which it can be processed as data. This work gets done almost invisibly as part of the routine work of psychiatric professionals. Psychiatrists, psychologists, social workers, and psychiatric nurses learn their specialized roles in training institutions, which are part of a national, and in most instances an international, professional structure. This training process standardizes the ways in which psychiatric care is organized and how patients are talked about, treated, and categorized. Using the textbooks, journals, and other media of their profession, psychiatric professionals learn to think and talk psychiatrically, to describe what is happening in the terms of their discipline, and to recognize and name patients' problems properly. They learn thus to produce the kinds of accounts that go into the work of psychiatric bookkeeping, and they learn, of course, to construct the kinds of accounts of people implied by psychiatric and psychological ideologies such as those described by Meredith Kimball.[25] Psychiatric discourses coordinate and standardize the ongoing practices of different professionals in particular sites and across sites.

As part of the same process, psychiatric professionals learn how to relate to people in the kinds of situations they will encounter them in—the various settings of ward and office, of coffee room and hallway, of lecture theater and convention hotel, that are the typical occasions of psychiatric encounter. They learn how to relate to members of their own professions and to those of others, and they learn how to talk *to* patients and how to talk *about* patients and how to talk *to* patients so as to be able to talk *about* patients.

We have seen in the previous chapter the operation of the ideological circuit as a property of hierarchic organization. Terminologies and methods are far from arbitrary. The terms and methods of accounting for and describing what is being done set the forms under which people recognize what they do and what others do as properly actionable. Gene Errington,[26] in a study of the workings of a police phone room, has shown how the problems callers telephone in with are shaped by the officer who takes the call into forms that fit the various possible "bureaucratic" responses—including, of course, the response of doing nothing. The world that people live in and in which their troubles arise is inscribed in the systems set up to control it by fitting them and their troubles to standardized terms and procedures under which they can be formally recognized and made actionable. These processes are intrinsic to the workings of professional and bureaucratic forms of organization. They are essential to the making and implementing of policies, including policies about what kinds of patients shall be admitted to a facility and therefore what kinds of numbers and statuses (marital status, age, and so on) will turn up in the final and simplified accountings of the government statistics.

Professional and bureaucratic procedures and terminologies are part of an abstracted system. Abstracted systems are set up to be independent of the particular, the individual, the idiosyncratic, and the local. Hence the specialized forms of training referred to above. Hence also the continual processes of working up and maintaining the standard set of terms, procedures, and so on, which are part of the work done in conferences, journals, and other forms of professional communication. In actual operation, however, the abstracted forms must be fitted to the actual local situations in which they must function and which they control. In practice the abstracted system has to be tied into the local and particular. Psychiatric agencies have to develop ways of working that fit situations and people who are not standardized, don't present standardized problems, and are not already shaped into the forms under which they can be recognized in the terms that make them actionable. What actually happens, what people actually do and experience, the real situations they function in, how they get to agencies—none of these things is neatly shaped up. There is a process of practical interchange between an inexhaustibly messy, different, and indefinite real world and the bureaucratic and professional system that controls and acts upon it. Professionals are trained to produce out of this an order, which they believe they discover in it.

Psychiatric agencies articulate the bureaucratic and professional structures to the local setting. The application of psychiatric methods of making accounts gets worked out in the actual situations that arise in the community. Local conditions and the troubles characteristic of them—the isolation of a housewife living in a trailer in a northern company town; the psychic and physical exhaustion of women overburdened by caring for children under conditions of poverty; the man who keeps himself going at the pulp mill by drinking himself blind every night; the young man whose efforts at autonomy from his family are treated as sickness; the lesbian teenager confused by the contradiction between her sexuality and the public orthodoxy of heterosexuality—such recurrent social situations create typical local uses for psychiatric facilities. An interface of routine operating develops, which transposes these recurrent and characteristic local uses into the psychiatric and administrative terms that make them actionable.

Different kinds of psychiatric agencies are set up with different capabilities and more or less specialized services. The latter are built into staffing patterns, types of premises, budgets, locations, and so on. As agencies become articulated to the local community their capabilities and services become part of a social organization that determines their actual uses, the kinds of problems that reach them, what we might describe as their administrative constituency (how agencies such as police and welfare use them), and their clientele. The uses of available agencies are the outcome of what the agency offers, the kinds of problems in the community that it can handle, and the fit that is created between the two by the social connections of referral, health insurance, welfare, police practice, word-of-mouth, and so on. The transposition of what happens and is happening to people where their problems originate into recognizable psychiatric forms is done in part by the social organization that connects agency and patient. There is a process of working up that is not done by any particular individual, but is a concerted action in which agencies such as welfare, the police, the patient herself, or her relatives are involved before she ever gets to the psychiatric facility. Further work is done by the various personnel of the agency: receptionists, social workers, and nurses, as well as psychiatrists. They shape up events and people in a whole variety of ways by routinely standardizing the settings in which they are observed, by asking them and others standardized questions, by isolating them from their personal and idiosyncratic situations, by controlling what they can say and how it is listened to, and so on. Much of what is really part of their lives and their experience simply disappears in this process. It ceases to be visible. How they came to the agency isn't visible except, perhaps, as a brief formality. The kinds of uses they or others are making of the agency also disappear.

People working professionally in psychiatric agencies and similar organizations come to categorize people's problems as types in relation to the kinds of actions to be taken. Types are an integral part of a process that fits the abstracted terms of the profession or bureaucracy to the actual situations.[27] They work as a matching process that assembles, selects, and organizes within a specialized context. The individual is already distant from her biography and her lived situation. She is encountered and experienced as a patient in the special settings of office, ward, foyer of hospital, interview room, or the like. She is encountered in the form of a case history already written and through forms of interview that disclose only those pieces of her life that fall into slots. She is encountered also, in the context of the routine performance of professional work, as part of what the psychiatrist (or other professional) has to get through that day. The experiences that are recurrent for the psychiatrist and that he has learned to name and describe as types of patients result from the characteristic local uses of the agency, but do not include them.

The clinical entities of mental illness are formalizations of types originating in the interrelation between clinical experience and the theories and systematic investigations of psychiatric discourse. They provide for psychiatrists (and others) a template to which the patterning of their experience is to be fitted. Here are two passages from autobiographies describing events that could be, but have not been, fitted to such a template. They are followed by a passage from a clinical description that shows the template to which they could be matched.

Margery Spring Rice, in *Working class wives*, published in 1939 and reflecting the Depression years in England, gives this account by a working-class woman:

> This constant struggle with poverty this last four years has made me feel very nervy and irritable and this affects my children. I fear I have not the patience that good health generally brings. When I am especially worried about anything I feel as if I have been engaged in some terrific physical struggle and go utterly limp and for some time am unable to move or even think coherently. This effect of mental strain expressed in physical results seems most curious and I am at a loss to properly explain it to a doctor.[28]

This is an account of subjective experience—insider's knowledge. The passage brings forward from an experience during the Great Depression only that aspect that is relevant to the topic here. I have already changed the character of the description by changing its relation to its original (textual) setting and have taken for granted whatever selective and editing operations went on at the point of its production (which was, of course, before the invention of tape recorders). It is a passage that could be fitted to the psychiatric diagnosis of depression, at least as it has been written up for the layperson in Sir David Stafford-Clark's *Psychiatry today*. He describes a "withdrawal of interest," a "slowing of mental and physical activity" sometimes to the degree of complete lack of response to what is going on outside the patient.[29]

The *clinical description* or its lay analogue can be understood as a set of instructions for how to select and form an account of someone "suffering" from this condition. Thus the generative structure conforms to the characteristic form of the case history. The protagonist is "the patient" (a term that can be fitted like a sack over anyone's head); the clinician commands a vantage point from which he can treat both insider's and outsider's knowledge as if they were (a) equal and (b) his. The behavior is described so that it is quite detached from the contexts in which it is lived. The terms used to describe behavior do so as if it had no "doer"—"there is a withdrawal of interest." The terms generalize in a way that makes them capable of describing a wide range of actual and various instances.

Using this procedure, the passage above could be made over into a clinical description (in the next chapter, the methods of this reconstruction are explored in detail). Does Margery Spring Rice's respondent speak of "mental illness" in the original? I think not. She speaks of arduous work, commitment to sustaining children, exhaustion, perhaps of fear and anxiety, of an unbearable load that is daily borne. She shows us strength rather than illness, a strength beyond the capacity of the body to bear it. Only when the grid of the psychiatric story is imposed on her experience is it given the form of mental illness.[30]

Again, I emphasize that I am not doing away with the actualities of people's experiences that underlie diagnoses of mental illness. Rather, what I want to bring into view in this example and examine in greater detail in the following chapter is the way in which the ideological organization works to produce for the attention of psychiatry a version that is both heavily controlled by established and professionally sanctioned schemata and *specifically inattentive* to the actual matrices of the experience of those who are diagnosed. Rice is describing, through the voices of her "respondents," the experience of working wives under conditions of severe economic deprivation. Her respondent's periodic inability to move or think coherently arises in that context. Yet the psychiatric procedures for description cannot admit it.

The actual conditions of people's lives do sneak into psychiatry, of course, but by the back door. The process is something like this: Clinical descriptions and methods of descriptions are elaborated and modified as psychiatrists and others begin to frame as descriptions the types they discover in their working experience. Different kinds of practice generate different experiences and different typological knowledge. The nature of the psychiatrist's working experience is a function of how the psychiatric agency or service is articulated to the local community and its organization of access. Thus the clinical types found in textbooks and journals are constructed out of the relation of psychiatry to the actualities of the community.

Psychiatry maintains a constant relation to a world that is constantly changing and evolving new situations that produce troubles coming within psychiatry's jurisdiction. A change in the basis of psychiatric experience resulting from establishing a different type of agency and creating thus a new psychiatric constituency will have the same effect. Psychiatric responses to changes learned and dealt with in actual local situations appear as new clinical insights, the description of variant clinical entities, the evolution of new methods of treatment (for example, family therapy), and so forth. The process is diagramed in figure 5.3.[31]

These descriptions, theories, and practices of therapy are not confined to the professionals. In various ways, and often intentionally (an educated clientele is easier to handle than an uneducated), these kinds of information are fed into the general knowledge about psychological problems available through women's magazines, television dramas, courses in mental hygiene, and Psych 100, as well as into the training of such professionals as teachers, social workers, and others. In this way, my seeing my own experience, as a matter for psychiatric care, or you seeing yours, comes about from knowing how to describe it and look at it in these ways. The same goes for my seeing or your seeing someone else's behavior in such ways. To be able to make such a description is to know how to make what I feel or what you feel or what she is doing into a matter that is psychiatrically actionable. The reality of mental illness is a recycled reality.

The statistics, then, do represent something real about the troubles which people have, but what is real cannot be separated from the professional and administrative operations that make those troubles actionable. These operations make over, tidy up, sort out, and shape what is actually happening with people into properly recognizable forms. If you are dealing with a "well-educated" population, much of the shaping will have already been done before the patient gets to the agency.[32] The people who are counted in the statistics are entered by these processes into a system that eliminates the situational variations, the contexts, the actualities, and the recurrent social conditions characteristic of a given community, industrial structure, class system, and so on. Any psychiatric agency comes to be organized in relation to a definite constituency or set of constituencies. This constituency is in part organized by its own policies, by the uses it comes to serve, and by how access to it is controlled. The bookkeeping of the agencies that Statistics Canada compiles is the end product of these processes. What Chesler and Gove and Tudor have done is to take these stripped-down bits of information and try to reattach them to situations in which they arose; to patch them together again into some kind of simulacrum of the form they had before they went through the meat grinder.

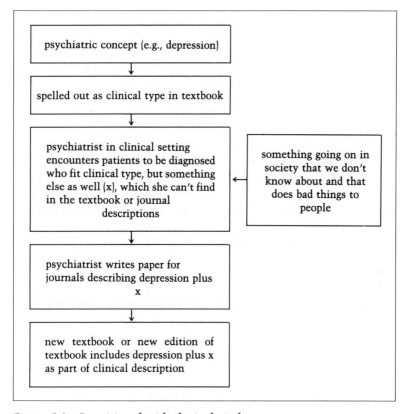

Figure 5.3   Repairing the ideological circle

◖ Thinking It

Differently

The foregoing discussion locates the issue of women and mental illness at the juncture of what is going on in people's lives, the locally specific organization of practices, work, and relating in which people's experience of the world is embedded, and the extralocal apparatuses of psychiatry. The latter are part of the textually mediated relations of ruling of contemporary society; they include the distinctive custodially structured medical facilities, the professions (psychiatrist, psychologist, psychiatric social worker, psychiatric nurse), the academic and professional discourses as ideological and knowledge resources, and the relevant legal powers, privileges, and conditions. Though at the beginning of the chapter I questioned the feminist interest in finding women's oppression as a cause of mental illness, I too am persuaded of the political nature of the relation between women and psychiatry. A while ago in a conference on women and the state, I sat in on a workshop run by activists in organizations of self-styled "psychiatrized women." Of all the workshops in the conference, here were the women who were still unbelievably angry and still totally unwilling in any way to trust the psychiatric establishment. Indeed, a painful split developed in the group between organization activists and women, themselves at one time psychiatrized, who had moved into professional or other "helping" roles in an attempt to improve the way women are treated in the psychiatric system. The organization activists saw the latter as having gone over to the other side. Of course, not everyone who is treated psychiatrically experiences it in just this way, but it was clear that everyone present who had been "psychiatrized" in some form or another knew where the anger came from.[33] It arises at this juncture where, as described in the previous chapter, the powers of psychiatric institutions enforce their interpretations and dispositions on the everyday lives of individual people. It is therefore a political issue; for women it is also a question of patriarchy.

The model "oppression → mental illness" does not adequately explicate the organization of these relations. Indeed, I think we have to set aside the issue of mental illness, of what it is that may be going on in the minds and feelings and bodies of women who are hospitalized for mental illness or treated as outpatients with psychotherapy or mood modifying drugs. Instead, the political and patriarchal dimensions of psychiatric institutions must be explored as an intervention of extralocally organized powers into a local order that an individual disrupts and disorganizes in some way. The patriarchal character of psychiatric institutions is overdetermined. The standpoint of men is built into the traditions of its theorizing and knowledge; that effect is reinforced by the continued predominance of men, particularly in the dominant psychiatric profession. Beyond that, however, psychiatry participates in and reinforces the patriarchal character of locally produced orders, such as families, as a routine effect of its operation.[34]

I'm not arguing that there is no mental illness in the sense that there are no states of psychic disturbance or disorganizations of action and behavior that go beyond our own capacities to deal with and that lead us to seek help from powers beyond ours. But we need not be mystified by the medicalization of these powers. We don't need to deny the significance of medical science to recognize also that psychiatric care and treatment is *always* implicated in the control and regulation of local social orders. My aim here, then, is to explicate the ways in which this jural and political relation determines women's experience as psychiatric patients.

Earlier in this chapter I described the interactional procedures that suspend the patient's capacity as subject. The thread of invalidation or discounting recurs again and again in experiential accounts. The patient, in assuming the status of a diagnosed, hospitalized person, is thereby formally accorded a new moral status, one that excludes her from participation as subject in the making of everyday realities. The loss of that social capacity is pointedly described in Barbara Findlay's account of her experience: "Perhaps for me the worst part [of hospitalization] was having no credibility. The basic assumption of the hospital was not only that we—the patients—were 'sick' but also that we were 'unable to cope.' Under that rationale they controlled every part of our life. And of course no one believed me—about anything. The golden truth about me carried no validity, and made no difference, unless it came from the lips of the shrink himself."[35]

Here is the importance of the experience of the "subjects" in Rosenham's study, who, having established that their sanity was unblemished, spent time in mental hospitals in California without being detected by the staff as impostors (yet patients noticed).[36] For staff, it is the status of patients, not their behavior, that governs how they are "read." The person so defined no longer functions as subject in the participants' local realities. Findlay experienced a denial of her lesbian sexuality that treated it as extraneous to her, as a sickness working on her. She could make no claims about herself that would be honored.

It is this dimension of the psychiatric relation that I want to bring into focus. However hard psychiatry works to establish itself as a purely medical function, a claim recently dignified by advances in biochemical knowledge and the development of medication specific to some types of psychoses, this "other business" of psychiatry is always also present, inextricable from the medical and inevitably contaminating it. With whatever modality, psychiatry acts to control people who have come to be seen as breaching, disrupting, or disorganizing the everyday/everynight and taken-for-granted accomplishments of a recognizable world. Mary Douglas in *Purity and danger* has given us a brilliant analysis of an everyday social ordering of the world as a specific symbolic mode, a particular social artifact that constitutes its own opposite, its negation, its other; its very symbolic coherence creates its peculiar possibilities for disorder and disruption. She analyzes the dietary prohibitions and other seemingly irrational prescriptions to be found in Leviticus as anomalies defined by the distinctive coherences of a moral order, and hence as generated by, marking the boundaries of, and preserving a social order as a coherent moral universe.[37] Though I'd want to rephrase her analysis more in terms of practices than concepts and symbols, I follow her formulation of the self-created fragility of the social orderings we participate in and thus create and renew. People rely on each other; they trust each other to create the normality on which they rely. This isn't just a matter of expectations or norms, it's a matter of how people's doing and saying is condition, context, and "what happens next" to a subject's doing and saying. To get on with things, to carry on in an ordinary way, depends continually on the normal texture and substance provided by others' doings. Psychiatric institutions take up, are called in, when someone disrupts and disorganizes the on-going work of producing everyday normality, and ordinary measures of bringing her back into line don't work.

To describe the interdependence of people's accomplishment of everyday/everynight realities is not, however, to suppose that they are equal in power and control over those realities and how they participate in them. The stories of "psychiatrized" women are dramatic and painful stories of inequalities in power and the connivance of particular powers with psychiatric institutions in opposing the overt or implicit alternative versions of the subject herself. The story she would tell, if taken seriously, if heard fully and properly, and particularly if heard and taken up as a basis for making change, would disrupt the locally established order of home and family. As Judi Chamberlain has written, "Like the single soldier who claims that it's everyone else who is out of step, and just as ineffectually, so I struggled against everyone else's conception of what I was and what I should become."[38]

Psychiatry is a recourse for people in positions of power in a threatened local order who seek to sustain their working version of the world. In providing "objective" grounds for repudiating alternative versions, it authorizes the local order. We can see this process of repression in an episode in Diane Harpwood's novel *Tea and tranquillisers.* The novel is a diary of the everyday life of a young housewife with two small children whose husband, hardworking and affectionate, gives no help with children or housework. The episode in question tells a story about the telling of a story; first she tells us what happened, tells her own story; then she tells us the story as told to the physician, scripted by her husband and told by her.

Saturday 28th I left home tonight, flew the nest, scarpered. I'd had E-nough and enough they say is as good as a feast, or in my case a glut. So the atmosphere in the old homestead has been a trifle chilled tonight.

I've been on my feet since half-past six this morning and my bum has scarcely come into contact with a chair all day. I've been making beds, tidying up, changing shitty nappies, tidying up, washing shitty nappies, tidying up, preparing, cooking and clearing up after breakfast, lunch and tea, washing the kitchen floor which is permanently filthy with bits of petrifying food and assorted muck carried in on everyone's shoes, except for today, when it was clean for a while. All of the aforementioned chores were carried out with the pack. The "enfants terrible", they were today, "et moi" have surged around the house in a scrimmage.

This evening I bathed the children, they soaked the new carpet which has lain in a string-bound roll since last September when we bought it. I brought them down to say goodnight to Daddy. I always do that to make sure they remember his name. I put them to bed, I tidied away the toys and went to make myself a drink which I intended to drink in solitude, in a chair that contained only me. He heard me, must have been the lid of the kettle, and he spoke to me. "Are you making a cuppa, love?" he said. So blinded was I by rage, the shock of hearing his voice and the thwarting of my plans to make something solely and only for me for once that I picked a jar of jam from the pantry shelf instead of the jar of coffee, and I dropped it. It shattered, scattering splinters of lethal glass and smearing red jam all over my shining clean floor. It was the last straw, the bitter end, the death blow to my self-control and I let rip, shouting obscenities about him sitting on his backside blind, deaf and dumb to everything going on around him, and crying my eyes out. He said I'd only dropped a jar of jam for Chrissakes. That did it. I told him to piss off but, while he was still standing with his mouth open, I did. I flung on my coat and slammed out of the house in my slippers. . . . I didn't know where to go, where was there to go?[39]

Later, David, her husband, suggests she should see a doctor and volunteers to make the arrangement himself. We see in her account of the interview with the physician how her husband's version of what happened becomes the version told by her in the doctor's office. The second story is very partial; though told as "what happened," it is in fact recentered from her to her husband; it includes only those sequences in which he is directly involved. The "official version" drops out her story of the daily routine of work in which frustrations and denials of her own desire accumulate, spilling over when her moment of gratification is thwarted; it drops out everything that would make sense of what was happening and of her anger with her husband.

> [David] came home at half-past five this evening and took us all in the car. . . . Panicked at what to say to Dr. Andrews so did as David suggested and described last Saturday night, the bolt for freedom the tears etc. because I'd dropped a jar of jam. It must have sounded ridiculous. He seemed to know what was wrong immediately, didn't say much, too busy, standing room only in the waiting room. He looked into my eyes, told me to hold my hands out in front of me, wrote a prescription, told me how and when to take the pills and he wants to see me again in a fortnight. I don't know what he's prescribed or why he prescribed it. I was too confused and embarrassed at wasting his time to interrogate him but I feel a bit better because he seemed sure he could help me.
>   David says he'll nip into Benton tomorrow to pick up my prescription.[40]

The heroine herself borrows her story from her husband, producing an account of her behavior from his viewpoint. Told thus it does indeed lack sense: the accidental dropping of a jar of jam precipitates an extraordinary outburst of rage against her husband. This version is received unquestioned by the physician and on this basis he prescribes a tranquilizer. His prescription ratifies the husband's standpoint. It does not change the heroine's situation, only the emotions she feels.

The diagnostic practices and concepts of psychiatry organize, validate, and objectify such suppression. It is here we might perhaps find the underpinnings of women's predominance in the categories of neurosis and affective psychosis. Consider again the instance of "depression" referred to above. Depression is specified by a collection of "indicators"—feelings of sadness, of guilt, of futility; crying; loss of interest, of energy; social withdrawal; sleeplessness; and so on. The concept extracts states of subjectivity or behavioral indicators from the actual settings of the patient's experience. In the previous chapter

I described how the organization of the medical establishment produces the patient in the physician's office stripped of the contexture of her life. That is the organizational complement of the conceptual stripping organized by the diagnostic procedure. The concept organizes a reconstructive procedure in the clinical setting as a physician or other professional questions and observes the patient, or questions the patient's family members, assembling a story that specifically discards the "other" story, the story that grasps the contextures of feeling and setting in an individual's life and is spoken from her standpoint as subject. In the context of treatment, psychiatrists may act to police standardized versions of normality. Barbara Findlay in her autobiographical account reports one psychiatrist who "felt I should lose weight and present myself in a more attractive manner. He told me that I chose unattractive clothes—my wardrobe was basic and practical, and there were no frills. He wanted me to date more often, to become involved with men."[41]

Though I have moved away from the conception of mental illness and from the model "oppression → mental illness," I cannot withhold my sense of how this political relation may destroy and disorganize our ability to participate actively as subjects and perhaps even over time may destroy our ability to function as subjects for ourselves at all. The isolation of mood, emotion, feeling, from the contextures of life are particularly significant here. For emotion isn't a state of mind or feeling; it tends to action. The conceptual detachment of emotions and states of mind from lived actualities disconnects them from possibilities of change, of action, and of power. The psychiatric work of defining emotions, moods, feelings, as what has to be treated (by psychotherapy, tranquilizers, shock, and so on) isolates them from prospective action, indeed seeks to "take out" (by medication or other means) people's energies, particularly rage, that press against human obstacles for change. A woman's resistance, her struggles, her efforts to move away from her suffering and toward she cannot always tell what, are expressed in action and speech disrupting and disjunctive with the locally sanctioned everyday/everynight realities. "Symptoms" are like springs forced from the rock—the logic of their movement and energy is not visible to the eye. The medical or psychiatric official in treating the patient, affirms the established order she disrupts. She is not heard as subject; she is insulated further from taking part in the making of a different order. Therefore, in her struggles to move she has no touchstone, no feedback, no possibility of efficacy, no possibility of developing a context of action and response in which she could make sense to others and to herself. Conceive, then, an intensifying spiral of disorganization, embedded in and accelerated by a psychiatric context that denies validity to feeling, to action, to speech,[42] as desire for and efforts to remake a given ordering of the lived world.

CHAPTER

6

NO
ONE
COMMITS
SUICIDE

❚

TEXTUAL
ANALYSES OF
IDEOLOGICAL
PRACTICES

◗   The Ideological Rupture

     in Consciousness

"She committed suicide" and "she killed herself" have the same meaning. They may, it appears, be used interchangeably with respect to what they denote, though the contexts of their use may supply a secondary set of conventions preferring one usage to another. Otherwise, they appear to be substitutable for one another so far as meaning is concerned. Nothing more or less appears to be said by the one than is said by the other. But between them lies a disjuncture, not apparent at the semantic level, that is a property of social relations in which these two phrases, exemplifying different language "games"[1] or "speech genres,"[2] are embedded.

Suicide has long been a focus of sociological work, as J. Maxwell Atkinson shows us in his account of the debates around the indeterminacy of the phenomenon and the ways in which sociologists have sought to give it determination.[3] In the textual discourse of the social sciences, we make use of categories such as suicide to denote the phenomena of which we would speak. Category and phenomenon seem wholly at one with one another. In this context, the choice between "she committed suicide" and "she killed herself" becomes merely stylistic or conventional. Both refer to the same "event," assumed to exist prior to or independently of the process of inquiry.

An alternative procedure is to take up the terms of our discourse and re-embed them in the social relations that were their original home. They have their specific work, their specific usages, which are not necessarily descriptive or referencing usages at all.[4] Here, then, our strategy is aimed at opening up the gap that social scientific discourse ordinarily seals over. We will explore and anatomize the dialogic order[5] of social science and psychiatry, examining ideology as a method of superseding, substituting, and suppressing the accounts that people create out of the recollection of experience with the accounts of professional discourse. This move, the ideological move, is more than a literary event; it is also a move that subordinates the individual within the relations of ruling.

At the point of someone's suicide, there is the sharpest sense of disjuncture between any formal account of that death and how that death has been experienced by those involved. That disparity, that severance, can also be found when we read experimental accounts of an attempted self-killing, such as that provided by Sylvia Plath in fictional form in *The bell jar*[6] and in poetic form in "Lady Lazarus."[7] Plath's poem is indeed deeply ordered within the conflicting relations of this rupture. The act of self-killing itself becomes in the context of institutional intervention a performance; she is at their disposal, to be raked over, anatomized; the projected flight and victory is ambiguously an escape via a different death from which there is no return; it is both an escape from repetition and an escape from the tyrannical scrutiny of male rulers. The institutional paraphernalia of "motives," "reasons," "clinically identifiable states of mind," let alone the more strictly legal questions of intent and hence responsibility, are in contradiction with the lived experiencing ending in self-killing.[8]

We are concerned here with a break in the social consciousness between how people experience, tell, and make sense of what is happening from within the particular times and places of their lived actuality and a formalized impersonal mode of knowing articulated to (and indeed an integral part of) an apparatus of ruling. This disjuncture is the focus of our inquiry. Since "experience" comes into view only in its telling and as a method of telling, we shall take up this disjuncture as well as the imperium of the institutional discourses as different modes of telling "what happened." The difference is more than that discussed by R. S. Peters, who contrasts a person's reasons for doing something and *the* reasons, where the latter are features of a formal discourse warranted by and accomplished in the work of experts.[9] We will explore the contrasts here as a relation between the ideological practices of the social relations of ruling and the everyday forms of talk in which events are told in primary narrative form[10] hugging an experienced actuality.

In the context of an actual self-killing the presuppositions of people's relations are called into question. The problem of whether it was indeed as I saw it, of the disparities between how it was experienced and how it comes to be represented, has a sharpness deriving from the power of the experience itself. I am not going to argue that it is the business of sociology to express experience. Rather, I am taking up as the problematic of the social organization of knowledge the relation between the original and fundamental location of consciousness, of knowing, in an experiencing individual at the center 0 of her system of coordinates, as Schutz describes it,[11] and an abstracted system of representing "what actually happened/what is" in which the subject is canceled in favor of expressions such as *suicide*. In these the individual and her act disappear in a category externalized and made apt as a constituent of the discourses of a professional intelligentsia. The apparent synonymy of reference in the expressions "she killed herself" and "she committed suicide" disappears if we work with these reflexively, for then we find them located differently in relation to the actuality that both intend. The first is the language of everyday discourse, whereas the second is in the ideological mode—it embeds the story in the relations of ruling within which an act becomes suicide.

◪   Ideology as

an Actual Practice

In the previous chapter, the concept of mental illness was substructed, that is, analyzed "behind" or "beneath" the ideological rupture that accords it a textual reality separate from the social relations that are its actual ground. There and in chapter 4, we were exploring our invisible but deep dependence on the bureaucratic, professional, and other forms of formal organization and organizational practices that bring phenomena into being in their relations to an everyday world they organize and regulate. We cannot find an everyday world beyond the categories without examining the organizational processes that do the work of transposing actual happenings, experiences, goings on, events, states of affairs as actualities, into an objectified system of records defining and defined by the jurisdiction and objectives of formal organization. Our thinking, our theorizing, our knowledge of society and social relations appear then as a precarious structure erected on a formidably organized apparatus mediating to us a world of which we claim to speak.

While it is not at all clear that "she killed herself" necessarily commits us to a language that speaks from a specific location and from within the knowing of a specific subjectivity, it *is* clear that "she committed suicide" does not. The latter form arises and belongs in an institutional form of ruling mediated by documentary forms of knowledge. "She committed suicide" is a form of factual statement provided for by the apparatus of governing, administering, and managing. As we saw in the last chapter, a relation is created between objectified and universalized systems of administration and the actualities always local, always particular, always individual, and inexhaustibly various.

This applies also to the work of the coroner's office in the determination of a death as suicide. That office is a state agency. It has a definite legal mandate. It is integral to the state system of control over the use of physical violence by its citizens and its control over the record keeping relevant to maintaining vital statistics, public health information, and so on. Suicide as a coherent type of act or event or type of death is framed in terms of these interests. The particulars of a death are organized and selected as accountable in terms of a frame of reference that is a feature of a social relation. The requirement that the set of descriptive categories be exhaustive with respect to the deaths of which account must be made[12] is a requirement of the state to ensure that every death within the jurisdiction of a given national entity be sanctioned. The set of categories, the development of methods of filling categories and of articulating descriptive categories to a lived actuality to constitute "what actually happened" as an organizational practice, arise in and as a part of an operation of the state and professional extensions of state interest. They are integral to the organization of the state and to other apparatuses and relations of ruling.

Suicide is not and cannot be simply a characterization of a death. Rather, it is an account of a death made warrantable and recorded in the work of a state agency. It expresses a relation between state interests, the established frame of reference in which those interests are realized as an array of legally warranted categories, and an event that is constituted as such by practical activities of agents of the state. "Suicide" as a phenomenon is generated in the same social relational complex as that which generates the demographic data discussed in chapter 4—the work organization of hospitals and of medical records, the production of death certificates, the workings of coroners' courts, police work, and the legislative and administrative processes that maintain, articulate, and regulate these.

There is a division of labor here: on the one hand, the professional and administrative organization of work that accounts for someone's death as a suicide; on the other, the secondary work of an intelligentsia, organized in discursive relations, reflecting on, systematizing, and generalizing from information constructed in multiple local sites. The theorizing—indeed, the knowledge—of a professional intelligentsia builds upon and makes sense out of the prior administrative work of producing organizational forms of knowledge, generally for organizational purposes, surely within organizational schemata of relevance, and conforming to their processing technologies, and so forth. Legal, administrative, and clinical records, data from the courts, newspapers, government statistics—these are the terms of our knowledge of the world. Our world as members of an intelligentsia is literate, documented, and secondhand.

This suggests an ideological organization at a more general level in the society, built into this characteristic division of labor between the institutional apparatuses that operate directly in people's everyday lives and a discursive work and organization that generalizes, systematizes, and theorizes. The first, as a byproduct of its operations, methodically transforms the particularities of people's experience of the everyday/everynight world into "data" (meaning "givens"). The second enters those worked-up data into the theorizing and synthesizing operations of social science. Some social sciences, notably sociology and anthropology, have also developed and relied on methods of investigating that construct data beyond that generated in the relations of ruling. But to a very great degree, particularly in sociology, the "independent" collection of data is profoundly rooted in a conceptual order expressing the same relations as those that generate the "facts" of suicide, crime, demographic statistics, the gross national product, unemployment statistics, and so forth.

But the categories and concepts float free; they can be taken to intend an actuality directly, uncomplicated by awareness of the complexity of the institutional apparatus of ruling that intervenes between the lived actualities and the surface of the text that the social scientist reads. Social science has developed methods of investigating the congruence of its theoretical schemata and the actuality they intend, using methods that preserve fully the autonomy of theory while testing its capacity to organize data of a determinate form. The theoretical work of the social scientific discourse develops, refines, tests, and renews the conceptual schemata that bureaucratic, managerial, and professional organizations use for *their* practical purposes. In the context of suicide, Atkinson has shown us how the sociological and psychiatric discourses have provided coroners with motivational analyses that are entered into the work of determining the character of a death:

> A . . . general conclusion is that the process of investigating sudden deaths involves the coroner in a process of *explanation*. If the clues available allow him to construct an explanatory model which seems to fit a particular type of death, then the verdict will categorize that death accordingly. Thus, if he cannot adequately explain why a person should have committed suicide, then another verdict will be recorded. (As contrasted with accidents) he is involved in a more complex form of explanation because the legal need to establish intent necessitates the search for a motive or reason why the deceased should have taken his own life.[13]

Atkinson makes clear that the process of investigation that produces the informational basis of the coroner's verdict (largely the work of the police) is directed toward the interpretive schemata that serve the coroner in analyzing what he finds and arriving at a determination of what has happened. The same relation can be discerned in Garfinkel's account of the Los Angeles Suicide Prevention Center[14]—indeed, the very presence of the researcher in that setting displays this relation.

Atkinson's findings in his study of the relation between commonsense and social scientific theorizing about suicide demonstrates the extent to which both methods and content are shared among those participating in a variety of roles in the ideological process.

> The evidence . . . shows that it is not just coroners and coroners' officers who theorize about suicide but that witnesses and, by implication, newspaper reporters engage in similar practices. . . . The analysis of the newspaper reports . . . showed that such reports tell the reader not only *that* particular deaths were suicides but also give a version of why the suicides took place. In addressing the *why* issue, causal rela-

tionships and other trends are referred to which seem in large measure identical to those contained in the writings of experts. Given the reliance of suicidologists on data derived from official sources and on other evidence obtained from witnesses to suicidal events, it is easy to understand how it is that the experts "discover" findings and construct theories which are already known and used by ordinary members of society.[15]

Our business here is the explication of these relations and the ways in which we as social scientists enter into them or have entered into them. In these interrelated practices we can see a division of "mental labor" among members of the professional intelligentsia working in various institutional contexts. The articulation of different segments of these social relations are not obvious, yet they create the actual links between a lived actuality and the event as it becomes known in the documentary forms in which it circulates for further work. Whatever else may be going on in this interchange between the professional discourse and the institutional structures of state control, it is a process that continually integrates, circulates, feeds back, and coordinates the changing relations of the bureaucratic apparatus to the actuality of everyday life. The phrase "she committed suicide" gives us entrée to that ideological process; the phrase "she killed herself" does not.

The process with which we are concerned is diagramed in figure 6.1, which sketches the relation between the actualities that may be spoken in the language of everyday life as "she killed herself" to the transformative, nominalizing language of ideology, "she committed suicide." It is in the latter term that it becomes available to us as practitioners of a specialized professional discourse.

As members of a professional intelligentsia, we are entered into the process twice over. It is indeed fully rather than partially reflexive. Partial reflexivity involves the explication of the theorizing, categorizing, and conceptual practices of sociology as features of settings;[16] a second partial reflexivity recognizes the placing, person, and values of the researcher.[17] Full reflexivity is achieved when we recognize our entry into the social relations of which we speak so that we can address our own practices as sociologists as well as grasp how we may enter these processes at the other end of a chain of organized social activities. Full reflexivity enables us not only to speak of members' methods, relying, as Roy Turner has pointed out,[18] upon our own knowledge, but also to speak of —and, of course, also address critically—our own methods as members.[19]

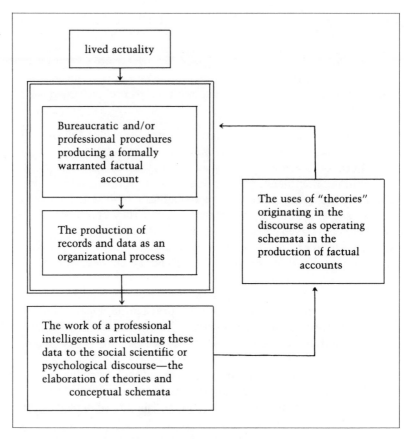

Figure 6.1   The actuality-data-theory circuit

🔖   An Investigation of Texts
as Constituents of Social Relations

This chapter explores the break between the experienced and the ideological by contrasting the characteristic structuring of "primary" narratives, that is, narratives that draw directly on experience as a method of production, with the procedures for constructing ideologically ordered narratives. A collection of texts will be used to enable us to explore our own knowledge of methods of operating on primary narratives to produce ideological accounts. Analysis of the texts is not textual analysis in the sense of an exclusive focus on what is there for us in print. Rather, texts are seen as constituents of social relations, and hence, by exploring our own knowledge of how to operate the interrelations among them, we explicate both our own practices and a segment of the social relations in which those practices are embedded and which they organize. Thus, this investigation takes up our relation as social scientists or psychologists to the process diagrammed in figure 6.1 at the juncture between "lived actuality" and the professional and bureaucratic production of facts, where our discursive schemata generated by our work enters the process of constructing the textual realities of ruling.

The materials made use of in this investigation tap this process at various points. They consist, at present, of a collection of texts; in this chapter they explore how psychiatric schemata operate on primary narrative texts to produce the "case," and in the following chapter they explore how the reader participates in the structuring of Quentin Bell's telling of the period leading up to Virginia Woolf's suicide as a period of developing mental illness. These exhibits bring into this text the actual structure of the relations they are embedded in. They are like laboratory specimens rather than illustrations. Through them we dissect our own practical and tacit knowledge of how to operate them, *not as idiosyncratic but as attributes of social relations.* Their capacity to appear as specimens differs therefore from the laboratory model. They are not isolated but are treated as bringing something like a knot to the surface of this text, trailing the segments of social relations in which the specimen is embedded along with it. In marked contrast to the laboratory, the social scientist is not separated from what she explores. Rather she knows how to trace the configuration of the knot because she participates in the relations it pulls into the text.

This method of investigation builds on the commitment to women's standpoint enunciated in the first chapter of this book. The exhibits and the relations they knot into the text are explored from inside, as experienced. Interpretation or analysis does not rely on their cogency, happiness, rhetorical effectiveness, or a contingent conjunction with how you or I see it. Analysis relies rather on processes and practices that are not private, that others, particularly those likely to read this, already know how to do. In spelling these out, I am only tracing on a map pathways that are already familiar, or, if unfamiliar, easily followed. It is from texts such as these and the textual discourse to which they are articulated that I have learned the interpretive practices I use, and they are not private. It is to texts such as these that such interpretive practices will apply as operators of the text, and they are not private.

A brief account of the concept of "social relation" as it is used here is needed. The usage is derived from Marx, though he does not use it quite as I do.[20] Integral to a materialist analysis of social processes, it identifies the actual practices of individuals and their articulation in forming a social course of action. Different individuals, different individual courses of action, enter into relations through which they are organized vis-à-vis one another. The division of labor here is not seen as an allocation of social tasks to individuals as roles that are components of a socially organized entity. Rather it is an actual process in which the generality and intersubjectivity of social phenomena are accomplished. The production of goods for a market, the exchange of those goods for money, the further sequence of exchanges, and the final entry of those goods into use—this is a sequence in which many individuals and many individual courses of action play their part. It is a process of actual activities in a temporal sequence. Its different moments are dependent upon one another and articulated to one another not functionally but as sequences in which the foregoing intends the subsequent and in which the subsequent "realizes" or accomplishes the social character of the preceding. Thus, Marx points out that a particular commodity is not realized as such by virtue of being a good produced for the market. If it is still haunting a warehouse, its character as commodity is ghostly. Its realization as *commodity* depends upon its sale.

The concept of social relation as used here does not identify a special class of social phenomena. Rather, it is an analytic device isolating in the phenomena, magnified and brought into focus for examination, the social courses of action of which they are constituents. For example, an ethnomethodologist might address a specific segment of courtroom talk, say, an interruption, as an instance of a general class of speech events, receiving the immediate setting of the courtroom as the temporal and spatial boundaries of the event. By contrast, the method of inquiry deployed here would treat the interruption as a feature of a social relation not fully present in the courtroom or to observation. Courtroom talk is directed towards the production of a formally warranted record of the proceedings. The record has a definite legal status and legal uses. Those responsible for it are the judge and the court recorder. The record is then available to lawyers at a later stage for the purposes of making appeals and the like. Courtroom interruptions are handled in specialized ways that clarify what was said and who said what *for the record.* They take on a distinctive character in the context of a social relation. Thus "social relation" as an analytic device explores the activities of a particular local setting or, as here, textual instances drawn into the analytic text, as articulated to social courses of action beyond the immediate time, place, and complement of people. "Social relation" enables us to go from the moment of "observation," in which the phenomenon arises for us in our here-and-now, to an analysis that discloses how it is organized by and articulated to foregoing and subsequent moments in a social relation. The textual exhibits analyzed below give access to interpretive practices integral to the social relations of ruling diagramed in figure 6.1. They are exhibits of the interpretive practices that articulate ruling to the actual settings that it governs, regulates, and coordinates. They are exhibits of interpretive practices of ruling that we participate in.

◼ Encoding Living Actualities

into the Relations of Ruling

The overall process of going from what actually happens, via the ordering work of encoding, to an account intending a particular interpretive method and schema can also be represented in a diagram. Figure 6.2 charts the relation between the "lived actuality" box and the formal organizational process in figure 6.1. In a sense, a lived actuality never happens, for it is always lived; what is, happens, or has happened arises only at the point where a recording is made, a story is told, a picture is taken. The ontological problem of correspondence between descriptive terms and objects or events is bypassed, as indeed it should be, in that "what actually happened/what is" arises only at that moment of reflection where experience is intended by an account or encoding aiming at an account. The process going from encoding to account constitutes "what actually hap-

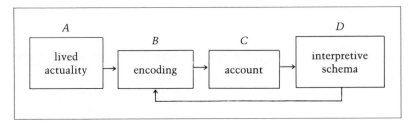

Figure 6.2   From actuality to account

pened" as that which is referenced in the account. Members' methods of constituting what actually happened in this relation are among those investigated by ethnomethodology. Among them, of course, are such members' methods as the categorization devices analyzed by Harvey Sacks.[21]

The encoding process (B) goes from an actuality (A) to an account (C). It involves selecting terms and grammatical and logical connections that express the appropriate sequencing. The arrow from D to B represents this relation. The selecting and ordering of instructions, as well as criteria of appropriateness, derive from the interpretive schema that the resulting account intends as its operating schema (the arrow from C to D). These enter, or may enter, into the encoding stage (arrow from D to B).

The different components of the diagram could represent a division of labor stretching the process over a complex sequence of practices ordered as a social relation. Thus, in what will be described as the primary narrative mode the experiencer (at A) and the encoder and teller of the tale (B and C) are one and the same, and the hearer or reader enters at the interpretive moment (D). In contrast, when someone kills herself in a contemporary setting, there may be some overlap in the process in terms of those involved at A and B, but the encoding and construction of the account (B and D) will be largely the work of the "authorities," including the police, the coroner and others. The "readers" whose interpretive schemata are intended may be news reporters, social scientists, professional colleagues and associates, and the family and friends of the person who killed herself, as well as the official recordkeepers of the state. All this at point D, where we too are located as we take up our work.

The analysis of texts aims to discover in the text the social relations of which we are practitioners. Through our analysis we seek to explicate our own tacit practices discovered in features or properties of a text. The "subjective" process is objectified in an explication of the text. The analysis of texts explicates what we know how to do. This presupposes that the text intends an interpretive schema, which we command. Where the text intends a schema we do not know how to operate and cannot learn, the text is effectively dead to us. The text can be said to intend an interpretive schema (though not necessarily a particular interpretation) when such a schema enters into the process of producing the text. In the process of writing, making corrections, in thinking again about how to address a topic, in thinking through a topic so that it can be first thought, then expressed, adequately, clearly, and well, a text is developed that depends upon and intends the interpretative schema that has entered normatively into its creation. In the production of the text the same circular process is at work as that which arises between text and reader. Hence the text can be said to intend interpretive procedures as those practices and methods of reading which will read it for the sense intended.

Sense is accomplished in the reader's silent transaction with the text. It is the reader who brings the text to life as meaning. The relation between text and reader takes the form almost of a special kind of inner speech, a "conversation" within the reader. It is in that sense subjective. Nonetheless, it is also clearly social. The reader uses interpretive schemata in finding the sense of the text. These she has learned as a member of her society participating in determinate social relations, including those of the discourse in the context of which her interpretive work is done. The inner conversation in which the reader plays the part both of text and reader is a material moment in a social relation. It implicates interpretive processes embedded in that social relation and integral to its organization.

The problem of the subjectivity of the effective sense of a text seems insoluble if we isolate the moment in which a particular reader and a particular text connect. In isolation the interpretive schemata appear as skills, attributes, informational resources, and biographical features that the individual reader brings to the text, and hence as attributes of the particular reader. The effective sense of the text as it arises in any particular reader does, of course, depend upon the particular reader's interpretive resources and commitment. But by treating that relation reflexively and embedding it in the actual social relations to which it is articulated, schemata can be relocated as features of social relations. The reader's engagement with the text can be examined with respect to the social relations to which it is articulated.

This is often a matter we don't attend to because in the social relation in which our own work is embedded we confront the text as our object. The text arises as an object in this relation of working. Its character as an object of that work becomes thematic in our consciousness. It does not appear before us in its active transactional being, as a moment in a sequence of practices concerted as a social relation. Our gaze, oriented toward the enterprise of inquiry, is not self-regarding. We do not in the orientation of our work recognize how at this moment, too, the text is taking on a distinctive character in the context of the social relations of our work and that this relation organizes what we bring to bear upon the text as interpretive practices. The relation of this moment to the discourse operates as a controlling framework selecting and subordinating the practice of our investigation to its relevances.

In analysis, therefore, we should be concerned to locate the controlling frameworks and interpretive schemata provided by the social relation that the text originally intended (was written to intend). Substantive nouns such as *novel*, which represent themselves as descriptive categories applied to types of text, are constituents of a social relation articulating writer, publisher, and reader—pieces of its organization. They are terms used in the everyday practices of the social relations of the literary marketplace. The relation of reader to text and the interpretive schemata she will bring into play are "selected" by her knowledge of this text as novel and her knowing whatever it is she knows how to do as a method of reading the text as fiction. The text and the interpretive practices of reading fiction are not seen as a social relation because the organization of social relations is an unobservable process located in the production, marketing, and distribution process relating writer and reader, or the organization of storage of texts, which structures the relation between the present reader and the writer who is dead. Telling children a story at bedtime is an observable form of relation between the teller of the tale and its hearers. But the anonymities of organizational and market relations are no less real. Furthermore, the reader has been prepared, in terms of what she has learned, to enter this relation and to know how to operate it. We can imagine how it would be possible to read a novel as a factual account. We can imagine—because it sometimes happens that we find a novel that is "autobiographical," where we attempt to deal with this double mode of reading—moving from bracketing the referential process when we read in the fictive mode to using it as we read in the factual mode.[22] The professional social scientist or historian reading the text of a Cretan storage inventory, an industrial time sheet, a court record, or the like, is reading in it the context of her relation to the professional discourse and hence under a set of interpretive practices that will not ordinarily read the text as it was read in its original setting. Often such texts are read as if they were descriptions referring to an actuality encoded in the text. But that itself is a particular interpretive strategy that has its home in a discourse. The procedure indicated here requires an examination of the relevances and schemata of the social relations into which the text is entered and hence of how it is read in the contexts in which it is used. That is to explicate the social relations of the interpretation the text intends.

Our major focus here is the ideological practices entering into the production and interpretation of factual accounts. The analysis of ideologically formed, factual accounts makes visible a phase of the extended relations of a division of labor among different sections of a ruling apparatus. The texts on which we will work are situated in various ways in relation to psychiatric discourse. Only one, to be explored in the following chapter, is an account of suicide. But all display the operation of a clinical mode of a type that is of very general use by coroners, among others. That this mode of making factual accounts of a biographical sequence is ideological will not be a matter of definition, categorization, or coding. Rather, ideological properties will be explicated through analysis.

◪   "Primary" Versus Ideological

Organization of Narrative

The experienced becomes social in members' methods of telling and hearing or reading. Ideological practices in constructing and interpreting factual accounts are one method. They are distinctively the mode in which the universalized terms of textual discourse, bureaucratic organization, or the like are inserted into local accounts, reconstructing them as instances within the abstracted jurisdiction of the ruling apparatus. The ideological method can be viewed as a special case of the documentary method of interpretation described by Mannheim[23] and developed by Garfinkel.[24] Here is Garfinkel's account of the method:

> The method consists of treating an actual appearance as "the document of," as "pointing to," as "standing on behalf of" a presupposed underlying pattern. Not only is the underlying pattern derived from its individual documentary evidences, but the individual documentary evidences, in their turn, are interpreted on the basis of "what is known" about the underlying pattern. Each is used to elaborate the other.[25]

His description of the interrelation of pattern and parts does not precisely hold for the ideological circle; his concept is broader. Some of the instances he makes use of do not involve treating events as documents of the schemata of a textual discourse. For example, the documentary method of interpretation includes the conversational process, "the everyday necessities of recognizing what a person is 'talking about,' given that he does not say exactly what he means."[26] But he also brings forward examples of a quite different kind:

> It [the documentary method] is recognizable as well in deciding such sociologically analyzed occurrences of events as Goffman's strategies for the management of impressions, Erikson's identity crises, Riesman's types of conformity, Parsons' value systems, Malinowski's magical practices, Bales' interaction counts, Merton's types of deviance, Lazarfeld's latent structure of attitudes, and the U.S. Census' occupational categories.[27]

This kind of documentary method is what we are addressing as the *ideological circle.* The circle arises as a product of two phases: an interpretive method analyzing the occurrence of events as documents of an "underlying" schema originating in a textual discourse— for example, Goffman's strategies for the management of impressions, or Parsons's value systems—and the uses of the schemata identified by "Goffman's strategies" or "Parsons' value systems" as procedures for selecting, assembling, and ordering those facts or observations as their documentation.

Explication of this process as the ideological circle locates it in the context of social relations, in which the textual discourse structures the transliteration of the everyday world of particular persons, places, and events into the abstracted generalizing language of bureaucratic and professional organization—of textual discourse and action. The diverse and particular can then be treated as *instances* of the same concept—for all practical purposes.

In identifying ideological methods, the contrast drawn is not between ideological and scientific, between biased and unbiased (objective), procedures for generating or reading accounts. We do not suppose that there is one objective account of "what actually happened" against which other accounts may be measured. The lived actuality remains a resource in memory in a relation of reflection through which "what actually happened" arises. Here ideological practices in encoding and constituting "what actually happened" will be contrasted with procedures which are directly expressive of the lived actuality in experience. The latter we will call "primary narrative" modes of expression. The difference is not one of accuracy, completeness, or truth. It is one of methods of telling and interpreting.

Ideological practices in the construction and reading of factual accounts can be characterized in a preliminary way as follows: the interpretive schemata selecting the terms and generating the grammatical, logical, and causal connections of the account originate in a textual discourse (a "conversation" mediated by texts) rather than being constrained by connections arising as expressions of the lived actuality. Hence, the selection of terms and connectives (of various types) is instructed by and conforms to an ideological "grammar," a set of rules and procedures derived from the textual discourse. These are or are derived from interpretive schemata made use of in the reading of the text: they are the schemata of the textual discourse and must have been learned as such if the text is to be intelligible to the reader. Such practices in generating and interpreting texts may be contrasted with the interpretive and generative practices of the primary narrative mode.

Distinctive methods of telling and hearing characterize a telling of experience that intends, is grounded on, and conforms itself to the lived actuality. Again, I stress that the primary narrative is merely one mode, and no claim is made for the greater accuracy of accounts made in it. It does, however, set up a relation between the narrative and the lived actuality different from the ideological. In developing a description of primary narrative I draw upon a study of oral narrative by Labov and Waletzky in which their general conception of narrative conforms to ours of primary narrative. They define narrative as follows: "Narrative will be considered as one verbal technique for recapitulating experience, in particular, a technique of constructing narrative units which match the temporal sequence of that experience." And further: "We have defined narrative informally as one method of recapitulating past experience by matching a verbal sequence of clauses to the sequence of events which actually occurred."[28] Their restriction of narrative to the recapitulation of past experience is too narrow a definition for general use, but it corresponds to our definition of *primary narrative.*

Labov and Waletzky are concerned with developing an analysis of the structural framework of experience-based narrative in which the temporal sequence is central. "The temporal sequence of narrative is an important defining property which proceeds from its *referential* function."[29] Their analysis identifies units or clauses of the narrative, establishes the temporal sequence of events, and relates the sequencing of narrative clauses to the sequence of events. The original sequence of events is normative vis-à-vis the sequencing of narrative clauses in that it provides a base against which the actual placing of narrative clauses can be evaluated. Deviations of narrative from actual sequences identify displacement sets. The range of displacement of a clause in its narrative location compared with its temporal location in the actual sequence can then be evaluated. Their analysis relies on the referential function of the narrative in that they depend upon how the narrative constitutes and references an actual sequence of events as the original against which the sequence of narrative clauses is compared. We know, therefore, in an ordinary and unproblematic fashion that (to use an example of theirs) what happens if the man running from his attackers trips after he reaches the other side of the street is different from what happens if he trips before he gets there: "and they was catchin' up to me / and I crossed the street / and I tripped, man" is a different sequence from: "and they was catchin' up to me / and I tripped, man / and I crossed the street."[30]

We find the difference through a referencing operation that introduces our own experience of an everyday world as a resource against which we can check out the alternatives. Using such interpretive methods, the reader is able to "correct" or fill in an unspoken piece in the second sequence. There is something missing between "I tripped" and "I crossed the street" that we insert quite smoothly as we read. When we try to express this transitional work of the reader as a specific narrative clause, we have addressed our own experience as a resource. The normative role of experience becomes equivocal.

Alternative, interpretive decisions are possible. I first gave this missing piece expression as a narrative clause in this way: "and I picked myself up before they caught me." Later it occurred to me that I had read "I tripped" as meaning that the subject fell. But perhaps he did not fall. Perhaps he recovered himself. Whatever the interpretive decision, the alternatives depend upon the reader filling in from a background knowledge of her experience not present in the text and not correctable from it. Primary narrative privileges the reader to draw upon her experience as an interpretive resource. Interpretations are, in principle, to be checked against the original experience that the narrative "recapitulates." An ideological account does not proceed in this fashion.

The way in which an experienced actuality governs the primary narrative can be seen in the following passage from an oral history of women's lives. The text is from a transcription of a tape-recorded interview. In it we can see the processes of checking back to (remembered) experience to establish events, the order of events, their context, the presence or absence of particular individuals, and so forth.

> Yes, and Douglas came to the hospital about half past eight in the morning, and he told me afterwards that when he went home, like it was—no, it must have been earlier than that, I don't know whether he was allowed in or something—but he said that he was out early in the morning, and somebody came and asked him the time, and he had to tell them that his wife had just had a baby! He was so thrilled he had to tell somebody. I thought it was lovely. I've got an idea that this incident took place when I was just coming out of hospital with my second child & yet it can't have—anyway, we had her home, but do you know—this is something that *kills* me—it was nothing except. . . . I think we had my aunt with us—I don't remember why we had her, but I think she was with us—she must have been, because what I am going to tell you concerns her. Now we had this very nice flat, it had one bedroom and a very nice living-room, and directly Douglas came in. . . . I had to have it on the side of the bed with him, with her there, and I was trying to fight him off, but it was no good—I mean he must have had it in his mind while I was away. Just ten days! Just coming out of hospital.[31]

We can see here how the teller of the tale references her experience in developing the narrative. It is clearly a narrative that has not been told in this form previously because the sorting out and ordering is going on as the narrative is told. The proper sequence derives from memories of experiences that have not been already ordered in the narrative mode. The procedure involves establishing narrative claus-es and then correcting against a lived actuality now imperfectly re-membered. The teller of the tale works up the narrative sequence by referencing the events and establishing the order in which they must have occurred. She also draws upon an unexpressed context to deter-mine whether the events happened when she was hospitalized with her first or second child. These processes are visible in moments such as "and he told me afterwards that when he went home, like it was—no, it must have been earlier than that," "I've got an idea that this incident took place when I was just coming out of hospital with my second child and yet it can't have—anyway," and "I think I had my aunt with us—I don't remember why we had her, but I think she was with us."

As we have seen in chapters 2 and 4, the ideological procedure is very different. What actually happened has to be produced as a for-mal record. It is investigated. Someone does the work of asking questions, or observing, or making use of whatever methods of cull-ing from the actuality what we will describe as the "particulars." The resulting account, or an earlier stage of the account at the point of encoding, represents the selection, assembly, and ordering of "the particulars."[32] This term is borrowed from its usage in courts of law. The particulars are the description of what happened, as prepared by the police on the basis of which specific charges are brought. They are not a neutral description. They represent what happened in a form that will intend a particular legally defined offense. Other information introduced must conform to the charge, which provides the critical relevances and boundaries. Hence, new interpretation must also intend the conceptual agenda provided by the charge. The question of what really happened is not an issue. The particulars represent the actuality intending the charge. Questions of truth and falsity, of guilt and innocence, are addressed to the particulars in relation to the charge. The particulars are organized by the charge intended. In this way "what actually happened" has been worked up so that it can be "entered" into the legal process as a formal charge.

The term "the particulars" identifies a moment intervening be-tween the actuality as people have lived it and the completed ac-count. It freezes for examination a moment (not always as distinctly apparent as it is in the legal context) at which the work of selecting, assembling, and ordering governed by the discursive schema is com-pleted and an array of particulars has been set up that will go forward into whatever kind of account is finally made. Selecting and assembling the particulars involves a process of examining the informational resources to find those that are relevant to a particular scheme. Sometimes the particulars are identifiable only as constituents of the completed account. Sometimes they appear as a distinct textual moment, supplied without interpretive connections. The latter remain to be contributed at a later stage in the process of reading, either when the final account is made, or by the reader in her course of reading.

The two modes have been presented here as independent of one another. However, the ideological procedure in practice often works on material given originally in primary narrative form. Primary narrative accounts become the raw material for the ideological transformation. People tell the police, the coroner, the psychiatrist, and so on, what happened. In so doing they draw their experience, reference it, and correct their account of what happened in its terms. Experienced police interrogators rely on just this feature of primary narrative in techniques of cross-examination. An invented story has neither an actual sequence that can be referenced again and again nor that contextual extension from which additional resources can be drawn to supplement any given version. Primary narrative forms the raw material of an ideological version. Atkinson provides an account of this process from an interview with a coroner:

> Normally, I don't think I could really take a story, even from you now, so that every word you said would be in story-book form, it would be impossible. I've got to try interviewing some people, they don't know what I want so I've got to ask them . . . the way these statements have been taken is question, answer—er—question then answer. Sometimes you get, particularly some elderly women, and they bloody go on and on, so I've got to interrupt them. But I must admit, in this very one I've got here—um—she was rambling on a bit, back and forwards, and he, I was taking the statement off him and she was chipping in. You get two sides of the tale then. And you think, "Well now, how do I play this?" So rather than taking two statements, one against the other— you're only going to end up with two negative statements, one against the other. So you bring it all into like a proper perspective as you think it is. It's a nice, well it's a nice story-book finish. Sometimes I get mixed up. I've read it through myself and then I'll suddenly scrap it and say, "Well, that's no flipping good" and start again.[33]

Methods of constructing primary narrative and methods of reading it both differ from the ideological. In telling, primary narrative depends on actual experience, whether of a single narrator or of more than one. The narrative sequence depends on an actual series of events. The ordering of that series is constituted in the telling. The reference procedures as an interpretive work are also distinctive. The reader's interpretive work draws upon her own experience in articulating the teller's experience. This relation is expressed in such phrases as "I knew just how she felt," "something just like that once happened to me." Difficulties with the narrative are characteristically located at points where the reader's experience doesn't serve to fill out the narrative clauses and to smooth transitions between them. They are resolved by questioning the teller about her experience. She is the only authority.

In contrast, the ideological form of narrative proceeds in a fashion that depends upon the reader's or hearer's grasp of the appropriate interpretive schema of the professional or other textual discourse. Indeed, accounts may be produced, as we shall see, consisting only of the particulars, so that the interpretive connections remain to be supplied by the (expert) reader. Knowledge of the interpretive schemata of the textual discourse enable her to read into the text the connections that will add up to "what it says." Alison Griffith, in her analysis of the ideological uses of the concept of the "single parent family" in the educational system, describes just this process. It is marked here by an actual break in the relation that is part of the division of labor between "lay" and expert.

> The report written by the teacher about a child she feels should be in another classroom setting is as concrete a document as possible. *The concreteness is achieved through examples of the child's behavior.* The teacher is very often aware of what the problem is, but she cannot put a diagnosis in her report. *Rather, what is included in the report are symptoms of a particular neurotic or psychotic dysfunction in such a way that the psychiatrist will come up with the diagnosis which the teacher already knows* [emphasis added].[34]

The emphasized sentences identify the practice of preparing what we are here calling "the particulars"—the concrete examples of the child's behavior, as symptoms of particular neurotic or psychotic dysfunctions—to intend a *particular* interpretation. The interpretation may not be present in the report, since the diagnosis is the prerogative of the psychiatrist.[35] If the reader does not know the schema intended by the ideological account, the particulars assembled in the account will not make sense. The reader must know the schemata of the discourse to read in connections that are not explicit.

🔖 Ideological Narratives

Anatomized

Let us see how ideological versions are constructed by examining procedures involved in applying the "assembly instructions" of professional discourse to a primary narrative text. First, the narrative. Here is a passage from Phyllis Knight's "autobiographical biography" as told to and edited by her son, Rolf Knight. It describes a period of her life in Germany before and during World War I.

> My mother worked most of the time, either running a small store or working as a seamstress. My father was a printer and he used to make a good salary, but he used most of it up himself on his different schemes and only gave my mother a few marks a week for the household. So she had to earn the money to support us herself. Very many times I remember her sitting late at night by the coal oil lamp sewing dresses. She sewed to make some extra money and made clothes for us children too. I must say, whatever other flaw she had, she always tried to dress us nicely and she took us out every afternoon for long walks in the park to get some fresh air. . . .
>
> By the time I could understand things, when I was nine or ten or so, my father wasn't contributing very much to the household. When he was in a good mood he might bring home five pounds of the cheapest meat. Sometimes he gave a few marks for the rent, often nothing. And he treated my mother pretty rotten. . . .
>
> We children didn't realize how badly he was treating our mother then. Sometimes we would find her sitting in a corner staring vacantly across the room. There wasn't the slightest opportunity or place for privacy. It didn't bother us kids too much but it must have been hell for her because she hardly ever got out. She used to sit behind the door some times, in a space between the wall and a large wardrobe. There she would sit, still and staring. We kids would open the door quietly and peep in. "Is Mama still sitting there?" "Yes, still there." No supper,

no light, nothing. She'd sit there for hours sometimes. Contemplating I don't know what, either mayhem or suicide I suppose. She never said anything about it and it was certainly not one of the things that we kids would ask about.[36]

We will find the assembly instructions to be applied to the above text in a passage from a psychiatrist's account of depressive illness. It is an account written for the lay person. A technical account might differ in substance as well as in expansion, but the use of a lay account allows us to recover the methods we ourselves use in assembling particulars to intend a textual discourse. The passage has been abridged to only those sections providing assembly instructions applicable to our primary narrative.

[Depression is characterized by] some blunting and withdrawal of interest from the outside world, a general slowing up of mental and physical activity so the patient thinks and responds to questions only with difficulty and after a struggle, and may even display a hesitation and retardation in movement as well as in thought. . . .

In some cases [inertia and retardation of response] may go on into a condition of complete stupor wherein the patient sits or lies motionless and unresponsive, completely aware of what is going on around him but no longer able or disposed to do anything about it.[37]

Applying these assembly instructions to the primary narrative discards those elements to which the clinical account of depression does not apply while retaining those that do. Thus we omit the passages describing how hard and consistently Phyllis Knight's mother worked, how she provided for her children and kept them neat and healthy in a situation of great poverty exacerbated by the oppressive behavior of her husband. The clinically interpretable particular is found in the passage where she is described as sometimes sitting behind the door, "still and staring," without response to the children, without eating or preparing food for them. Thus, this passage is constituted as a particular intending the schema of clinical depression as described in the psychiatrist's account. Of particular relevance is Stafford-Clark's description of "a condition of complete stupor wherein the patient sits or lies motionless and unresponsive." When we return to the primary narrative with the assembly instructions derived from the clinical description, we can then find "depression" in the primary narrative account. We set up this relation using the procedures of an ideological circle. We discard those aspects of the primary narrative that do not "belong" and retain only those that do. We then have locked the two together, schema and particulars, so that the latter can "find" the former and the former will interpret and describe the latter. In this way the actual is entered into textual discourse. (I am not suggesting that these particulars are sufficient to arrive at a clinical judgment of depression. I am exemplifying the method only.)

The selection, assembly, and ordering of particulars provides also for the distinctive interpretive properties of the ideological schema. In discussing a second exhibit, the case of Harriet, we also work with a relation between a psychiatric text and a set of particulars. In this sequence, the work of going from primary narrative to particulars has already been done. It is mediated by the case record on which a psychiatric resident's case history is based. The case record consisted of a loose assemblage of records from admission interviews, diagnostic interviews, ward notes, interviews with relatives, and treatment prescribed and given. Much of this, in various ways, originates in primary narrative or consists of primary narrative partially worked up into forms intending psychiatric schemata.

The sequence we are looking at begins this time with the particulars in the form of an extract from a case history prepared by a psychiatric resident for formal clinical presentation. The particulars of the case history intend an interpretive schema that is named in the heading but the connectives that would link the particulars into a coherent ideological narrative are not made. Hence, the case history as an assemblage of narrative items is ordered by a schema of discourse that is not available in the narrative itself. The extract from the case history (with names, dates, and some factual details changed to ensure anonymity) is followed by a second account I wrote to provide other material about the case that was not included in the case history; it is based on notes made by the psychiatric resident from the case record in the course of preparing the case history. By providing additional materials that are not available in the case history, we can recognize more clearly the operation of selection and assembly procedures provided by the extract from a psychiatric textbook that follows. The latter provides the discursive schema that would both instruct the selection of particulars and read connectives into the case history's collection. Finally, I have written an account of the case that represents the product of such a reading. It integrates particulars and schema into a single ideological narrative.

First, the resident's case history:

A Case of Recurrent Psychiatric Disturbance Involving Para-natal Factors

The history of the first hospitalization followed by an account of the patient's course and subsequent admissions. Harriet delivered her first child in 1970. The pregnancy and post-partum course was without complication and described by the patient as a happy period of her life.

The patient felt well until 1976 when she was 4 months pregnant with her 2nd child. She began lying awake at night worrying "that God was going to punish me for this unnatural insemination with the birth of a deformed child."

For eight months previously Harriet and her husband had undergone investigation for infertility and artificial insemination using the husband's sperm was finally employed. Shortly afterwards Harriet became pregnant.

A male child was born in June 1976. Harriet breast fed the infant for three months until her pediatrician, being concerned about the baby's poor gain in weight, recommended bottle feeding. The patient was upset by this because "being a good mother meant breast feeding for 8 months."

After switching to bottle feeding Harriet began having nightmares and her husband noticed her becoming increasingly exhausted with her attempts to force feed the infant and her persistent worrying about its welfare.

Recall the account in Diane Harpwood's novel, cited in chapter 5, of a housewife's outburst against her husband and its ground in her frustration and exhaustion in the face of an inequitable division of household work. Harriet's story, her primary narrative, may have been something like this, brokenly told in the course of sessions with her psychiatrist. But his case history is based upon a case record that would include much more: nurses' observations, perhaps an interview by the social worker with the family, possibly an interview by the psychiatrist himself with the husband. Her story cannot be reconstructed, though we know it must have been there. Nonetheless, I want to try to reveal the psychiatric work that has been done on Harriet's buried story. I have therefore assembled a simple narrative based on the case history, using a sequencing procedure conforming to "real-life" constraints—for example, that insemination precedes pregnancy—and relying on internal evidence of motivated connections, as between the baby's failure to gain weight in the first few months and the doctor's concern about his lack of progress. I have numbered its narrative clauses for ease of reference in the ensuing discussion:

1 Harriet and her husband underwent investigation for infertility. Harriet was inseminated artificially and became pregnant.

2 The early months of the pregnancy were very difficult. Harriet was sick much of the time and it seemed likely she would lose the baby. She was placed on medication.

3 By the fourth month she was beginning to feel that something was very wrong. She lay awake at night worrying that "God was going to punish me for this unnatural insemination with the birth of a deformed child."

4 The baby was carried to full term but weighed barely more than five pounds at birth.

5 The baby was difficult. He cried a lot, was wakeful at night, and put on weight very slowly.

6 At three months Harriet's pediatrician became disturbed by the baby's slow weight gain and suggested that Harriet stop breast feeding and start the baby on formula.

7 Harriet was very upset. She had felt that breast feeding was very important and that good mothers breast feed until eight months.

The resident's case history and my pseudo-primary narrative are different in order and selection of narrative clauses. The resident's narrative opens with general instructions for reading what follows: it is to be read as a narrative of an illness. As a procedure for ordering narrative clauses, "illness" selects as its first clause the first appearance of symptoms—Harriet's transition from wellness to illness in the fourth month of pregnancy with her second child. The illness appears as worry about the impiety of artificial insemination. This ordering procedure displaces from its logical place in the experiential order the instance of artificial insemination that Harriet's term "unnatural insemination" refers to (note that my reading of Harriet's reference to artificial insemination involves looping back from this displaced clause to an expanded interpretation of what is presumably her term). In my version of the narrative, this clause appears at the beginning of the sequence, conforming to its experiential order. In the case history, the displacement of this clause provides for a nonnarrative reading, that is, the clause is not read as part of the sequence of narrative clauses. Conceive of the preamble as instructions for interpreting what follows. They could be rewritten as "Read what follows as the narrative of an illness!" The clause referring to the artificial insemination is then not read as part of the narrative of the illness. It becomes a detour providing the reference for Harriet's worries. It establishes that they are not delusional in this respect; she actually did undergo artificial insemination.

My narrative introduces information that is lacking in the resident's case history. It includes references to Harriet's sickness during the pregnancy (for which she was given medication), to the baby's smallness at birth, and to his being "difficult" in the early months of life. This information could have been there. I took it from what was available in the resident's extended notes based on the case record. Its omission from the case history provides for the symptomatic reading of Harriet's worries. Deprived of local occasion, the worry that God would punish her for the unnatural insemination with the birth of a deformed child appears to come from nowhere, to have no ground. In the resident's background notes I could find material to make up clauses that can be read to occasion Harriet's behavior, that is, to provide for it out of the context of illness as a frame, thus letting it lapse back from the ideological circle into the local and locally motivated connections of the primary narrative form. Their absence from the case history means that Harriet's worries lack context. They don't make sense. They are thus available as symptoms to be interpreted in terms of the underlying psychiatric schema. But if the occasions for her worries were included, a competing narrative practice could take over. The reader, drawing upon her ordinary working knowledge of how she'd add things up in her own contexts of action, could work within her experience in reading into Harriet's. Artificial insemination (the reader might think) is no doubt a nasty, impersonal experience. Who knows, in these days of the lies and deceptions of those in authority about the consequences of high technology, whether it might not be bad for the child? The early months of Harriet's pregnancy were difficult—so different from the first. She was given medication to help keep the baby. What about the effects of *that*? Such considerations as these come readily to hand in locating Harriet's experience in the same known world that I inhabit. It is a characteristic procedure of the interpretive work involved in the reading of a primary narrative that the reader feels entitled to deploy just such resources of "what anyone knows."[38]

Occasioning is an interpretive procedure situating the individual's behavior in an experiential context. It is typical of primary narratives. It selects, assembles, and organizes contexts peculiar to the specific narrative. It summons what a reader takes to be commonsense knowledge. Using this procedure, we can see Harriet's behavior as arising out of her lived situation.

Note, then, that in the absence of the occasioning clauses there are connective lacunae in the case history. Harriet's worrying appears unmotivated. Her fears about the child's deformity arise without an intelligible connection to her life and experience. The absence of connectives in the case history, or of occasions permitting primary type inferences to be made as connectives by the reader, has these effects: (a) to provide for its reading as mentally ill behavior by depriving it of contextual instructions and allowing it to stand as anomalous,[39] (b) to provide for its reading as a symptom for which an underlying pattern is to be sought (hence, summoning the documentary method), and (c) to permit and provide for the insertion of the warranted connectives of the psychiatric discourse.

Our third extract is from a textbook account of a type of "affective disorder associated with pregnancy and childbirth." The title of the case history referring to "para-natal factors" locates this as a relevant schema of interpretation.

There are . . . no specific mental disorders related to either of these periods. Latent or repressed psychological material may, under the stress of maintaining physiological homeostasis and of the emotionally significant situation, prove too great for the patient's ego resources with the result that psychopathological reactions occur. What her pregnancy unconsciously means to the mother is of significance, as is the birth of her child. Doubtless, it reanimates the patient's old attitudes toward her own mother and may revive old complexes of bodily harm or injury. Sometimes the patient expresses delusions indicating hostility for either the husband or the child, thus reflecting a conflict about married life or motherhood. Rejection of the child may be expressed by a delusion that it is dead, by abusive treatment of it, or by fear that something will happen to it.[40]

This is the schema intended by the case history. It treats the latter's particulars as its documents or indexes. The relation of intention is set up when the schema instructs the assembly and ordering of particulars. Let us apply this textbook account, using the pseudo-primary narrative as a substitute for the case record, treating it as that resource from which a collection of particulars is made up. To clarify how the schema operates on the pseudo-primary narrative resources to produce a case history intending it, I have translated the procedure into a set of instructions as follows:

1   Using the textbook's clinical description, isolate a passage that selects as its "document" at least one item of information about the patient from the pseudo-primary narrative. This passage will serve: "Rejection of the child may be expressed by a delusion that it is dead, by abusive treatment of it, or by fear that something will happen to it." It provides models of the kinds of behaviour that can be interpreted as documents of the schema "rejection of the child": the delusion that it is dead, abusive treatment of the child, or fear that something will happen to it.

2   Look back to the pseudo-primary narrative to find a clause or clauses that can be thus categorized. Clause 3 is a good candidate: "She began lying awake at night worrying that 'God was going to punish me for this unnatural insemination with the birth of a deformed child.'"

3   Reinterpret the clause in relation to the theory embedded in the textbook account. The theory transforms fear into rejection. The clause then functions as a particular documenting "rejection of the child."

4   Omit information providing occasions for the selected particulars. The narrative connectives (the sickness of a difficult pregnancy) linking Harriet's fear that her unborn child will have something seriously wrong with it will make a sensible context to the experience of artificial insemination. So these must go. Omit clause 2 of the narrative.

Procedures such as these produce the particulars of the case history and make visible how the connections to the schema are drawn and, hence, how the case history can be interpreted as an instance of "recurrent psychiatric disturbance *involving para-natal factors.*" At the point of reading (or hearing) the case history, those who know the psychiatric schema and how to apply it can read the connections into the particulars. Using this schema to select clauses 1, 3, 6, and 7 from the pseudo-primary narrative and adding some additional materials from the resident's notes, a fully "psychiatrized" story can be told that unites particulars and schema, very much as they could be united as the reader interprets the particulars of the case history in terms of the schema:

Harriet's relation to her own mother had been deeply unsatisfactory. She had felt unloved and rejected. Her mother had showed her no warmth. When she herself became a mother, old conflicts surfaced. Her rejection of her role as mother arose from her unsatisfied need for her mother's love. Rejection of her own role as mother was expressed in hostility toward the child, a hostility appearing as fears that the child would be born deformed and later in an obsessive concern with its welfare. It also appeared in irrational anxieties about her inadequacies as a mother.

The suppression of "occasions" and the cutting off of inferential connectives as *her* reasons[41] opens the particulars to the insertion of ideological connectives derived from the psychiatric discourse. Discarding as particulars the information that occasions and hence makes sense of Harriet's fear that her child might be born deformed permits us to treat that clause as an instance of the category "rejection of the child," and hence as a document (or indicator) of the syndrome "affective disorder associated with pregnancy and childbirth." "Rejection of the child" can now be inserted as the motive for her fear. *The* reason has been substituted for *her* reasons. Harriet's capacity as subject has been subdued.

This is the ideological procedure. The ideological circle as a method of producing an account selects from the primary narrative an array of particulars intending the ideological schema. The selection and assembly procedure discards competing reasons (*her* reasons) and permits the insertion of ideological connectives. The resulting collection of particulars will intend the ideological schema as its "underlying" pattern. The process of selecting and assembling the particulars creates an array in terms of the criteria "Does the schema apply to this?" and "Is this describable or interpretable by the schema?" The resulting factual account may be entirely accurate, but the order that provides its grammar, its logic, and the connectives sequencing its clauses will be provided by schemata originating in the discourse rather than by an explication of actual social relations. We have seen, moreover, how the ideological method works a transformation on narratives speaking from people's actual experience so that the active presence of subjects is discarded and the objectified version entered into the relations of ruling is installed as the authoritative account. These are the practices that make over the telling of the actual and everyday/everynight world into the forms that subjugate it to the objectified relations of ruling.

The question of the synonymy of "she killed herself" and "she committed suicide" was posed at the beginning of this chapter as the point of entry into an investigation of the contrast and contradictions between the primary narration of experience and ideological practices of writing and reading. I have tried to show how these different practices of reading and writing texts enter the reader (and are entered by the reader) into different social relations. The appearance of a text before us conceals the situation of its reading and writing in such relations and hence conceals how our practices of reading organize our participation in them. Each text appears to us as if it stood at the same distance from us. We seemingly can substitute one text for another without changing our relations. The social relational shifts go on, so to speak, behind our backs. They are invisible to us because they are immanent in our methods of reading and hence in how the sense of the text arises for us. Our two terms "she killed herself" and "she committed suicide" appear synonymous on paper, and the social relations into which "she committed suicide" is entered are present only in the methods of reading that we bring to bear. For as members of an intelligentsia we know how to do that kind of reading, and in doing that kind of reading we enter those textually mediated relations of ruling to which ideological practices are integral.

Our investigation here has required that we take a step that Marx could not take in his analysis of ideology, for it was not yet there. History in his time had not yet developed the actual forms in which such relations could emerge in the differentiated forms in which they could be thought. Here ideological practices are not only in texts, they are functional constituents of a ruling apparatus. Ideological circles transpose actual events, located in specific places and performed by real individuals, into the generalized forms in which they can be known, knowable and actionable within an abstracted conceptual mode of ruling and organization.

These abstracted modes of ruling—the administrative and managerial practices of government, professional organization, and business, as well as the extensive systems of textual discourse—are characterized by a determinate form of social consciousness in Marx's sense of language as practical consciousness. It is a form of social consciousness in an objectified mode, specifically independent of particular subjectivities located in particular places. It is constituted in such a way that it can be spoken, thought, and written by anyone (given that they know how). Why they are, where they are, and with what feelings they speak, read, or think make no difference.

The practice and organization of ideological circles, integral to this form of social consciousness, coordinate and transpose actualities and the subject's experience of those actualities into the textual forms of the discursive and institutional consciousness. Ideological practices organize the interchangeability of actual events, the treatment of individuals (whether persons or events) as equivalent "for all practical purposes," and the coordination of processes and events occurring in different places and at different times. They bring them into a coherent relation to the objectives, interests, and relevances vested in a given discursive or organizational form. Organizational forms are increasingly standardized nationally and supranationally. Thus, for example, the local work of taking in mental patients or determining a type of death is brought into a coherent relation with similar local work elsewhere whose product enters the textual discourse. These provide the virtual realities that are the ground of professional and academic discourses, while the latter provide the schemata controlling the ideological circles that produce the virtual realities.

Figure 6.1 described the relation between lived actuality, the process of inscribing that actuality into the records of formal organization or academic or professional discourse, and the feedback process linking the work of an intelligentsia to the work of the inscriber. We have seen the same circuit at work in the relation between a clinical situation, the writing of a clinical account, and the formulation of a particular syndrome in the psychiatric discourse. The local events of psychiatric hospital and the discursive order of the profession intersect in the ideological circle. Here, then, we can see the latter as a matter not just of an individual practice but of a division of labor in the organization of ruling whereby discourse coordinates multiple local sites, subjugating local actualities to its abstracted governance.

CHAPTER

7

IDEOLOGICAL METHODS OF READING AND WRITING TEXTS

A SCRUTINY OF QUENTIN BELL'S ACCOUNT OF VIRGINIA WOOLF'S SUICIDE

☙ The Interrelation of Ideological and

Primary Narrative in Bell's Story

In this chapter I want to explore further the disjuncture between an
ideological method of writing texts and the primary narrative of experience, by giving greater emphasis to the part the reader plays, as a
participant in social relations, in the reading of the text. The text
used here consists of the last ten pages of Quentin Bell's biography of
Virginia Woolf, describing the months leading up to her suicide in
April 1941.[1] It consists largely of narrative based on primary sources
of various kinds—letters, diaries, and recollections—describing
Woolf's domestic life, her work, her friendships and professional relations, and finally the events leading up to and including her suicide.
Bell gives this primary narrative an ideological "gloss," interpreting it
in terms of an underlying course of mental illness eventuating in
suicide. The investigation explicates the shift to an ideological relation whereby the reader assumes the interpretive mantle of psychiatric discourse (at least in its lay version), the breaking of the local
connectives of primary narrative, and the substitution for them of
ideological connectives.

The ideological work is examined as a practice of reading. The
reader activates the text using her own knowledge to eke out the text
in reconstructing the primary narrative as a manifestation of mental
illness. The analytic focus here is upon the shared ideological work
of reader and text in which the ideological circle is completed only as
the reader contributes the missing schema and interpretive movement. Analysis of Woolf's biography discloses the transformative

work of the ideological circle and the process of replacement of primary narrative connectives, contexts, and subject-object relations with characteristically ideological forms. The transformative work is reader's work, arising as the reader engages with the text in a course of reading. At one moment meaning rests in the primary narrative mode, and at the next the ideological operation introduces a new level of meaning, modifying and reinterpreting the primary narrative retrospectively and prospectively, and laying down a governing schema for the interpretation of what has been told and what will follow. Beyond explicating features of the text, the analysis aims to bring out the distinctively ideological transformations that obliterate the presence of Woolf as a human subject embedded in her particular circumstances; excise the active presence and individuals as subjectivities in action, feeling, and experience; and substitute the connectives and constituents of the schemata of the textual discourse for the "natural" connectives and moments of primary narrative.

I selected this text for analysis because I could already see in it the dim forms of a phenomenon that my analytical work will explicate. These became visible to me because I read Bell's biography as a feminist who has written critically of psychiatry. That standpoint led me to question the way in which the concept of mental illness provided a coherence otherwise lacking between the events of the last year of Virginia Woolf's life and her suicide. I sensed the interposition of an ideological process linking the text into those specific forms of social relations constituting the ruling apparatus of this social form. As I read, certain passages locked the text into my "background knowledge" of nontechnical psychiatric discourse. In seeing what was going on I found that as a reader I brought into play resources not in fact present in the text. These operated on events told at the primary narrative level[2] to gloss or reinterpret them in a way that established a coherent movement or sequence leading up to Woolf's death.

Indeed, without this ideological gloss it may well be seen that the only available "occasion" for her death was her husband's decision that she should be told by a physician that she was mentally ill and his arranging with a physician friend of theirs to examine her and tell her of this. In his autobiography Leonard Woolf tells us that the step of telling her of the gravity of her mental illness was taken with full knowledge that it might precipitate her suicide. The decision to do so was finally taken in the context of fears that her state of mind was already such that she might kill herself anyway—perhaps, indeed, had already made one attempt. "Yet one had to take a decision and abide by it, knowing the risk—and whatever one decided, the risk was appalling."[3]

On the day following that examination and that sentence Virginia Woolf killed herself.

Our focus here will be on sequences in the text that are brought under the governance of the schemata of psychiatric discourse. The passage in Bell's biography that interests us begins with the summer of 1940, after the collapse of France and the evacuation of the British army from Dunkirk. An invasion of Britain was expected imminently. Since Leonard was Jewish and both Virginia and Leonard were socialists, they were fearful of what would happen to them in such an event and made plans to commit suicide. After a while, fears of invasion declined and even in the context of air battles and bombing raids life took on a more routine character—the completion of a novel and other writings, contacts with friends and relatives, housekeeping, professional contacts, and so on. And then came the final few weeks leading up to Virginia's death in April 1941, which, at least as Bell tells the story, occurred without intimations of this in her daily life.

The primary narrative does not provide a rationale for Woolf's suicide. We cannot find in it the motivational linkages that would make sense of her decision to kill herself. The coherence of the narrative of her last few months of life with her death is managed quite differently by inserting an ideological structure that overrides and reconstructs the primary narrative level of meaning.

Figure 7.1 exhibits the characteristic circularity of the ideological process, in which the reader intervenes to complete the cycle. The operation as a whole depends on the active participation of the reader, who not only "activates" the text by reading it but also draws into the interpretive work her practices of reading as a participant in the relations ordering the exclusions of mental illness.

The ideological circle diagrammed in figure 7.1 is a series of steps representing a moment in a social relation. It begins with the original events, the lived actuality, as they are recorded in various media, some of which, such as letters, are themselves part of that lived actuality and subsequently play a new role as resources in the work of making a biography. The text is the product of that work, appearing before the reader in synthetic form, seamless, and without traces of its making. It describes Virginia and Leonard Woolf's fear of invasion, their return to

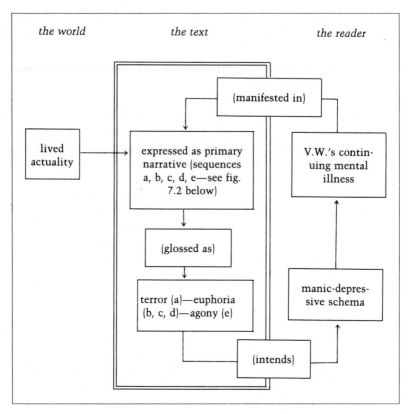

Figure 7.1   The ideological circle in operation

relatively normal routines, and finally Virginia's suicide. It provides a meta-order by glossing the narrative as a triadic sequence in which terror is succeeded by euphoria, which is in turn superseded by agony.[4] This gloss intends the schema of manic-depressive psychosis. That term is not used in the text. It is, however, waiting in the wings, so to speak, for the reader to supply it. That schema has already been established in the interpretive canon of Virginia Woolf's life by a televised interview with Leonard Woolf done by Malcolm Muggeridge some years ago.

The next step involves the reader's participation in the relevant phase of public textual discourse or in the coprofessional margins of psychiatry or both. In either case the reader can plug the interpreter "mental illness" into the reading of the primary narrative, linking the present narrative sequences to others earlier in the biography when Woolf's mental illness had been described. The primary narrative thus comes to stand, via this interpretive loop in which reader and text cooperate, as a manifestation of the course of her mental illness.

Bell's biography has already established that Virginia Woolf suffered from recurrent episodes of mental illness. In these passages our "knowledge" is brought forward as a governing schema for the ordering procedures to be introduced by the reader here. The sequence leading up to her suicide is identified as a recurrence of the illness. That illness has been "witnessed" in a characteristic way by the formation of the circle of those close to Woolf.[5] It has been legitimated with reference to consultation with professional experts. Thus her mental illness has already been objectified for us. That objectification establishes mental illness as a proper and warrantable interpretive procedure for her. She comes under the jurisdiction of the psychiatric discourse. Hence, mental illness and its subschemata may be applied to the accounting of her behavior without further jural process. That discourse is already in place as a "cognitive domain"[6] within which the reader's subjectivity may be located in reflecting upon the text. The reader thus engaged has entered the social relations of psychiatric discourse and now deploys its methods of reading to understand the text.

The work of interrelating the documented events of the year preceding Virginia Woolf's death to her decision to kill herself is performed by two key passages, which, together with some fleeting references elsewhere, "carry" the relating schema so that it can be traced through material in which it is not manifest. This relating schema organizes the events from the summer of 1940 as a sequence—a countdown—leading to her death. The first of the two passages follows a paragraph reporting Leonard and Virginia's apprehensions concerning the Nazi invasion and their plans for suicide. The paragraph in question implies that the direct experience of air battles had a "therapeutic" effect, displacing "imagined" with "actual" dangers.[7]

The second passage occurs after lengthy sequences describing the various domestic annoyances of Virginia Woolf's life, the destruction of family residences in London, and her exchange with her nephew, Benedict Nicolson. It describes her as passing from a "mood of apprehension" to one of "quiet imperturbability,"[8] then ties that into an overall sequence inclusive of her death, a sequence of "terror," "euphoria," and "agony," which is attributed to the "workings of her mind." Following this passage is an account of the state of the war and the diminished likelihood of a German invasion. Later, fleeting references to the events of the weeks immediately preceding her death—for example, "When did the laughter end and the darkness begin?"[9]—knit those events back into the governing frame of alternating moods set in place by this second passage.

Both passages are inserted into sequences having a primary narrative structure and intending primary narrative interpretive procedures. In the sequences intending a psychiatric schema the organization of meaning (arising between reader and text as the reader's work) is supplied from the professional discourse rather than arising as biographical connections understood by the reader to refer to an experienced world. Entering the subject (that is, Virginia Woolf) into the clinical mode introduces an ideological procedure that suspends the primary narrative interpretive procedures indexing a world of experience wherein moods, feelings, responses to circumstances, conditions, settings, situations, and so on are located in biographically particular relations. The connectives supplied in the primary narrative mode, corresponding to "her reasons" as contrasted with "the reasons"[10] and to the "occasions" (identified as omissions from the clinical history in chapter 6) are suspended. Readers' interpretive practices referring to Woolf's point of view, her feelings, and her responses to events do not apply. Rather, the clinical subject, as a textual construct, enters states of mood, feeling, mind, and so on, which constitute an illness or a course of illness. These states preempt the expression of her subjectivity; they subsume instances of such expression embedded in the primary narrative sequences. The latter then come to stand as documents of the underlying pattern supplied by the psychiatric discourse.

In the course of reading Bell's text we pass from primary narrative to its ideological interpreter and hence to an interpretive practice that reflects both prospectively and retrospectively on the primary narrative, setting it into a superordinate interpretive frame. The primary narrative does not yield directly and simply a set of particulars that will intend a manic-depressive interpretation, or indeed any particular clinical description. For such an interpretation to be made, an ideological gloss is needed. Figure 7.2 describes the transformative work of the two passages described above as a stacking effect in which we can distinguish an intervening band or level of ideological gloss belonging neither to the discourse not yet to the primary narrative mode. This band has the effect of restructuring the primary narrative and hence mediating its relation to the schema of psychiatric discourse. Figure 7.2 shows, for example, how the discussion of suicide is first lifted out of its actual context (in relation to Leonard, in relation to the threat of invasion), then entered into the frame of mental illness in general, and finally given the intermediary gloss of a "mood of apprehension," bringing it into conformity as a constituent of the "terror, euphoria, agony" schema intending the manic-depressive interpretation.

Figure 7.2 identifies the ideological circle as a series of transformations passing from primary narrative to the schemata of the professional discourse. The first step, the primary narrative level, is represented on the left by a, b, c, d, and e: (a) the Woolfs' fears; (b) the plans they made to kill themselves should the Nazis invade; (c) the destruction of the family residences in London, a quarrel with Virginia Woolf's sister, and an exchange with Woolf's nephew about his political views; (d) Woolf's work on her novel and its completion, meetings with friends, and correspondence; (e) the visit with Leonard's friend Octavia (a physician), who tells her that she is mentally ill and then Virginia's death. The second step of connecting glosses mediates the primary narrative and the ideological mode, step 3, which intends the psychiatric interpretation. The glosses redescribe the primary narrative sequences and reformulate its connectives as constituents of a possible description of a mental illness. Step 3 builds on and subsumes the glosses at step 2, reconstructing them as a movement between "terror" or "agony" and "euphoria." Step 3 thus fits the sequence of steps 1 and 2 to the schema of manic-depressive psychosis at step 4. Bell never says, "Virginia Woolf suffered from a manic-depressive psychosis" (though Leonard Woolf did in the interview with Malcolm Muggeridge referred to above). So step 4 is the reader's work. She must know how to go from the contrasting states formulated at step 3 to a reading in terms of manic-depression. This is what I was able to do. But even if the reader doesn't complete the sequence just as I did, the more general schema of "mental illness" is already available as schema for reading at step 4. The sequencing of the primary narrative has now been brought under the governance of a schema in relation to which it may be read as a countdown leading to Woolf's death.

Thus the representations of the primary narrative come to be understood as exhibiting the alternating mood states of an underlying mental disorder. The reader is enabled to treat the primary narrative as a surface and the conceptual order of the clinical discourse as a

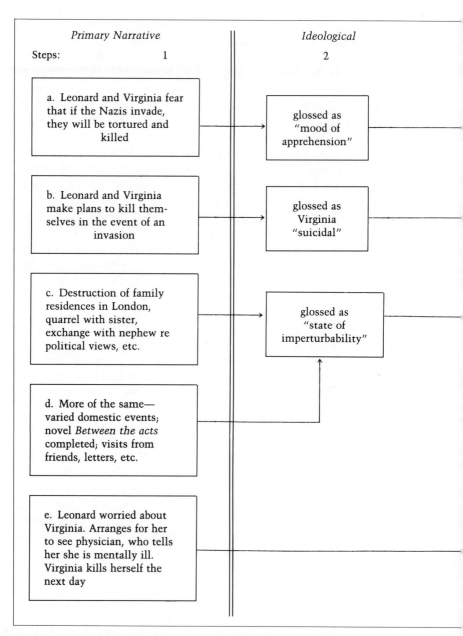

Figure 7.2   The construction of the ideological circle in the countdown to Virginia Woolf's death

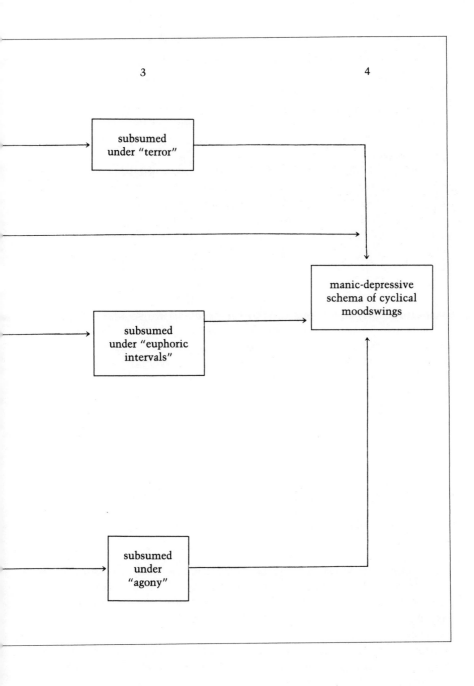

movement underneath that surface. This structure sets aside the potential problem of the lack of any account of Virginia's mental illness given on the basis of the primary narrative alone. The search for such a direct relation is lost in inconsistencies, such as treating Leonard Woolf's plans for suicide in an entirely different mode from Virginia's, or oversimplifications, such as glossing the period from (approximately) September 1940 to the beginning of 1941 as a "euphoric interval."

The way in which the organization of the text establishes primary narrative features as a surface and the ideological discourse as "behind the scenes" can be seen in the following passage: "Shattering, nerve-wracking though such experiences [air battle] must have been, unfit though Virginia was to be at the periphery, let alone the center of a battle, I think that the effect may have been therapeutic. From the time when she came literally under fire, the talk of suicide ceased."[11] Here a contrastive structure[12] establishes the normative character of "shattering, nerve-wracking" experiences vis-à-vis a deviant (probable) effect construed by the psychiatric discourse (inserted here by the use of the term *therapeutic*). In this way the "commonsense" interpretive practices of the primary narrative mode are rejected in favor of an interpretation from the psychiatric discourse contradictory to common sense.

◗ How the Reader's Interpretation of Primary Narrative

is Reshaped by the Ideological Operation

The diagrammatic representation in figure 7.2 is atemporal. But the actual operation of the text as the reader enlivens it in a course of reading is temporal. Sequence and succession are integral to effects arising as an experience of reading.[13] In analyzing how the text works as a course of reading, we shall work with the notion that the active, temporal relation between reader and text involves procedures and steps conforming to those laid down by Marx and Engels as a method of producing an idealist version of history (see chapter 2). In this context, we will examine the transformation from primary narrative to ideological as a sequence—or, perhaps better, a transformative operation—in the course of reading. The production of an ideological version is an active process, an active relation between text and reader. Figures 7.1 and 7.2 represent the completed procedure. But they also represent the ideological circle as a process, the different levels of which enter into an active, dual relation with one another. It is a transformative process arising in the course of reading and an interpretive process selecting, ordering, and reassembling the particulars retroactively. Our focus, then, is on a course of reading in which primary narrative connections are superseded by or reconstructed to manifest the connections of textual discourse.

Substituting ideological terms and "grammar" for those of primary narrative is an operation taking place in time. The act of reading moves in two directions: forward, in which the transformative process is at work in the course of reading, and reverse, in which the higher-order ideological formulation retroactively subsumes, can be substituted for, and supersedes the primary narrative clauses. Failure to recognize these two movements as distinct is a source of confusion in Kress and Hodge's[14] interesting but problematic attempt to equate the "kernel" sentences of the ideological form to a "theory of reality" and to analyze ideological formulations as transformations of kernel sentences. Their notion is that it is possible as a syntactic investigation to trace back through the ideological form to an original "theory of reality" embodied in a kernel sentence. But the movement, the transformative process, going from the primary narrative form (their kernel sentence?) to the ideological form is distinct from the movement by which the ideological form appropriates, subsumes, and generates as its particulars the primary narrative clause or clauses. Once completed, the ideological form supersedes the primary narrative clauses on which its transformative work was done. The latter are not recoverable through it. Referring to figure 7.2, we can see the two movements as the course of reading. Bell's biography lays down first the primary narrative (step 1) and then the ideological schema (step 2) that operates on it. This is the transformative process. Once the ideological schema is in place the primary narrative is brought under the governing frame of the textual discourse of mental illness, thereby organizing the countdown (steps 3 and 4). Primary narrative occurring after the passage introducing the triadic organization of "terror," "euphoria," and "agony" is read "under the sentence of death." That is the interpretive completion of the circle.

Thus the two movements are phases or moments of the ideological circle. In Bell's text the reader first encounters the primary narrative sequences, then their ideological transformations. Then a retroactive movement of interpretation brings those primary narrative sequences under the interpretive authority of the ideological schema. At this point, in other words, the reader, in thinking back over what has gone before, now knows how to shape up the primary narrative so that it will document the underlying pattern. For example, when I checked back from the paragraph in which Woolf's suicidal impulses are "cured" by the experience of air fighting to see the difference between her talk of suicide and Leonard's, I found in the preceding paragraph the phrase "Virginia refers frequently to the question of how and when they should make an end of themselves."[15] I knew how to construe that as a particular intending a psychiatric schema. Retrospectively, I could understand it as obsessive preoccupation with suicide on Virginia Woolf's part. Such knowledge of how to take up primary narrative clauses and construe them as constituents of the ideological discourse often comes to light in the context of arguments about a text. It locates that reading and discussion of the text in the social relations of the relevant discourse.

When we examine the transformative process as a course of reading, the distinctive features of the ideological mode can be traced as operations on the primary narrative clauses. The two passages on which we have focused reconstruct the account of suicide, detach it from the contexts in which it originally arose, and relocate it in relation to a mental illness and hence under a different set of interpretive rules. Virginia's thoughts of killing herself, as contrasted with the discussions she shared with Leonard, are thereby deprived of a warranted occasion and are connected to her illness via the language of "cure" and "therapy." The transformations are a process analogous to that of the "three tricks" of Marx and Engels' account of an idealist method of representing history (see chapter 2). The actual subjects of action disappear, the connectives and occasions of the primary narrative are discarded, and the formal connectives of the textual discourse are inserted.

This movement from primary narrative to ideological interpretive procedures allows statements in the two modes to contradict one another without apparent conflict. Thus, when Virginia and Leonard Woolf are discussing the possibility of committing suicide should there be an invasion, care is taken to establish that their fears are not illusory. By contrast, in the ideological passage where Virginia is sole

Step 1	Leonard and Virginia	discussed the question	of suicide (p. 216)[16]
Step 2	Virginia	refers frequently	to how and when they should make an end of themselves (p. 216–7)
Step 3	ø	the talk of	suicide (p. 217)

Figure 7.3   The course of reading: Transformations 1

subject, these threatening dangers become "imagined dangers" contrasted with the "actual dangers" of air battle.

The failure of that contradiction to connect relies upon a course of reading during which a shift is made from primary narrative to ideological mode. Leonard and Virginia's talk of suicide then comes under the jurisdiction of primary narrative interpretive procedures, whereas Virginia's part in that talk is brought under the interpretive jurisdiction of the ideological schema of mental illness. The movement from one to the other is managed in a course of reading in which a series of shifts deletes Leonard's presence and give "the talk of suicide" a symptomatic reading. Thus Bell can conclude his interpretation of Virginia Woolf's experience of air battle with the words "From the time when she came literally under fire, the talk of suicide ceased."

Figure 7.3 represents the transformative process as a sequence of steps recovering the transformations as a course of reading. Ø represents the disappearance of a subject who was part of the action in its previous description. The course of reading is from the top down. At step 1 Leonard and Virginia are together engaged in talking of suicide. At step 2 Virginia alone is doing the talk. Leonard has disappeared. At step 3 both of these become nominalized as "the talk of suicide." The nominalized form enables the talk itself to become the grammatical subject and to enter into relations independently of the explicit presence of the subject or subjects to whose actions it refers. In these transformations we can see the force of nominalization as a device extracting "behavior" from its relation to a living subject. It can then be entered into relations framed by the schema of the discourse rather than the primary narrative. This operation on the primary narrative reproduces the "information" at the ideological level so

This happened	Connective	Then this happened
threat of Nazi invasion	meaning to a Jewish socialist and his wife	planning to commit suicide

Figure 7.4   The text's work: Making connections 1

that the ideological form can be substituted for primary narrative's clauses.

The ideological discourse also suppresses the connectives and occasions of the primary narrative and substitutes for them the connectives of the textual discourse. The term *connectives* is used here to identify the types of linkages set up in "this happened, then this happened" sequences. That type of sequence may be supplied with connectives of meaning or subjective connectives. For example, the threat of Nazi invasion has specific meaning for Leonard and Virginia. They feared what would happen to a Jewish socialist and his wife if the Nazis invaded (fig. 7.4).

The ideological procedure substitutes for the local connectives of primary narrative connectives supplied by discourse. This is how discursive structure is inserted into accounts of actualities. In this case, the discursive connectives are causal, formal, or mechanical. For example, the relation between the experience of air battle and the "talk of suicide" is made through a causal connective—the relation of therapy to cure (fig. 7.5). In another instance, we find a "mechanical" connective linking Woolf's states of mind (fig. 7.6).

The ideological operation separates the feelings, actions, and thoughts of people from the actual individuals as subjects. It detaches them from the actual situations and circumstances of their lives in which those feelings, actions, and thoughts arise. In going from the primary narrative to its ideological reflection in the psychiatric mode, a "behavior" or a "state of mind" is entered into causal, for-

This happened	Connective	Then this happened
Virginia came literally under fire	(therapeutic effect)	the talk of suicide ceased

Figure 7.5   The text's work: Making connections 2

This happened	Then this happened	Then this happened
terror	euphoria	agony
Connective	the workings of her mind	

Figure 7.6   The text's work: Making connections 3

mal, or mechanical relations as if it were external to the subject, who now becomes the *site* of "this happened, then this happened" sequences. The transformative process discards both the subject's presence in the act or feeling and the particular situations and circumstances of his or her life that might occasion such acts and feelings. This effect can be examined as a course of reading in the reconstruction of Leonard and Virginia's fear that Nazi invasion would mean humiliation, torture, and death for both of them. This threat occasions their joint plans to commit suicide. In figure 7.7 this is summarized in the sentence "Leonard and Virginia were afraid that they would be tortured and killed if the Nazis invaded." The ideological reflection of this is the "mood of apprehension" that Virginia is described as passing from sometime in the fall of 1940. The nominalization of "Leonard and Virginia were afraid" as Virginia's "mood of apprehension" deletes the unwanted subject (Leonard), suspends her active subjectivity, and deletes the immediate personal occasion and its more general historical setting. It permits the insertion of the informational content of the primary narrative clause into a form that in the paragraph that follows intends the manic-depressive schema. It necessitates also the insertion of a new connective, "was passing from," which relates the subject externally to her own state of feeling.

The new connective substitutes for what is missing now, namely, the meaning and occasion of that meaning, which might otherwise be where one sought first for reasons why Virginia ceased to be afraid.

Leonard and Virginia		were afraid	that they would be tortured and killed	if the Nazis invaded
ø	Virginia	was passing from a mood of apprehension	ø	ø

Figure 7.7   The course of reading: Transformations 2

In fact, there *were* changes in the situation that occasioned the fear and the plans for suicide. During August and September of 1940 it was becoming clear that a successful Nazi invasion was no longer a high probability and that Britain's capacity to resist was greater than had been feared. If this information were added into the formulation "Leonard and Virginia were afraid that they would be tortured and killed if the Nazis invaded," the occasion for their plans for suicide is eliminated. If the Nazis will not invade (or not invade successfully), Leonard and Virginia are no longer afraid that they will be tortured and killed. Hence, they are no longer planning to commit suicide. However, the transformative process reconstructing primary narrative at the ideological level deprives us of the opportunity of making these connections. The isolation of the state of mind (the "mood of apprehension") from its occasion; the suppression of the connectives of meaning (why Leonard and Virginia were afraid and planned suicide); the suppression of the "occasion" (threat of Nazi invasion); the deletion of the second subject, Leonard, and the attribution of the suicidal disposition to Virginia; these are the transformative processes that when completed have reconstructed the information as constituents of a clinical problem located in the psychiatric text. *After* this work has been done (and it is completed in the first third of the sequence) it is possible to reintroduce the historical "context" that was the original occasion for Leonard and Virginia's plans to commit suicide, namely, the war and the fear of Nazi invasion. At this point the state of mind and the historical context are brought into an externalized relation rather than linked essentially as they are through the original connectives of meaning in the primary narrative form. They are now represented as independent but contingent: the happier phase of the "terror, euphoria, agony" sequence can be directly related to public events.[17] If this had been introduced prior to the ideological transformations, the elaborate organization of the countdown could not have gotten underway and we would be left with the rawness and suddenness of the account of the last few days of Virginia's death.

The introduction of the ideological schema and its method of operating on primary narrative clauses creates an interpretive stability. It suspends the process identified by Garfinkel and Sacks[18] whereby each next moment accomplishes the sense of what has gone before so that, as Wilson[19] has pointed out, the definition of social events is essentially open to revision at each next moment of the social process. The ideological circle binds that process of revision through the capacity of ideological schemata to subsume concretely disparate particulars retroactively and prospectively and to "sort" in such a way that what does not fit is discarded. The binding of the interpretation is, of course, the collaborative work of the reader, who now knows how to go to work on what follows and what has gone before.

I want to emphasize that we are not just talking about reading and writing texts, nor of how people go about constructing and interpreting different kinds of narratives. These textual "moments" are to be seen as embedded in social relations; the moment of writing or reading enters the subject as an active participant in those relations. Textual discourse—the material organization of an intelligentsia—is an organization of social relations lacking the identification of specific jurisdiction with definite physical premises. It interpenetrates other and generally hierarchical forms of ruling—government, management, professional organization, and so forth. It provides for interchange among those working in organizations with varying functions and objectives and within varying institutional spheres. The psychiatric discourse, for example, intersects with universities, hospitals, the work of the coroner's office, private psychiatric practice, and mental hospitals, with open linkages into the general textual discourse of the intelligentsia and the mass media. These relations, as they surface in the texts of suicide and psychiatry, were examined in the previous chapter. Here we have taken up the reflexivity of these processes. We have been concerned with our own, with *my* own, participation in a textual discourse and how that is drawn into an interpretation of an ideologically ordered text. This moment of reading is a moment of active participation in the lay margins of psychiatric discourse. Bell relies on his readers' participation in this discourse; indeed, he makes the join for us—the reader has only to take it up. The selective, ordering, and transformative operations of the ideological circle are embedded in the social relations to which they are articulated and which they articulate.

There are definite ways in which the narrative practices through which subjects speak directly to us from the ground of their experience may be analyzed and transliterated so that they become the documents of a discursive schema. When I use the term *primary narrative*, I do not have in mind only the way a telling of what happened is grounded in the experience of the teller. An implicit or broken primary narrative is also present in the work of Atkinson's coroner constructing his narrative on the basis of two primary accounts and his own questions. But systematic approaches to questioning such as those used in psychiatry or in the structured interviews of sociological methodologies predigest primary narrative so that it is already construed as documents to the discursive schema. Here, then, we can see a second aspect: Bell's narrative also borrows (in a quiet way) the institutional authority of psychiatric discourse. It is the discursive schema of the relations of ruling that controls the narrative. Once the schema is introduced, as we have seen, other records of Woolf's subjectivity are subdued to it. The process of subduing the subject's experience-based narrative to the professional discourse (here the discourse of psychiatry) can be summarized as follows. In these processes we find again the lineaments of the Marxist account of methods of constructing an idealist version of historical processes.

1   The ideological operation severs the relation of the events of interest to the particular local and biographical settings in which they arise. Conditions, situations, circumstances, settings, and events are linked in primary narrative explicitly or implicitly in the subjectivities of actors— their feelings, thoughts, responses, and so on. In other words, subjects' acts, feelings, what they or others said, provide the connectives between different stages of the action and the contexts in which action goes forward. The inner texture of the action is the expressed or imputed consciousness of the original teller or tellers of the tale. Of course, a given text, such as Bell's biography of Virginia Woolf, contains more than one layer of narrative even in its simpler constructions. But when Bell writes of Virginia and Leonard's fear of Nazi invasion, we can see that buried here is an original primary narrative in which the connectives are the Woolfs' consciousness. They were not afraid in general—they were afraid of Nazi invasion. That invasion was a direct and special threat to a socialist couple, where one was a Jew. Their consciousness, their fear of Nazi invasion, and the immediate context of a present danger provide the local cogency of this passage. Ideological transformations break that inner relation, suppressing, as we have suggested in relation to mental illness in chapter 6, the active presence of the subject as an organizer of the relations of relevance admitted to discourse.

2   Acts, utterances, and expressed feelings are reconstructed as constituents of a course of illness or a psychic syndrome. They are extracted thereby from their participation in the localizing and particularizing configurations of meaning characterizing the primary narrative form. Here again we find the same device we explicated at the end of chapter 5, namely, the extraction of a state of mind or feeling from actual contexts, activities, and utterances.

3   This transformation discards the grammatical subject. A characteristic device is nominalization, as when Woolf's fear of Nazi invasion becomes a "mood of apprehension." Or recurrent acts or feelings may be categorized as constituent states, as when we saw how the description of Phyllis Knight's mother as sitting behind the door, not moving or speaking, may be reconstructed as a symptom of a depressive state. In the construction of states the subject as experiencer or actor is suppressed. Hence the particularizing organization provided by a subject's consciousness is disrupted. What the subject did, said, or felt can be resituated in a course of illness or psychic syndrome. The constituted states are available to function as either subject or object of sentences. The subject may be described as *suffering from* what she feels or does or thinks. What she does, says, or feels becomes something external to her that acts upon her or happens to her. Such an externalized relation has its typical syntactic forms as when Woolf "passes from" a mood of apprehension to a state of imperturbability.

4   Such transformations excise the localizing and particularizing linkages of meaning that organize the primary narrative, suppress the presence and activity of the experiencing subject, and constitute selected utterances and actions as states or symptoms that are constituents of the schemata of the textual discourse.

5   The reconstruction of utterances, acts, and feelings as constituents of a course of illness or a syndrome locks a segment of a reported actuality into a schema that produces its own connectives. Connectives are those features of a narrative providing for "this happened, then this happened" sequences. When what an individual does, says, or feels has been reconstituted as a constituent it is directly entered into schemata with its characteristic connectives. In this way the connectives of the textual discourse are substituted for the particularizing connectives of the primary narrative.

6   The framework provided by a course of illness or a psychic syndrome is endogenous. It is conceptualized as independent of particular biographical contexts and local settings. As such it provides a mode of interchange coordinating observations in a variety of local settings. A coroner working in one place can find features of what has happened recognizable as properties of a formalized course of events that is the same as that used elsewhere by other coroners. In these and analogous ways accounts of local events, situations, states of affairs, and so forth are structured by the relevant universalized conceptual controls of a textually mediated discourse.

Thus the ideological circle as a methodology of such transformations inserts the conceptual forms of the discourse as an organizer of the account. The reader knowledgeable in the ideological practices at work, as I am here, actively participates in this process; she comes to think the objectified version that has been inserted and thus to share unwittingly in the suppression of the subject's voice. Edwin Lemert has described a dynamic that he suggests is distinctive as a lead-in to the development of full-blown paranoid delusions. The individual is progressively enfolded in an increasingly closed circle of friends, co-workers, or relatives, all of whom are agreed that he is becoming mentally ill, all of whom are talking with one another about this, all of whom treat him as someone who is mentally ill, and *none* of whom tell him what is going on. Lemert calls this the dynamic of exclusion.[20] The process is capped and authenticated when validated by the psychiatrist. The dialectic between the subject's version and the "normal" version is then objectified by practices just such as those we have been examining. My own sense is that this process is not confined to the paranoid experience.[21] I think, indeed, that Bell's biography is an organizer in just such a process, drawing the reader who knows how to read the psychiatric as a governing frame into its professionally validated frame. We consent. We are active as readers. We go along with it.[22] The subject's voice is silenced, sealed over; its objectified invalidation validates the "normal." This is the dynamic so marvelously realized in Woolf's novel *Mrs. Dalloway*, when Septimus Smith, whose madness is to see the other side of the heroic masculinities of Empire (to be later explicitly attacked by Woolf in *Three guineas*), encounters the doctors. Those complacent and authoritative men manage the margins of "sanity" and madness, sustaining war, empire, heroism, and family life as normal, right, and real against Septimus's experience of their other side—despair, horror, and meaninglessness.[23] They are indeed the angels of darkness themselves, and it is their coming that Septimus escapes by killing himself. And perhaps Virginia Woolf, too.

CHAPTER

8

CONCLUSION

■

In the women's movement in North America, we began with consciousness raising. We began with a struggle with and within language. When we had named our issues, formulated the sources of our oppression, explored the multiplicities of what it is and has been to be a woman, and gone on to create, theorize, and challenge, the struggle did not cease because the relations within which the struggle goes on have not ceased. Gail Scott's contrast between the mothertongue and the domination of the fathertongue, with which this book opened, expresses the ongoing currency of this struggle.

This volume brings together the thinking and investigations I've been doing that originated in the dramatic moment when I discovered in my own life that there was a standpoint from which a woman might know the world very differently from the way knowledge had already claimed it. Of course, for centuries and still today, here and globally, women care for children, cook, do housework, and make other contributions to survival. It isn't that we weren't conscious or that we ceased to be subjects when we were at home doing the work of caring and cleaning. The extraordinary moment came when we saw that this was a place from which we could speak to and of the society at large, moving into a terrain of public discourse that somewhere along the line had been appropriated by and ceded to men.

What we awoke to in the women's movement was the alienation of utterance. We became aware of modes of speaking, writing, and thinking that took our powers of expression away from us even as we used them. Beginning to speak from a site of consciousness that had not already been made over and subdued was a violent, exciting, and extraordinarily consequential moment. This is the moment I have tried to work from and remain with. I sought first to see how to work from outside the conceptual and methodological procedures that objectify knowing as knowledge, when everything we know how to do as members of a North American intelligentsia reinstates exactly the problem we tried to escape. I resorted to Marx because I had discovered in *The German ideology*, when I was doing a naive and happily untutored reading of his work in the 1960s, that he wasn't doing at all what established sociology was doing with the notion of ideology. He was struggling to develop a method of reasoning and investigation that would connect up concepts and theories with the actualities of people's lives and with how people put them together in and through their actual activities. He was developing methods of reasoning and inquiry about historical and social process that express actual organization and relations. In so doing, he worked with the concept of ideology, treating it not as meaning, sense, or signification, but as practices or methods of reasoning.

I've turned this aspect of Marx's method toward exploring the complex of activities that draws our powers and practices of reasoning into objectified knowledges integral to our ruling. The standpoint of women is in a new place. We begin from the site of our experience, with the ways in which we actually exist, and explore the world from where we are. The standpoint of women pulls Marx's strategies of inquiry into a new and marvelously flexible form, just as taffy is pulled and becomes elastic in the pulling. Marx's version of materialism is reshaped and transformed when we take up a standpoint in local actualities to explore as insiders (for this, indeed, is the only way they may be known) the social relations that tie the local and particular into the generalized and generalizing relations that determine and organize the local and particular.

I'm striving for a sociology that will open up and expand how we know the world of our experience. What is there for the sociologist exists in and only in particular people's activities in definite places and times. What is there for us is produced or accomplished in people's ongoing and co-ordered practices. The ordinary objects of our world, such as tables, chairs, and sidewalks, are distinctive orderings of actual activities. Tables, for example, aren't just distinctive physical shapes; they collect and cue definite, actual practices; they call for separations between floor and foot level and a surface apt for the upper part of the body. A table as a mere physical form stripped of its social organization can be imagined if we think of a small child peeing on a table surface, or if we remember how a table appears to children from the underside, or, turned upside down, how it can be used to simulate a boat in play. A table as a social organization is visible too in how someone moving into a new living space might use a packing case as a table before her belongings are unpacked: she has a friend coming to dinner; she puts a cloth on the packing case and a water glass with a flower on it in the center. Children learn by example and instruction the practices differentiating the table surface from others. The table surface organizes meetings of people around it; it differentiates the body parts above and below it, stashing away the lower part of the body and allowing the talking heads to function with a discreet suppression of legs and genitals under the table; tables organize distances among people; they establish discrete territories for temporary appropriation in cafés and restaurants; and so forth.

But it's misleading to focus too much on objects as paradigmatic of the ontology of the social. Rather we should grasp entities as moments in social relations; we should grasp how the property of being an entity itself is a specific form of socially organized practice. A gift, for example, is an entity that comes into being as a definite sequence of organized practices, again one that becomes visible as you teach it to a child. I remember the pretences and play I used as a single parent to introduce my young son to practices of giving me a gift at Christmas, pretending that I did not know what I was getting, that I was pleased and surprised when I opened the package I had helped to wrap. A gift arises in a relational practice. So do commodities. As Marx showed, they come into being only in the relations of exchange of money and commodities. And they fall out of existence at the termination of that process, just as groceries are groceries only until they are stashed away on the kitchen shelves. And here knowledge has been explored as a set of social relations. We move from a focus on the object thus constituted to the relations in which that object arises and through which we are being related to it. Useful as it is to begin with "entities," it is the relations coordinating people's actual sequences of action that must be central to our investigation, for it is these actual activities that bind them into the extending sequences coordinating activities among many individuals and across multiple sites.

A social ontology grounded in the ongoing coordination of people's actual activities does not presuppose order, organization, or relations. These are not given; they are always in process. They arise as people coordinate their activities. Generalized social relations are definite modes in which people's activities have come to be organized, and they are daily and nightly both reproduced and changed as people's local activities articulate to, coordinate with, and are determined by them. Such an ontology means that inquiry and investigation are inextricably joined; it means that the work of inquiry is a process of discovery and that its conceptual articulation is governed by, and seeks to express, actual social organization and social relations.

◖   The Reflexive

"Critique-through-Investigation"

Speaking of the world from the standpoint of women calls for methods of knowing that encompass the disjuncture itself, including the social relations of objectified knowledge. The critique of sociological methods of constructing objectivities is developed in this book as a method of inquiry enabling escape from the surfaces of textual discourse into the actualities of people's lives, and hence our own. The materialism that I've developed from Marx understands thought, concepts, textual work, and what is ordinarily thought of as meaning as what people do, as existing in time, and as integral constituents of social relations and organization. Constituting these phenomena as *culture* or *meaning* converts the practices of actual people, integral to everyday courses of action, into a timeless, dislocated space of mere language, mere thought. By contrast, an insider's strategy takes concepts, ideas, ideology, and schemata as dimensions and organizers of the ongoing social process that we can grasp only as insiders, only by considering our own practices.[1]

An essential step of this materialist method is to grasp that the text is always in the actual, and that if it constructs a world apart from the actual, it does so as actual people read in actual settings. Our practices of reading and writing the world of social relations, whether as cultural theory, sociology in its varieties, or political economy, conceal beneath them the depths of textual realities and other textual forms that mediate people's actualities. The textual realities constructing the relation of knowing at the surface are substructed by relations and apparatuses of ruling that mediate people's local actualities and specific factual accounts entering textual time.

The placing of the "feminine" in the texts of poststructuralism and deconstruction presupposes just such a textual surface. It is only on this terrain that women are absent, other, without the passage into discourse that the sexuality of men accords. Speaking from the margins determining the boundaries of masculine speech, the feminine disrupts and disorganizes the discourse of modernity. Thus the feminine has been appropriated by the male speaker as leverage in the unseating of modernity.[2] This theorizing of femininity gives women nowhere to come from that is not already defined by men, and we can have nowhere else to come from so long as we remain on the reading side of the text. But the standpoint of women, as I've grasped it, situates the subject in women's lives, in people's lives, not on the textual surface. From the site of her own experience in a two-week course of seminars given by Derrida in Toronto some while back, Lola Lemire Tostevin writes: "Derrida likes to question the masters, in his classes master and students stay in their respective places. In Derrida's seminar women remain seminally divided. Keep to the margins to bear witness to what he tells."[3] The textual surfaces of discourse obliterate the structures of power sustaining their coherence and authority. It is just those relations of power mediated by textuality that I've sought to explore in these chapters.

The critique of sociological method developed here is more than formal; as a critique of sociology as actual practices, it has already moved critique into the mode of inquiry. Such an inquiry moves beyond sociology, for sociological objectifications are a special case of (and depend on) the objectified knowledges of the relations and apparatuses of ruling. Taking up critique-as-inquiry and inquiry-as-critique as an insider adds a further dimension. Inquiry becomes an essentially reflexive critique. For the relations explored here can be grasped only as we are insiders participating in them. At the same time, in exploring them we bring into view not just our actual practices of thinking, reasoning, reading, making sense of accounts, and so forth, but the social relations we participate in by doing so. In this way, as insiders, relations that our own practices are embedded in can be made explicit and examinable through inquiry.

Introspection turns us toward ourselves and does not give us access to practices tied in and organized by a complex of relations beyond ourselves. Working as an insider means that inquiry into "how things work," into the actualities of socially organized practices, makes what we are part of visible. In exploring social organization, we explore our own lives and practices. Thus critique is investigation and investigation is a reflexive critique, disclosing practices we know and use. As a method of inquiry it has powers to disclose just how our practices contribute to and are articulated with the relations that overpower our lives. In exploring the reading of Quentin Bell's account of the months leading up to Virginia Woolf's death, we saw how we ourselves might be joined through our practices of reading with the doctors from whom Septimus Smith, and perhaps Virginia Woolf also, sought escape.

Here I've worked where I've been most familiar, namely, in the area of mental illness. Using this method of reflexive inquiry, I've explored the relations organizing the textual realities that mediated what I could know of "mental illness" as a sociologist, other than through experience and accounts of experience. I had struggled in my prefeminist life to find ways of addressing these experiences—my own experience of psychotherapy, others' experiences written in the very considerable literature of personal accounts of mental illness and treatment. Until the women's movement opened up women's standpoint as a place to speak from, there seemed no point of entry that did not convert what was primary in people's experience to mere illustrations, subdued by the authorized voices of psychiatry and sociology. Much of this book has been working through from a number of different angles the complex of relations and practices that organize psychiatric knowledge to exclude or subdue the actualities of people's experience. I have been working against an enemy that I was also part of, to discover how it worked so that I could discover how I was, and am, tied in to the relations of ruling in my practices of thinking about and speaking about people who are mentally ill and those who work with them. Renouncing such methods of speaking and writing is not by any means just a matter of a personal transformation.

This insider's feminist materialism directs us toward grasping how our local and particular moments are entered into extended, generalized, and generalizing social relations. It exposes the ideological practices in which we in the women's movement formulate women's issues as constituents of the relations of ruling. Gillian Walker has described and analyzed the first struggles of women against men's use of violence against women in the home,[4] the arguments and debates about their conceptualization ("battered women," "wife assault," "wife abuse," and so forth), the contexts "in and against the state" within which debates went on, the contradictions between naming for mobilization in the movement and naming oriented toward jural and administrative action by the state, the successes of the movement in Canada in securing government action, and the ambiguity of the feminist successes in shaping a government committee report on "family violence" that made practical gains while at the same time shifting the locus of control and initiative from women's organizations to the relations of ruling.[5] The concept of "family violence" displaces the centrality of women. Recently a friend told me of a conference on family violence she attended as a representative of a rape relief organization. Discussion groups were organized to include representatives of organizations concerned not only with violence against women but also with violence against children, sexual abuse, violence against senior citizens, and other issues subsumed under the term. Hence the distinctive issues for women could not emerge, and indeed, participants were told that they should not let feminists have it "all their own way."[6]

Adele Mueller has investigated how feminist struggles to have women represented in the development policies of the U.S. government evolved into the effective controls coordinating "Women in Development" thinking and research with U.S. development policies in the third world. Research is produced in accord with those policy interests rather than the interests and concerns of women subject to development. Mueller shows the conflicts embedded in the process as women researchers, working in the field in direct relationship with third-world women, seek to represent the concerns and interests of the latter, only to find that the standardized conceptual practices of the field, the forms required of research, and the internal political process of government-funded conferences effectively silence them.[7]

These ambiguities are a permanent feature of our politics. The method of inquiry developed in this book proffers no simple solutions. A reflexive critical inquiry following the path taken here explicates how we are connected, through the socially organized practices of knowing, into the relations of ruling, whether as super- or subordinates. It enables us to explore how our practices of knowing articulate us to, and are themselves articulated to, the generalized and generalizing relations of the society we live in, and in particular how we may be caught up in the relations of ruling and be confined, in our knowing, to the surfaces of the text.

The insider's materialism I have put forward is intended to deepen and expand our access to the actualities of our lives and what we are caught up in without knowing it. The particular analytic strategies I've used are sometimes technical. The technical practices are not an orthodoxy; they are not required, nor is the concept of ideology. There could be no irony greater than an ideological practice of the concept of ideology as I've used it here. The techniques of analysis and the concepts are there for your use. Feel free.

NOTES

Notes to the Introduction

1. Gail Scott, *Spaces like stairs* (Toronto: The Women's Press, 1989).
2. Dorothy E. Smith, "Women and psychiatry," in *Women look at psychiatry*, ed. Dorothy E. Smith and Sara J. David, 1–19. (Vancouver: Press Gang, 1975).
3. See John A. Clausen and Madeleine Yarrow, eds., "The impact of mental illness on the family," *Journal of Social Issues* (1955) 2, no. 4 (special issue).
4. These general ideas, rather rudely formulated and never published, are similar in some ways to those later formulated by Thomas Scheff in *Becoming mentally ill* (Chicago: Aldine Press, 1966). Scheff's thesis, however, unlike mine, considers mentally ill behavior to be learned responsively in a feedback process between "residual" forms of deviance and the resulting labeling of someone as mentally ill.

Notes to Chapter 1

1. Robert Bierstedt, "Sociology and general education," in *Sociology and contemporary education*, ed. Charles H. Page (New York: Random House, 1966).
2. Dorothy E. Smith, *The everyday world as problematic: A feminist sociology* (Boston: Northeastern University Press, 1987).
3. Jean Briggs, *Never in anger* (Cambridge: Harvard University Press, 1970).

Notes to Chapter 2

An early draft of this paper was presented at the Western Anthropological and Sociological Association meetings in Calgary in January 1972. The form it has now was prepared for presentation to the Department of Sociology, Queen's University, Kingston, Ontario, in April 1972. I am grateful to that department for the opportunity to prepare the version upon which this is based. It was published in *Catalyst* 8 (Winter 1974): 39–54.

1. Karl Mannheim, *Ideology and utopia* (New York: Doubleday/ Anchor, 1965).

2. See my *Everyday world as problematic*, chapter 3 in particular, for an elaboration of this view.

3. One possible result is the construction of a sociology of doubtful interest to anyone.

4. See Smith, *Everyday world as problematic*.

5. Sandra Harding, *The science question in feminism* (Ithaca: Cornell University Press, 1986).

6. Karl Marx and Friedrich Engels, *The German ideology* (Moscow: Progress Publishers, 1976).

7. Some interpreters, applying the sociological reading of ideology to Marx's work, have accused him of not recognizing the ideological character of his own work in taking the standpoint of the working class; see, for a notable example, Martin Seliger, *The Marxist conception of ideology: A critical essay* (Cambridge: Cambridge University Press, 1977). That Marx himself did not view his own work as ideological is treated in this literature as a peculiar aberration. It is a reading of his work that depends upon imposing on it the interpretive framework of a later sociology—laced with a degree of political prejudice—that has inhibited careful reading. In *The German ideology* the perspective he held and the theoretical enterprise on which he was engaged are clearly contrasted to ideology. It is hard for anyone familiar with his work, and with the strength and uncompromising intellect at work in it, to imagine that this is the ordinary inconsistency of a man blindly partial to his own theory. He saw his work as a science and science as a means of discovering how the world actually is.

8. In *The Grundrisse* Marx contrasts the method he has criticized in *The German ideology* (and later, with Proudhon as his object, in *The poverty of philosophy*) with his own. Here he goes back to Hegel as the founder of this method of reasoning about the world:

> Hegel fell into the illusion of conceiving the real as the product of thought concentrating itself, probing its own depths, and unfolding itself out of itself, by itself, whereas the method of rising from the abstract to the concrete,

reproduces it as the concrete in the mind. But this is by no means the process by which the concrete itself comes into being. . . . Therefore, to the kind of consciousness—and this is characteristic of the philosophical consciousness—for which conceptual thinking is the real human being and for which the conceptual world as such is thus the only reality, the movement of the categories appears as the real act of production—whose product is the world; and . . . this is correct insofar as the concrete totality is a totality of thoughts, concrete in thought, in fact a product of thinking and comprehending; but not in any way a product of the concept which thinks and generates itself outside or above observation and conception; a product, rather, of the working-up of observation and conception into concepts. (Karl Marx, *The Grundrisse: Foundations of the critique of political economy*, trans. Martin Nicolaus [New York: Random House, 1973], 101)

9.   The *German ideology* is, of course, the product of Marx's and Engels's joint work. The extensive critical treatment of the ideological practices of those there described as the "German Ideologists," however, is Marx's work; furthermore, the later methodological discussions developing this line of thinking are entirely Marx's. *The poverty of philosophy*, which follows *The German ideology* very closely and is by Marx alone, follows up the line of thinking developed there and, I believe, carried forward in the whole body of Marx's work that follows and in particular in the introduction of *The Grundrisse*. Engels, on the other hand, in his later work makes use of a somewhat different and sometimes contradictory version of materialism. These considerations make it appropriate, I believe, to address the thinking on ideology in *The German ideology* as Marx's work.

10.   I am bracketing for the time being Marx's central emphasis upon productive activity in the strict sense. I am also bracketing for the duration of this chapter his emphasis on development and upon historical change.

11.   See, for example, Linda J. Nicholson, *Gender and history: The limits of social theory in the age of the family* (New York: Columbia University Press, 1986).

12.   See R. A. Sydie, *Natural women, cultured men: A feminist perspective on sociological theory* (Toronto: Methuen, 1987).

13.   Marx and Engels, *German ideology*, 36.

14.   See Derek Sayer, *The violence of abstraction: The analytic foundations of historical materialism* (Oxford: Basil Blackwell, 1987), last chapter, for an excellent discussion of the epistemological issues raised by Marx's method.

15.   Louis Althusser, *For Marx* (Harmondsworth: Penguin Books, 1969).

16.   For an interpretation of Marx's ontology congenial to this, see Carol C. Gould, *Marx's social ontology: Individuality and community in*

Marx's theory of social reality (Cambridge, Mass.: MIT Press 1975), particularly chapter 1, on the ontology of society.

17.   Karl Marx and Friedrich Engels, *The German ideology*, ed. R. Pascal (New York: International, n.d.), 15.

18.   Karl Marx, *Capital: A critical analysis of capitalist production*, vol. 1, trans. Samuel Moore and Edward Aveling (Moscow: Progress Publishers, n.d.), 80.

19.   See Bertell Ollman, *Alienation* (Cambridge: Cambridge University Press, 1976).

20.   Mannheim, *Ideology and utopia*, 57.

21.   Ibid., 19.

22.   Marx, *Capital*, 65.

23.   Ibid.

24.   *Natural*, as Marx generally uses it, does not necessarily mean "of nature." Rather, it serves to differentiate what is consciously planned, the outcome of conscious agency or will, from what arises without conscious planning or thought.

25.   See Harold Garfinkel, in *Proceedings of the Purdue Symposium on Ethnomethodology*, ed. Richard J. Hill and Kathleen Stones Crittenden, Institute Monograph Series no. 1, Institute for the Study of Social Change, Purdue University.

26.   E. H. Kantorowicz's magnificent book, *The king's two bodies: A study in medieval political theology* (Princeton, N.J.: Princeton University Press, 1957).

27.   Michael Polanyi, *Personal knowledge* (New York: Harper, 1964).

28.   Marx and Engels, *German ideology* (1976), 19. These words could have been written by George Herbert Mead, whose account of mind and consciousness as a socially structured practice is complementary to Marx's account of consciousness.

29.   Ibid., 50.

30.   Ibid., 46.

31.   Ibid., 70.

32.   Ibid., 508.

33.   Hans Zetterberg, *On theory and verification in sociology* (Totawa, N.J.: Bedminster Press, 1965), 54-55.

34.   Durkheim's prescriptions systematically discount the subjectivity of the member of society as a constitutive component of the social fact; see Emile Durkheim, *The rules of sociological method* (New York: Free Press, 1964). See my analysis of Durkheim's method as among the founding "conventions" of sociological discourse in "Sociological theory: Writ-

ing patriarchy into feminist texts," *Feminism and sociological theory*, ed. Ruth Wallace (New York: Sage Publications, 1989).

35. Rom Harré, *Theories and things: A brief study in prescriptive metaphysics* (London: Sheed & Ward, 1961).

36. Marx and Engels, *German ideology*, 42.

37. Terence K. Hopkins, *The exercise of influence in small groups* (Totawa, N.J.: Bedminster Press, 1964).

38. Zetterberg, *Theory and verification*, 92.

39. Marx and Engels, *German ideology*, 107.

40. Ibid., 37.

41. Alfred D. Chandler, Jr., *Strategy and structure: Chapters in the history of American industrial enterprise* (New York: Anchor Books, 1966), 16.

42. For a full exploration of a methodology that defines its problematic as an expression of this relation between the experienced and the determinations of experience, see my *Everyday world as problematic*.

43. Norman Geras, "Fetishism in Marx's *Capital*," *New Left Review* 65 (1971).

44. James Q. Wilson, "Violence," in *Toward the year 2000*, ed. Daniel Bell (Boston: Beacon Press, 1969).

45. We have the beginnings of this kind of work in the sociological tradition that stems from symbolic interactionism, particularly in the study of deviance, where labeling theory has been a focus. More recently some of the work done in ethnomethodology, particularly that concerned with the procedures for constructing administrative records, makes the social construction of social facts its primary research focus. See Aaron Cicourel, *The social organization of juvenile justice* (New York: John Wiley, 1968), and Don H. Zimmerman, "Record-keeping and the intake process in a public welfare agency," in *On record: Files and dossiers in American Life* (New York: Russell Sage Foundation, 1969).

46. Marx and Engels, *German ideology*, 45.

Notes to Chapter 3

This chapter is a modified version of a paper originally published as "The social construction of documentary reality," in *Sociological Inquiry* 44 (1974): 257–68.

1. The notion of text here includes both the written (or otherwise inscribed) words or other symbols and its physical aspect—printed on paper and so forth. As is emphasized later in this chapter, the materiality of the text, both as practices of writing and reading and as an actual physical

form reproduced by definite technical practices, is an essential part of the analysis put forward here.

2. Though the social organization producing a factual account is isolated in this analysis, this has only an accidental similarity to Louis Althusser's notion of a scientific knowledge of society as a process of production in its own right. See his *For Marx*.

3. As Walter Benjamin takes the physicality of the work of art seriously in his study "The work of art in the age of mechanical reproduction," in *Illuminations* (New York: Schocken Books, 1969).

4. For the full version of this, see Dorothy E. Smith, "The active text," Chapter 5 in *Texts, facts, and femininity: Exploring the relations of ruling* (London: Routledge & Kegan Paul, 1990).

5. Don H. Zimmerman, "Facts as practical accomplishment," in *Ethnomethodology* (Harmondsworth: Penguin Books, 1974), 128–43.

6. Bruno Latour and Steve Woolgar, *Laboratory life: Social construction of scientific facts* (New York: Sage Publications, 1979).

7. See Alfred Schutz, "On multiple realities," in *Collected papers*, vol. 1, 207–59 (The Hague: Martinus Nijhoff, 1962).

8. See Michael Lynch, *Art and artifact in laboratory science: A study of shop work and shop talk in a research laboratory* (London: Routledge & Kegan Paul, 1985).

9. For a model of inquiry into the socially organized production and uses of factual documents, see Zimmerman, "Facts as practical accomplishment."

10. Marx, *Capital*, 77.

11. Lennard Davis gives a very interesting account of the differentiation of factual from fictional accounts in the seventeenth and eighteenth centuries. His interest is primarily in this as the origin of the contemporary novel, but he also has much of use to tell us of the emergence of facts and news; see Lennard J. Davis, *Factual fictions: The origins of the English novel* (New York: Columbia University Press, 1983).

12. E. H. Carr in his classic *What is history?* (Harmondsworth: Penguin Books, 1964) distinguishes between a "fact of history" and a story, however accurate, about an event occurring in the past. A fact of history has to be properly introduced into and established as part of the discourse of history as a discipline.

13. Dorothy E. Smith, "K is mentally ill: the anatomy of a factual account," in *Texts, facts, and femininity*.

14. See Michel Foucault, *Power/Knowledge: Selected interviews and other writings, 1972–1977* (New York: Pantheon Books, 1980), particularly chapter 5 ("Two lectures") and chapter 6 ("Truth and power").

15. See Norwood Russell Hanson's discussion of how statements fail to

be factual in *Perception and discovery* (San Francisco: Freeman, Cooper, 1969). He has a wonderfully trenchant presentation of the arguments between philosophers about whether facts are things in the real world that you can kick or whether they exist only at the level of proposition.

16. Carr, *What is history?*

17. See Hanson's discussion in *Perception and Discovery.*

18. Ludwik Fleck, *Genesis and development of a scientific fact,* trans. Fred Bradley and Thaddeus J. Trenn (Chicago: University of Chicago Press, 1979); see especially chapter 3, "The Wasserman reaction and its discovery."

19. See Zimmerman, "Record-keeping."

20. See Michael Lynch's brilliant study of graphic inscription as integral in domesticating the wild actualities of the natural universe to the measurement of science ("Discipline and the material form of images: An analysis of scientific visibility," paper presented at the meetings of the Canadian Sociology and Anthropology Association, June 1983, Vancouver).

21. "Chronotopy" is Bakhtin's term; see his *Dialogic imagination* (Austin: University of Texas Press, 1981).

22. See, for example, J. Thorpe, *Principles of textual criticism* (San Marino, Calif.: The Huntington Library, 1973).

23. I am indebted to M. L. Stephenson for the use of this material.

24. See Norman Holland, *The dynamics of literary response* (New York: W. W. Norton, 1975).

25. Melvin Pollner, *Mundane reason: Reality in everyday and sociological discourse* (New York: Cambridge University Press, 1987), 32–33.

26. This social organization may be the origin of the type of analysis of meaning that Wittgenstein pursued in the *Tractatus* (Ludwig Wittgenstein, *Tractatus logico-philosophicus,* trans. G. E. M. Anscombe [London: Routledge & Kegan Paul, 1961]).

27. Peter Eglin's study of readings of the two accounts of the street people–police encounter I have referred to displays this quite strikingly. Students reading the two accounts treated both as simple representations of what actually happened; see Peter Eglin, "Resolving reality disjuncture on Telegraph Avenue: A study of practical reasoning," *Canadian Journal of Sociology* 4 (1979): 359–75.

28. See Michel Foucault, *Power/Knowledge.*

Notes to Chapter 4

1. Don H. Zimmerman and M. Pollner, "The everyday world as phenomenon," in *Understanding everyday life*, ed. J. D. Douglas (Chicago: Aldine Publishing, 1971).

2. Ibid.

3. Hilary Graham and Ann Oakley, "Competing ideologies of reproduction: Medical and maternal perspectives on pregnancy," in *Women, health and reproduction*, ed. H. Roberts (London: Routledge & Kegan Paul, 1981), 52.

4. Similar processes are observed by Cicourel and Kitsuse in the context of a high school. Aaron Cicourel and John Kitsuse, *The educational decision-makers* (Indianapolis: Bobbs-Merrill, 1963).

5. See Bryan S. Green, *Knowing the poor: A case-study in textual reality construction* (London: Routledge & Kegan Paul, 1983), 154–58.

6. Cicourel, *Social organization*, 163.

7. Ibid.

8. Ibid., 144.

9. Canadian Mental Health Association, The Women and Mental Health Committee, *Women and mental health in Canada: Strategies for change* (Toronto: Canadian Mental Health Association, 1987), 59–60.

10. Ibid.

11. Cicourel, *Social organization*, 163.

12. See the Government Statisticians' Collective, "How official statistics are produced: Views from the inside," in *Demystifying social statistics*, ed. John Irvine, Ian Miles, and Jeff Evans (London, Pluto Press, 1979), 130–151.

13. Ann Oakley and Robin Oakley, "Sexism in official statistics," in *Demystifying social statistics*, 173–74.

14. See George W. Smith, "Policing the gay community: An inquiry into textually-mediated social relations," *International Journal of the Sociology of Law* 16 (1988): 163–83.

15. Patricia Groves, "Lawyer-Client interviews and the social organization of preparation for court in criminal and divorce cases" (Ph.D. diss., Department of Sociology and Anthropology, University of British Columbia), 152, 153–54.

16. Daniel Ellsberg, *Papers on the war* (New York: Simon and Schuster, 1972), 18.

17. Jonathan Schell, *The village of Ben Suc* (New York: Vintage, 1966), and *The military half: An account of the destruction of Quang Ngai and Quang Tin* (New York: Vintage, 1968).

18.   Schell, *Military half,* 181.

19.   For example, see Mark Baker, *Nam: The Vietnam war in the words of the men and women who fought there* (New York: Berkeley Books, 1981).

20.   During the 1960s attempts were made to break down these barriers to effective communication among psychiatric professionals and patients by redesigning them as what were called "therapeutic" communities. In my experience these failed to become generalized partly because they violated the professional relationships intersecting with the particular local contexts in which therapeutic communities were founded, and partly because they were in contradiction with the powerfully custodial functions of the psychiatric inpatient facility.

21.   I am reminded of seeing a documentary called *China: The roots of madness* some twenty years ago. It included much footage showing aspects of China during the twentieth century. One sequence, described as documenting the Long March, showed rather dim figures walking over a mountainside (they could have been anyone, anywhere). All of a sudden the bottom of the screen showed the warning "Unauthenticated communist footage."

22.   Elaine Buckley Day, "A 20th century witch hunt: A feminist critique of the Grange royal commission into deaths at the Hospital for Sick Children," *Studies in Political Economy* 24 (1987): 21.

23.   Ibid., 27.

Notes to Chapter 5

I am indebted to Yvana Christie for typing the original draft and for many helpful editorial notations, and to Steven Smith for helping me to check the table.

1.   Michel Foucault, *Madness and civilization: A history of insanity in the age of reason* (New York: Vintage Books, 1973), and *Discipline and punish: The birth of the prison* (New York: Vintage Books, 1979).

2.   Phyllis Chesler, *Women and madness* (New York: Doubleday, 1972).

3.   Ibid., 119–20.

4.   Adapted from table 6 of Statistics Canada, *Mental health statistics,* vol. 1, *Institutional admissions and separations* (Ottawa: Information Canada, 1970), 52.

5.   Ibid.

6.   Chesler, *Women and madness,* 120.

7.   Ibid., appendix, table 3.

8.   W. R. Gove and J. F. Tudor, "Adult sex roles and mental illness," in

Changing women in a changing society, ed. Joan Huber (Chicago: University of Chicago Press, 1973), 50–73.

9. Ibid., 69.

10. Ibid., 50.

11. Ibid.

12. Advances in medical knowledge about the biochemistry of the brain and its involvement in certain types of mental disorder make this distinction increasingly hard to maintain in its original simplicity.

13. Statistics Canada, *Mental health statistics,* 15.

14. See Statistics Canada, *Mental health statistics,* 44 (table 4).

15. Ibid.

16. Chesler, *Women and madness,* 33.

17. Chesler is careful to restrict what she says about the data to women's "involvement with psychiatry." In other contexts she speaks of how "some women are driven mad" by being "impaled on the cross of self-sacrifice" (ibid., 31), of madness as a "rite" that women "perform," and of "useless women" becoming "visible" as insane (33). Generally, however, she takes advantage of a variant of the model I describe, and this is certainly the method of thinking that others use in interpreting what she says.

18. Thomas Szasz, *The myth of mental illness: Foundations of a theory of personal conduct* (New York: Dell, 1961); Thomas Scheff, *Being mentally ill: A sociological theory* (Chicago: Aldine Press, 1962); R. D. Laing, *The divided self: A study of sanity and madness* (Chicago: Quadrangle Books, 1960).

19. Szasz, *Myth.*

20. Scheff, *Being mentally ill,* chapter 2, pp. 31–54 in particular.

21. Laing, *Divided self,* chapter 2.

22. Judi Chamberlain describes this experience; see Judi Chamberlain, "Women's oppressions and psychiatric oppression," in *Women look at psychiatry,* ed. Dorothy E. Smith and Sara J. David (Vancouver: Press Gang, 1975). See also R. D. Laing, *The bird of paradise or the politics of experience* (Harmondsworth: Penguin Books, 1967), 58.

23. Statistics Canada, *Mental health statistics,* 14, 15.

24. This picture describes the psychiatric process; the general bureaucratic procedure has been fairly extensively described elsewhere. For technical descriptions and analyses see Harold Garfinkel, *Studies in ethnomethodology* (Englewood Cliffs, N.J.: Prentice-Hall, 1967); Zimmerman, "Record-Keeping"; David Sudnow, "Normal crimes: Sociological features of the penal code," *Social Problems* 12 (1965), 255–76; Cicourel, *Social organization.*

25.   Meredith Kimball, "Women, sex role stereotypes, and mental health: Catch 22," in *Women look at psychiatry*. See also Elinor King, "How the psychiatric profession views women," in *Women look at psychiatry*.

26.   B. Gene Errington, "Negotiating the decision: What is a police matter?" (M.A. thesis, University of British Columbia, 1973).

27.   Sudnow, "Normal crimes."

28.   M. Spring Rice, *Working class wives*, cited in Sheila Rowbotham, *Women's consciousness, man's world* (Harmondsworth: Penguin Books, 1974), 75.

29.   Sir David Stafford-Clark, *Psychiatry today* (Harmondsworth: Penguin Books, 1963), 95–96. The passage is quoted in full below in chapter 6.

30.   David L. Rosenham's study "On being sane in insane places," *Science* 197 (1973): 250–58, provides instances of the same process of "reading" a clinical syndrome from the behavior of people who were admitted without psychiatric illness into mental hospitals in the U.S.

31.   This is a variant of J. Maxwell Atkinson's formulation in his "Societal reactions to suicide," in *Patterns of deviance*, ed. S. J. Cohen (Harmondsworth: Penguin Books, 1974).

32.   Smith, "K is Mentally Ill."

33.   Taking the standpoint of women means relying on women's experience. This is what I've done here. There's no sample, no attempt to generalize in the ordinary sense. I do not argue that the few instances I avail myself of are representative or typical. I'm proceeding in a different way, from the assumption that any such story bears ineluctable traces of the social organizations and relations that are integral to the sequences of action it retails. Where the teller of the story speaks of an experience with psychiatry or medicine, her story relies on social organization and relations that are generalized and extralocal. As we have seen, psychiatric practices are standardized; professional training and other institutions generalize and standardize; new approaches, techniques, knowledge, and so forth are produced in systematically standardized forms (hence the significance of double-blind experiments as a method of evaluating the efficacy of new drugs). Hospital practices and organization are also standardized, and there is an increasingly generalized conception of mental illness ensuring at least a minimal standardization of knowledge in the population at large. These are forms of social organization and relations that are implicit in though not necessarily overtly addressed in the stories. Social organization and relations are built into the language used and into the connections set up syntactically in the story. Therefore, I argue, we can find social organization in the accounts of experience (al-

though, of course, it is only partially present and in those aspects that have determined the storyteller's experience). The same principle applies to the uses of fiction, at least of certain kinds. My uses of accounts from experience rely on this provenance or ground. I seek to make explicit those properties of the social organization present but not explicated in the narratives that tie experience into the generalized and generalizing organization of psychiatric institutions.

34. I have not made a parallel analysis of the accounts of men hospitalized or otherwise in treatment for mental illness. I would expect to find there also the enforcement of patriarchy, though it would of course take a different character. This kind of analysis could also, I believe, be suggestively applied to the enforcement of other dimensions of the regime, such as class and race.

35. Barbara Findlay, "Shrink! shrank! shriek!" in *Women look at psychiatry*, 71.

36. Rosenham, "On being sane."

37. Mary Douglas, *Purity and danger* (Harmondsworth: Penguin Books, 1966).

38. Judi Chamberlain, "Struggling to be born," in *Women look at psychiatry*, 53–57.

39. Diane Harpwood, *Tea and tranquillisers: The diary of a happy housewife* (London: Virago, 1982), 12–13. See note 33 above for a discussion bearing on the use of fictional material.

40. Ibid., 18–19.

41. See Findlay, "Shrink!" 60.

42. Cf. Thomas Scheff's account of mental illness as an intensifying negative feedback system in *Being mentally ill.*

Notes to Chapter 6

1. Ludwig Wittgenstein, *Philosophical investigations*, trans. G. E. M. Anscombe (New York: Macmillan, 1953).

2. Bakhtin, *Dialogic imagination*, 291–422.

3. J. Maxwell Atkinson, *Discovering suicide: Studies in the social organization of sudden death* (London: Macmillan, 1978), 9–32. Suicide has, of course, been a focus for sociology and sociological debate since Durkheim's innovative theoretical and methodological work on that topic (Emile Durkheim, *Suicide* [London: Routledge & Kegan Paul, 1952]), and "suicide" has been the contingent center of more than one significant shift in the development of sociology. Though this chapter is not about suicide as such, it is situated in the methodological and epistemological

debate stemming from Durkheim's work. I take up the dialogue at that point where it has been shaped by the work of Harold Garfinkel (*Studies in ethnomethodology*), J. D. Douglas (*The social meanings of suicide* [Princeton, N.J.: Princeton University Press, 1967]), and Atkinson, who have moved away from a concern with the social determinants of suicide and rates of suicide to the problem of the social meanings of suicide and the socially organized forms of knowledge that constitute it as such.

4.   See Dorothy E. Smith, chapter 4, "On sociological description: A method from Marx," in *Texts, facts, and femininity.*

5.   This notion is from Mikhail Bakhtin, particularly from the essay on it in *The dialogic imagination.*

6.   Sylvia Plath, *The bell jar* (New York: Harper and Row, 1971).

7.   Sylvia Plath, *Ariel* (London: Faber and Faber, 1972).

8.   An analogous contrast between a formal account and an experienced actuality is given in a passage from Wolfgang Iser's analysis of Faulkner's *The sound and the fury:*

> When Quentin is walking through the suburbs of Boston, he is followed by a little girl. He wants to get rid of her and decides to take her home, but the girl does not know where she lives and so the two of them wander through the streets aimlessly and yet with a specific aim in mind. The desire to get rid of the child awakens in Quentin the memory of how he once used to worry about his sister Caddy; at the time he wanted to win Caddy's love, and now he wants to be free of the child. The dumb persistence of the child and the painful relationship with the sister run into one another, creating a new situation, of which the past and the present situations become mere shadow. . . . When finally Quentin is found by the girl's brother, taken to the sheriff, and accused of wicked intentions, he reacts with wild laughter, because he can only regard as absurd the reduction of his various thoughts to a single motive—especially of this nature. (Wolfgang Iser, *The act of reading: A theory of aesthetic response* [Baltimore: Johns Hopkins University Press, 1978], 147).

9.   R. S. Peters, *The concept of motivation* (London: Routledge & Kegan Paul, 1958).

10.   W. Labov and J. Waletzky, "Narrative analysis: oral versions of personal experience," in *Essays on verbal and visual arts*, Proceedings of the 1966 Annual Spring Meeting of the American Ethnological Society, ed. J. Helm (Seattle: American Ethnological Society/University of Washington Press, 1967).

11.   Schutz, "On multiple realities."

12.   Garfinkel, *Studies in ethnomethodology.*

13.   Atkinson, *Discovering suicide*, 143.

14.   Harold Garfinkel, "Suicide for all practical purposes," in *Studies in ethnomethodology*, 11–18.

15. Atkinson, *Discovering suicide*, 171.

16. Zimmerman and Pollner, "Everyday world."

17. Alvin W. Gouldner, *The coming crisis in western sociology* (New York: Basic Books, 1970).

18. Roy Turner, "Introduction," in *Ethnomethodology* (Harmondsworth: Penguin Books, 1974).

19. For a full development of this as a sociology, see my *Everyday world as problematic.*

20. See chapter 4 of my *Texts, facts, and femininity.*

21. Harvey Sacks, "Sociological description," *Berkeley Journal of Sociology* 8 (1963): 1–16.

22. Norman Holland, *The dynamics of literary response* (New York: W. W. Norton, 1975).

23. Mannheim, *Ideology and utopia.*

24. Garfinkel, *Studies in ethnomethodology.*

25. Ibid., 78.

26. Ibid.

27. Ibid., 78–79.

28. Labov & Waletzky, "Narrative analysis," 13, 20.

29. Ibid., 20.

30. Ibid., 21, 22.

31. Sheila Rowbotham, *Dutiful daughters: Women talk about their lives* (London: Allen Lane, 1979), 42.

32. See chapter 4. I learned this usage from Patricia Groves.

33. Atkinson, *Discovering suicide*, 173.

34. A. Griffith, "Single parents and education ideology," Paper presented at the Canadian Sociology Anthropology Association Annual Meetings, Saskatoon, 1979.

35. See Griffith, "Single parents," and chapter 4 of this book.

36. Phyllis Knight and Rolf Knight, *A very ordinary life* (Vancouver: New Star Press, 1974), 4–5. Abridged passages represented by dots in the extract concern the children alone or their relation to their father. They have been omitted for the sake of brevity.

37. Sir David Stafford-Clark, *Psychiatry today* (Harmondsworth: Penguin Books, 1963), 95–96.

38. Garfinkel, *Studies in ethnomethodology.*

39. See chapter 2 of my *Text, facts, and femininity.*

40. L. C. Kolb, *Modern clinical psychiatry* (Philadelphia: W. B. Saunders, 1977), 180.

41. Peters, *Concept.*

42. See Turner, "Introduction."

Notes to Chapter 7

1. Quentin Bell, *Virginia Woolf: A biography* (New York: Harcourt Brace Jovanovich, 1972).

2. I am using the term "primary narrative" for narratives constructed on the basis of actual experience, the connectives of which conform to the mundane linearity of experience and embed events in their mundane contexts. Primary narratives defined in this way are of varying complexity. Those investigated by Labov and Waletzky ("Narrative analysis") are restricted to narratives told by the person who experienced the events. I have extended the term to include "composite" narratives, that is, narratives assembled from the experience of more than one and presented as description, while preserving the same relation to actual events as narratives told by the person experiencing the events.

3. Leonard Woolf, *The journey not the arrival matters: An autobiography of the years 1939 to 1969* (New York: Harcourt Brace Jovanovich, 1969), 92.

4. Bell, *Virginia Woolf,* 221.

5. See D. Smith, "K is mentally ill," in *Texts, facts, and femininity.*

6. Schutz, "On multiple realities."

7. Bell, *Virginia Woolf,* 216.

8. Ibid., 221.

9. Ibid., 224.

10. Peters, *Concept.*

11. Bell, *Virginia Woolf,* 216.

12. See D. Smith, "K is mentally ill," in *Texts, facts, and femininity.*

13. See Stanley E. Fish, "Literature in the reader: Affective stylistics," in Fish, *Self-consuming artifacts: The experience of seventeenth-century literature* (Berkeley: University of California Press, 1972), 382–427.

14. Gunther Kress and Robert Hodge, *Language as ideology* (London: Routledge & Kegan Paul, 1979).

15. Bell, *Virginia Woolf,* 216.

16. Page numbers in the figure refer to Bell, *Virginia Woolf.*

17. Ibid., 227.

18. Garfinkel, *Studies in ethnomethodology;* Sacks, "Sociological description."

19. Thomas P. Wilson, "Conceptions of interaction: A focus of so-

ciological explanation," *American Sociological Review* 35 (1970): 697–710.

20. Edwin M. Lemert, "Paranoia and the dynamics of exclusion," *Sociometry* 25 (1962): 2–20.

21. See in particular D. Smith, "K is mentally ill," in *Text, facts, and femininity.*

22. See Stanley E. Fish, *Surprised by sin: The reader in "Paradise Lost"* (New York: St. Martin's, 1967).

23. I was fifteen when I read that Virginia Woolf had committed suicide. At the time it was reported that she had drowned, and although the implication was suicide, that was not distinctly asserted. I remember reading *Between the acts* some three years later and knowing at once not only that she had committed suicide but why.

Notes to Chapter 8

1. Which is not to say, of course, that we cannot learn this strategy. Ethnographers must.

2. See Alice Jardine's wonderful study *Gynesis: Configurations of woman and modernity* (Ithaca, N.Y.: Cornell University Press, 1985).

3. Lola Lemire Tostevin, "By the smallest possible margin," in *'sophie* (Toronto: Coach House Press, 1988).

4. The first, at least in this phase of the women's movement, for there were, of course, earlier struggles.

5. Gillian Walker's Ph.D. thesis, "Conceptual practices and the political process: Family violence as ideology," is to be published by the University of Toronto Press. Other aspects of this problem for the women's movement have been explored by Patricia Morgan in "From battered wife to program client: The state's shaping of social problems," *Kapitalstate* 9 (1981): 17–39, and Roxana Ng, *Immigrant women and the state: The political economy of voluntary organization* (Toronto: Garamond Press, 1988).

6. Thanks to Lee Lakeman for this account.

7. Adele Mueller, "Peasants and professionals: The social organization of Women in Development knowledge" (Ph.D. diss., University of Toronto, 1987).

BIBLIOGRAPHY

Althusser, Louis. 1969. *For Marx.* Harmondsworth: Penguin Books.

Atkinson, J. Maxwell. 1978. *Discovering suicide: Studies in the social organization of sudden death.* London: Macmillan.

———. 1974. Societal reactions to suicide. In *Patterns of deviance,* ed. S. J. Cohen. Harmondsworth: Penguin Books.

Bacon, Lord Francis. 1900. *Novum organum.* New York: Colonial Press.

Baker, Mark. 1981. *Nam: The Vietnam war in the words of the men and women who fought there.* New York: Berkeley Books.

Bakhtin, M. M. 1981. *The dialogic imagination.* Trans. Caryl Emerson and Michael Holquist. Austin: University of Texas Press.

Bell, Quentin. 1972. *Virginia Woolf: A biography.* New York: Harcourt Brace Jovanovich.

Benjamin, Walter. 1969. The work of art in the age of mechanical reproduction. In *Illuminations.* New York: Schocken Books.

Bierstedt, Robert. 1966. Sociology and general education. In *Sociology and contemporary education,* ed. Charles H. Page. New York: Random House.

Briggs, Jean. 1970. *Never in anger.* Cambridge: Harvard University Press.

Canadian Mental Health Association, The Women and Mental Health Committee. 1987. *Women and mental health in Canada: Strategies for change.* Toronto: Canadian Mental Health Association.

Carr, E. H. 1964. *What is history?* Harmondsworth: Penguin Books.

Chamberlain, Judi. 1975. Struggling to be born. In *Women look at psychi-*

atry, ed. Dorothy E. Smith and Sara J. David, 53–57. Vancouver: Press Gang.

Chandler, Alfred D., Jr. 1966. *Strategy and structure: Chapters in the history of American industrial enterprise.* New York: Anchor Books.

Chesler, Phyllis. 1972. *Women and madness.* New York: Doubleday.

Cicourel, Aaron. 1968. *The Social organization of juvenile justice.* New York: John Wiley.

Cicourel, Aaron, and John Kitsuse, 1963. *The educational decision-makers.* Indianapolis: Bobbs-Merrill.

Clausen, John A., and Madeleine Yarrow, eds. 1955. The impact of mental illness on the family. *Journal of Social Issues* 2(4) (special issue).

Davis, Lennard J. 1983. *Factual fictions: The origins of the English novel.* New York: Columbia University Press.

Day, Elaine Buckley. 1987. A 20th century witch hunt: A feminist critique of the Grange royal commission into deaths at the Hospital for Sick Children. *Studies in Political Economy* 24:13–39.

Douglas, J. D. 1967. *The social meanings of suicide.* Princeton, N.J.: Princeton University Press.

Douglas, Mary. 1966. *Purity and danger.* Harmondsworth: Penguin Books.

Durkheim, Emile. 1964. *The rules of sociological method.* New York: Free Press.

———. 1952. *Suicide.* London: Routledge & Kegan Paul.

Eglin, Peter. 1979. Resolving reality disjuncture on Telegraph Avenue: A study of practical reasoning. *Canadian Journal of Sociology* 4:359–75.

Ellsberg, Daniel. 1972. *Papers on the war.* New York: Simon and Schuster.

Errington, B. Gene. 1973. Negotiating the decision: What is a police matter? M.A. thesis, University of British Columbia.

Findlay, Barbara. 1975. Shrink! Shrank! Shriek! In *Women look at psychiatry*, ed. Dorothy E. Smith and Sara J. David, 59–71. Vancouver: Press Gang.

Fish, Stanley E. 1972. Literature in the reader: Affective stylistics. In *Self-consuming artifacts: The experience of seventeenth-century literature*, 382–427. Berkeley: University of California Press.

———. 1967. *Surprised by sin: The reader in "Paradise lost."* New York: St. Martin's Press.

Fisher, Sue. 1986. *In the patient's best interest: Women and the politics of medical decisions.* New Brunswick, N.J.: Rutgers University Press.

Fleck, Ludwik. 1979. *Genesis and development of a scientific fact.* Trans. Fred Bradley and Thaddeus J. Treun. Chicago: University of Chicago Press.

Foucault, Michel. 1972. *The archaeology of knowledge.* Trans. A. Sheridan-Smith. New York: Harper Colophon.

———. 1979. *Discipline and punish: The birth of the prison.* Trans. Alan Sheridan. New York: Vintage Books.

———. 1973. *Madness and civilization:* A history of insanity in the age of reason. New York: Vintage Books.

———. 1980. *Power/Knowledge: Selected interviews and other writings, 1972–1977.* Ed. Colin Gordon. New York: Pantheon Books.

Garfinkel, Harold. 1968. In *Proceedings of the Purdue Symposium on Ethnomethodology,* ed. Richard J. Hill and Kathleen Stones Crittenden. Institute Monograph Series no. 1, Institute for the Study of Social Change, Purdue University.

———. 1967. *Studies in ethnomethodology.* Englewood Cliffs, N.J.: Prentice-Hall.

———. 1967. Suicide for all practical purposes. In *Studies in ethnomethodology,* 11–18. Englewood Cliffs, N.J.: Prentice-Hall.

Geras, Norman. 1971. Fetishism in Marx's *Capital. New Left Review* 65.

Gould, Carol C. 1975. *Marx's social ontology: Individuality and community in Marx's theory of social reality.* Cambridge, Mass.: MIT Press.

Gouldner, Alvin W. 1970. *The coming crisis in western sociology.* New York: Basic Books.

Gove, W. R., and J. F. Tudor. 1973. Adult sex roles and mental illness. In *Changing women in a changing society,* ed. Joan Huber, 50–73. Chicago: University of Chicago Press.

Government Statisticians' Collective. 1979. How official statistics are produced: Views from the inside. In *Demystifying social statistics,* ed. John Irvine, Ian Miles, and Jeff Evans, 130–51. London: Pluto Press.

Graham, Hilary, and Ann Oakley. 1981. Competing ideologies of reproduction: Medical and maternal perspectives on pregnancy. In *Women, health and reproduction,* ed. H. Roberts, 50–74. London: Routledge & Kegan Paul.

Green, Bryan S. 1983. *Knowing the poor: A case-study in textual reality construction.* London: Routledge & Kegan Paul.

Griffith, Alison. 1979. Single parents and education ideology. Paper presented at the Canadian Sociology Anthropology Association Annual Meetings, Saskatoon.

Groves, Patricia. 1973. Lawyer-Client interviews and the social organization of preparation for court in criminal and divorce cases. Ph.D. diss., Department of Sociology and Anthropology, University of British Columbia, Vancouver.

Hanson, Norwood Russell. 1969. *Perception and discovery.* San Francisco: Freeman, Cooper.

Harding, Sandra. 1986. *The science question in feminism.* Ithaca: Cornell University Press.

Harpwood, Diane. 1982. *Tea and tranquillisers: The diary of a happy housewife.* London: Virago.

Holland, Norman. 1975. *The dynamics of literary response.* New York: W. W. Norton.

Hopkins, Terence K. 1964. *The exercise of influence in small groups.* Totawa, N.J.: Bedminster Press.

Iser, Wolfgang. 1978. *The act of reading: A theory of aesthetic response.* Baltimore: Johns Hopkins University Press.

Jardine, Alice A. 1985. *Gynesis: Configurations of woman and modernity.* Ithaca: Cornell University Press.

Kantorowicz, E. H. 1957. *The king's two bodies: A study in medieval political theology.* Princeton, N.J.: Princeton University Press.

Kimball, Meredith. 1975. Women, sex role stereotypes, and mental health: Catch 22. In *Women look at psychiatry,* ed. Dorothy E. Smith and Sara David, 121–42. Vancouver: Press Gang.

King, Elinor. 1975. How the psychiatric profession views women. In *Women look at psychiatry,* ed. Dorothy E. Smith and Sara David, 21–37. Vancouver: Press Gang.

Knight, Phyllis, and Rolf Knight. 1974. *A very ordinary life.* Vancouver: New Star Press.

Kolb, L. C. 1977. *Modern clinical psychiatry.* Philadelphia: W. B. Saunders.

Kress, Gunther, and Robert Hodge. 1979. *Language as ideology.* London: Routledge & Kegan Paul.

Labov, W., and J. Waletzky. 1967. Narrative analysis: Oral versions of personal experience. In *Essays on verbal and visual arts,* Proceedings of the 1966 Annual Spring Meeting of the American Ethnological Society, ed. J. Helm. Seattle: American Ethnological Society/University of Washington Press.

Laing, R. D. 1967. *The bird of paradise or the politics of experience.* Harmondsworth: Penguin Books.

———. 1960. *The divided self: A study of sanity and madness.* Chicago: Quadrangle Books.

Latour, Bruno, and Steve Woolgar. 1979. *Laboratory life: The social construction of scientific facts.* New York: Sage Publications.

Lemert, Edwin M. 1962. Paranoia and the dynamics of exclusion. *Sociometry* 25:2–20.

Lynch, Michael. 1985. *Art and artifact in laboratory science: A study of shop work and shop talk in a research laboratory.* London: Routledge & Kegan Paul.

———. 1983. "Discipline and the material form of images: An analysis of scientific visibility." Paper presented at the meetings of the Canadian Sociology and Anthropology Association, June, Vancouver.

Mannheim, Karl. 1965. *Ideology and utopia.* New York: Doubleday/Anchor.

Marx, Karl. n.d. *Capital: A critical analysis of capitalist production.* Vol. 1. Trans. Samuel Moore and Edward Aveling. Moscow: Progress Publishers.

———. 1973. *The Grundrisse: Foundations of the critique of political economy.* Trans. Martin Nicolaus. New York: Random House.

Marx, Karl, and Friedrich Engels. 1976. *The German ideology.* Moscow: Progress Publishers.

Morgan, Patricia. 1981. From battered wife to program client: The state's shaping of social problems. *Kapitalstate* 9:17–39.

Mueller, Adele. 1987. Peasants and professionals: The social organization of Women in Development knowledge. Ph.D. diss., University of Toronto.

Nicholson, Linda J. 1986. *Gender and history: The limits of social theory in the age of the family.* New York: Columbia University Press.

Oakley, Ann, and Robin Oakley. 1979. Sexism in official statistics. In *Demystifying social statistics,* ed. John Irvine, Ian Miles, and Jeff Evans, 172–89. London: Pluto Press.

Ollman, Bertell. 1976. *Alienation.* Cambridge: Cambridge University Press.

Peters, R. S. 1958. *The concept of motivation.* London: Routledge & Kegan Paul.

Plath, Sylvia. 1972. *Ariel.* London: Faber and Faber.

———. 1971. *The bell jar.* New York: Harper and Row.

Pollner, Melvin. 1987. *Mundane reason: Reality in everyday and sociological discourse.* New York: Cambridge University Press.

Polanyi, Michael. 1964. *Personal knowledge.* New York: Harper and Row.

Rosenham, David L. 1973. On being sane in insane places. *Science* 197:250–58.

Rowbotham, Sheila. 1979. *Dutiful daughters: Women talk about their lives*. London: Allen Lane.

———. 1973. *Women's consciousness, man's world*, Harmondsworth: Penguin Books.

Sacks, Harvey. 1963. Sociological description. *Berkeley Journal of Sociology* 8:1–16.

Sayer, Derek. 1987. *The violence of abstraction: The analytic foundations of historical materialism*. Oxford: Basil Blackwell.

Scheff, Thomas J. 1966. *Being mentally ill: A sociological theory*. Chicago: Aldine Press.

Schell, Jonathan. 1968. *The military half: An account of the destruction of Quang Ngai and Quang Tin*. New York: Vintage.

———. 1966. *The village of Ben Suc*. New York: Vintage.

Schutz, Alfred. 1962a. Commonsense and scientific interpretations of human action. In *Collected papers*, vol. 1, 3–47. The Hague: Martinus Nijhoff.

———. 1962b. On multiple realities. In *Collected papers*, vol. 1, 207–59. The Hague: Martinus Nijhoff.

Scott, Gail. 1989. *Spaces like stairs*. Toronto: The Women's Press.

Smith, Dorothy E. 1987. *The everyday world as problematic: A feminist sociology*. Boston: Northeastern University Press.

———. 1989. Sociological theory: Writing patriarchy into feminist texts. In *Feminism and sociological theory*, ed. Ruth Wallace. New York: Sage Publications.

———. 1990. *Texts, facts, and femininity: Exploring the relations of ruling*. London: Routledge & Kegan Paul.

———. 1975. Women and psychiatry. In *Women look at psychiatry*, ed. Dorothy E. Smith and Sara J. David, 1–19. Vancouver: Press Gang.

Smith, George W. 1987. *Occupation and skill: Government discourse as problematic*. Studies in the Job-Education Nexus, Occasional Paper 2. Toronto: The Nexus Project.

———. 1988. Policing the gay community: An inquiry into textually-mediated social relations. *International Journal of the Sociology of Law* 16:163–83.

Stafford-Clark, Sir David. 1963. *Psychiatry today*. Harmondsworth: Penguin Books.

Statistics Canada. 1970. *Mental health statistics*. Vol. 1, *Institutional admissions and separations*. Ottawa: Information Canada.

Sudnow, David. 1965. Normal crimes: Sociological features of the penal code. *Social Problems* 12:255–76.

Sydie, R. A. 1987. *Natural women, cultured men: A feminist perspective on sociological theory.* Toronto: Methuen.

Szasz, Thomas. 1961. *The myth of mental illness: Foundations of a theory of personal conduct.* New York: Dell.

Thorpe, J. 1973. *Principles of textual criticism.* San Marino, Calif.: The Huntington Library.

Tostevin, Lola Lemire. 1988. By the smallest possible margin. In *'sophie.* Toronto: Coach House Press.

Turner, Roy. 1974. Introduction. In *Ethnomethodology,* ed. R. Turner. Harmondsworth: Penguin Books.

Walker, Gillian. 1988. Conceptual practices and the political process: Family violence as ideology. Ph.D. diss., University of Toronto.

West, Candace, 1984. *Routine complications: Troubles with talk between doctors and patients.* Bloomington: Indiana University Press.

Wilson, James Q. 1969. Violence. In *Toward the year 2000,* ed. Daniel Bell. Boston: Beacon Press.

Wilson, Thomas P. 1970. Conceptions of interaction: A focus of sociological explanation. *American Sociological Review* 35:697–710.

Wittgenstein, Ludwig. 1953. *Philosophical investigations.* Trans. G. E. M. Anscombe. New York: Macmillan.

———. 1961. *Tractatus logico-philosophicus.* Trans. G. E. M. Anscombe. London: Routledge & Kegan Paul.

Woolf, Leonard. 1969. *The journey not the arrival matters: An autobiography of the years 1939 to 1969.* New York: Harcourt Brace Jovanovich.

Zetterberg, Hans. 1965. *On theory and verification in sociology.* Totawa, N.J.: Bedminster Press.

Zimmerman, Don H. 1974. Facts as practical accomplishment. In *Ethnomethodology,* ed. Roy Turner, 128–43. Harmondsworth: Penguin Books.

Zimmerman, Don H., and M. Pollner. 1971. The everyday world as phenomenon. In *Understanding everyday life,* ed. J. D. Douglas. Chicago: Aldine Publishing.

INDEX